Every Intellectual's Big Brother

LITERARY MODERNISM SERIES

Thomas F. Staley, *Editor*

George Orwell in early spring 1946.

Every Intellectual's Big Brother

George Orwell's Literary Siblings

⁓

John Rodden

UNIVERSITY OF TEXAS PRESS ⬥ AUSTIN

Requests for permission to reproduce
material from this work should be sent to:
  Permissions
  University of Texas Press
  P.O. Box 7819
  Austin, TX 78713-7819
  www.utexas.edu/utpress/about/bpermission.html

⊗ The paper used in this book meets the minimum requirements of
ANSI/NISO Z39.48-1992 (R1997) (Permanence of Paper).

Library of Congress Cataloging-in-Publication Data

Rodden, John.
    Every intellectual's big brother : George Orwell's literary siblings / John Rodden.
— 1st ed.
        p.   cm.—(Literary modernism series)
    Includes bibliographical references and index.
    ISBN-13: 978-0-292-71308-6 (cloth : alk. paper)
    ISBN-10: 0-292-71308-8 (alk. paper)
    1. Orwell, George, 1903–1950—Criticism and interpretation—History. 2. Orwell,
George, 1903–1950—Influence.   3. Orwell, George, 1903–1950—Political and social
views.   I. Title.

PR6029.R8Z7753   2006
828'.91209—dc22

2006024667

For Lynn,
who endured and prevailed

Contents

ACKNOWLEDGMENTS

This study originated in numerous conversations two decades ago with former colleagues of mine at the University of Virginia about George Orwell, cultural politics, and the vocation of the contemporary intellectual. At that time, the serious study of Orwell was riveted on the approach of 1984, and public discussion was largely limited to Orwell biography and to interpretations of his last novel, rather than to reflection on his ambiguous legacy.

I am especially grateful to three former colleagues from my Virginia days. First, Michael Levenson has been a close friend for a quarter-century, indeed a beneficent intellectual big brother. I am also deeply grateful to an emeritus Virginia scholar who shares in the liberal intellectual heritage that Orwell exemplified: Walter Sokel. Tom Cushman has remained a dear comrade, a generous supporter, and the model of a scholar who develops an argument without losing sight of the evidence on which it needs to be based.

A number of other people have kindly offered me their time, attention, and memories in interviews and in correspondence. I am particularly indebted to the many intellectuals with whom I corresponded and, in many instances, whom I interviewed. Their cooperation was invaluable, and their assistance with my research has been one of the most enjoyable aspects of this project. Those who shared reminiscences with me include Steven Marcus, William Phillips, Mary McCarthy, Alfred Kazin, Russell Kirk, Julian Symons, John Atkins, Kingsley Amis, John Wain, and Martin Green. In particular I would like to thank Diana Trilling, Irving Howe, Norman Podhoretz, Dennis Wrong, and Richard Kostelanetz for taking the time to explain to me their New York intellectual milieu.

Friends, colleagues, teachers, students, and editors have also assisted me during these years of research and writing. With particular pleasure, I thank Jack Rossi for his unfailing encouragement, scholarly example, and sage advice. Scott Walter, Jonathan Rose, and Peter Dougherty have proven themselves wise counselors and reliable allies. To Jeffrey Meyers, I extend my appreciation for his continuing interest as my work developed. I am obliged to Ian Williams for reading the sections on British intellectual life in this study. I am also pleased to thank Christopher Hitchens and Jim Sleeper for sharing their stories about and insights into contemporary intellectual life. Morris Dickstein and William Cain have been continuing and cherished sources of intellectual support and challenge, engaging me in dialogue and offering illuminating perspectives from their rich experience.

Finally, I am grateful to my teachers at La Salle University in Philadelphia, and also to my students at Virginia and the University of Texas, whose curiosity and skepticism have helped me strengthen the ideas herein. Their encouragement over the years has sustained me, and I have relied upon their expertise and suggestions in writing this book.

My deepest debt of gratitude goes to seven editorial interns, who volunteered their energy and enthusiasm to the realization of this book, working diligently and often tirelessly behind the scenes to check sources and assist with manuscript revisions. The laser-like ability of Zachary Kupperman, Megan Giller, and Jennifer Nation to catch factual as well as stylistic errors was indispensable. Jay Alejandre displayed extraordinary research skill and keen intellectual understanding of Orwell's work and heritage. Evan Autry and Matt Casey exhibited a special acumen for analyzing and organizing research materials. Mike Haydel furnished invaluable assistance in the final stages of preparing the manuscript for publication. Wielding an uncanny memory that enabled him to recall almost every line of dozens of pages, he showed unflagging tenacity as he delivered incomparable manuscript detail work. No research project could ask for more than the selfless dedication of these young people.

Several of the chapters in this book took shape with the steady encouragement and inspiration of James B. Schick, who, as editor of the *Midwest Quarterly*, has published several essays of mine. During his tenure as editor of *Society*, Jonathan Imber has also given me invaluable opportunities to develop my ideas in print.

In the course of writing this book, I have incurred a great many other personal as well as scholarly debts. I thank Paul Rodden and Cristen Reat for years of astute criticism, intellectual nourishment, and loving care. I am also indebted to my parents, John and Rose Rodden, the goodness and kindness of whom have proven to me again and again what is important in life, and to my brothers Edward and Thomas, who have furnished me unwavering emotional support over the years.

My deepest personal thanks goes again to Lynn Hayden, who sacrificed a great deal so that this book could come to fruition. Radiating a gentle Gulf Stream of warmth, she was patient, understanding, and cooperative beyond measure. Her faith and love have made this work possible.

"Orwell" Still Lives

I

In May 2003, I co-chaired, along with my friend Thomas Cushman, a three-day centenary retrospective on Orwell's work and heritage titled "George Orwell: An Exploration of His World and Legacy." The international event was hosted by Wellesley College, near Boston, and it was one of the biggest Orwell gatherings ever held, as close to three hundred participants gathered to discuss the iconoclastic British writer and to ponder how his writings remain pertinent in the twenty-first century.[1]

Our conference took place as the public interest in Orwell's life, which had peaked in 1984 with a spate of Orwell portraits and teledramas, was undergoing another sharp (if temporary) rise in 2003, highlighted by the appearance of two new full-length biographies and a new edition of *Nineteen Eighty-Four* introduced by Thomas Pynchon. Orwell's biographers and critics pondered and plumbed in excruciating, seemingly endless detail the complexities and ironies of Orwell's life.

But quite apart from this task, Orwell—or "Orwell," the outsized iconic figure elevated to world-historical status—possesses what I have elsewhere termed an *afterlife*.[2] And indeed, the most illuminating as well as the most heated conversations at the conference—which ranged from disputes about Orwell's antifeminism to speculations about his likely positions on the Bush administration's invasion of Iraq—addressed Orwell's ambiguous afterlife, reigniting old Left/Right controversies about his political stance and moral example that have repeatedly erupted since his death in 1950.

During the quieter moments of the conference, I spoke at length with Christopher Hitchens, Robert Conquest, Todd Gitlin, and other intellectual admirers of Orwell. Each of them emphasized Orwell's presence in their lives, reminding me once again that even if Orwell the man is dead, "Orwell" the writer (and the Icon) still lives—and still provokes arguments among literary and political intellectuals.[3]

Especially my conversations with Robert Conquest and Dennis Wrong, both of whom spoke about their early encounters with Orwell's work during his own lifetime, recalled my interviews with Orwell's friends more than twenty years ago. Orwell came alive for me at that time, when I interviewed Julian Symons and John Atkins, and also corresponded with George Woodcock, V. S. Pritchett, and other acquaintances of Orwell's—all of whom have now passed from the scene. My interest in Orwell during the "countdown to 1984" also brought me into contact with numerous intellectuals of the generation following his own, such as Russell Kirk, John Wain, Kingsley Amis, Irving Howe, Alfred Kazin, and Mary McCarthy. Alas, they too have passed on.[4] But, as the chapters in Part One attest, their intense engagement (or intellectual jousting) with Orwell is preserved in the pages of this book.

That topic—"Orwell and the Intellectuals"—is the central theme of this book. Given that my discussions with several intellectuals at the conference still bear immediate relevance to the international political scene in the twenty-first century, I have decided to include certain portions of the interviews conducted during the conference in Part Two.[5] The intellectuals who discuss Orwell in Part Two are, in some sense, Orwell's heirs, and so it seemed fitting to include their responses here as evidence of his ongoing influence and enduring relevance more than a half-century after his death.

II

Will Orwell—or "Orwell"—continue to engage readers deeply and provoke impassioned argument among intellectuals as the new century unfolds? Or was 2003 his swan song? Has Orwell's historical moment passed?

Every Intellectual's Big Brother touches on those questions. Indeed, it is possible that Orwell—and even "Orwell"—may vanish down the memory hole in the upcoming decades, perhaps well before 2050, the centennial of his death (and, coincidentally, the target date for perfecting Oceania's Newspeak). It is still too early to say.

But this much can still be said today: Whereas the historical moment of communism (or even socialism) has evidently passed, neither Orwell's literary voice nor his moral example—nor indeed his major books, *Animal Farm* and *Nineteen Eighty-Four*, which address those political ideologies—have yet lost their social relevance or literary power.

For Orwell's writings are about more than just "communism" or "socialism." Indeed, the era of communism is likely over, but not yet the specter of totalitarian technology or tyrannical language distortion. These historical developments, which emerged in the last century, persist in our own, and they have received rich and vital embodiment in Orwell's fictional masterpieces and best essays. So long as what might be called "the historical Will" of such developments continues to exert force, the pertinence of Orwell (and "Orwell") to cultural life in the twenty-first-century—and, above all, to the lives of his many intellectual heirs, including those featured in these pages—will also endure.

Every Intellectual's Big Brother

George Orwell and His Intellectual Progeny

I

George Orwell (1903–1950) was the foremost political writer of the twentieth century and the widely acknowledged contemporary master of plain
English prose. The following chapters orbit around Orwell's intellectual
legacy and cultural impact, focusing especially on his deep and ongoing influence
on the generations of Anglo-American intellectuals that followed him.

My chief intention in this study is to explore the politics of Orwell's reception
history as a dimension of cultural history, thereby to understand his unique and
enduring role in Anglo-American intellectual life. Orwell's reception in the mid-
to late twentieth century is the subject of Part One of this book, in which I take
the story of his complex heritage slightly further than I have in my previous two
studies of his reputation and legacy.[1] Each of these five chapters focuses on one
or more literary circles in London or America and shows how networks of interpersonal and institutional influence acted to burnish and expand Orwell's reputation. Key nodal points in these networks are the little magazines and literary
quarterlies (e.g., *Partisan Review, politics, Dissent, Modern Age*, and *Nation*), whose
editors or prominent contributors identified with Orwell and promoted his work.
I am especially interested in the ideologically conditioned responses to Orwell
by these intellectuals, in their political affinities with other writers and thinkers,
and in the close, impassioned, even familial relationship—ranging from reverence to reproach—that so many of them openly displayed toward Orwell.

Chapter One addresses the 1930s and '40s, discussing Orwell's distinctive "outsider" relationship to the London Left. Orwell was "not one of us," as an English
leftist derided Orwell, whom he excluded from the rather cliquish Oxbridge-
educated Left intelligentsia of their day. This chapter thereby highlights the ex-

emplary value of Orwell's life and work as a case study in the sociology of intellectuals.[2] The chapter locates Orwell within an intellectual milieu but determines
that Orwell was an "outsider" from the so-called Auden group of the 1930s intellectuals and intelligentsia. The argument relies on a close analysis of Orwell's
personal as well as his political history in order to understand his independent
stance and his views on the social function of a writer-intellectual.

Chapter Two is the lone section to address Orwell's reputation among an intellectual group that consisted primarily of poets and novelists: the Movement
writers of the 1950s (e.g., John Wain, Kingsley Amis, Robert Conquest, Donald
Davie).[3] The chapter highlights the image of Orwell as a writer and man of letters
(rather than a political intellectual), giving attention to his specifically literary
qualities as well as his ideological influence. Here again, we are reminded how
intellectuals bent Orwell and his work to their own aspirations. They projected a
man and writer in whom they wanted to believe; they reconfigured a figure that
could meet their professional and private needs.

We move across the Atlantic to New York in Chapter Three, examining the
elder two generations of the intellectual circle known as the New York Intellectuals, a highbrow, chiefly Jewish group clustered around *Partisan Review* (for which
Orwell wrote a wartime and early postwar "London Letter").[4] Norman Podhoretz
famously dubbed them "The Family," and he and others viewed Orwell proudly
as their English cousin. Our focus is on Orwell's reception by a leading member
of this New York group: Irving Howe, a prominent *PR* contributor, editor of *Dissent*, editorial board member of *politics*, and arguably the leading member of the
second generation of the New York Intellectuals. As we shall see, Orwell's work
was immediately accorded an enthusiastic reception by Howe and other *Partisan
Review* writers. (Orwell was even honored with the first Partisan Review Award
in 1949.) The lavish tributes from reviewers of the first editions of his American
works—from intellectuals such as Lionel Trilling, Diana Trilling, Philip Rahv,
and Podhoretz, among many others—exerted decisive influence on the development of his American reputation throughout the second half of the twentieth
century.

Chapter Four is devoted to Orwell's reception by Russell Kirk, the best-known
and most articulate voice of a much smaller literary-intellectual group, the American cultural conservatives associated with the literary quarterly *Modern Age*,
which Kirk founded in 1957. Here too, Orwell's positive reception by American
conservatives (the John Birch Society accorded him the dubious honor of selecting "1984" as the last four digits of its national phone number) served to highlight his image as the West's leading literary cold warrior of the postwar era.

Part One closes with an in-depth look in Chapter Five at Orwell's history of reception at the *Nation*. The chapter focuses particularly on the response of one-time *Nation* columnist Christopher Hitchens, a British expatriate active on the American intellectual scene who has often been touted (or reviled) as Orwell's intellectual successor.[5] I suggest that Hitchens, who strongly identifies with Orwell and has authored *Why Orwell Matters* (2002), exemplifies a way of becoming the Orwell of one's generation as the twenty-first century unfolds.[6]

"The Orwell Confraternity Today" is the subject of Part Two. Its cornerstone is a series of edited interviews[7] woven together to form Chapters Six and Seven, which in toto amount to a collective family portrait of Orwell's much younger siblings, i.e., of more than a dozen intellectuals and scholars who have strongly identified with Orwell and studied his work carefully. Their relative distance—whether a development attributable to intellectual independence or isolation—from the kinds of circles, networks, and coteries that we saw in earlier chapters is not just a reflection of Orwell's changing reputation, but also of the altered conditions of intellectual life in the twenty-first century. Nowadays, if one embraces Orwell, one does so largely on one's own, without the benefit and guidance of a group of like-minded thinking people who help form one's intellectual life. In a sense, the readers of Orwell featured in these chapters testify that single individuals, rather than groups around a literary hub such as a small magazine, are Orwell's siblings—and sometimes indeed sibling rivals—today.

Part Two of *Every Intellectual's Big Brother* ends on a very personal note in Chapter Eight, in which I attempt to speak in autobiographical terms about Orwell's role in my own intellectual life. Here and elsewhere in the book, I also elaborate on the figurative language of intellectuals' "fraternal" relationship to Orwell, whether as his literary siblings or his intellectual progeny. Like me, numerous other intellectuals have embraced one or both stances toward Orwell, or alternated between them, reflecting not just the unusually personal relationships that his literary persona invites, but also the kinds of writers and intellectuals who are powerfully attracted to him. The chapter also addresses the difficult challenge posed today for those who would seek to enter the tradition of the intellectual and man of letters that Orwell exemplified. I argue that, in order to embrace this tradition fully, one needs today to "adopt" an intellectual "big brother" (or "big sister") who will strengthen one's commitment to engage issues of wide public concern seriously—and thereby fortify one's resistance to academic careerism, literary professionalism, scholarly overspecialization, and both polemics ad hominem and punditry ad nauseam.

In the Epilogue, I take up an issue raised by Orwell's still-prominent, still-controversial reputation: the moral dimension of his status as an intellectual object of admiration—and detraction. Orwell's reputation has been claimed by those who seek to use him for the legitimation and sanction of all kinds of divergent political and intellectual programs. This process has led to a sometimes blind and uncritical fetishism of Orwell and his work. Yet, at the same time, there is a similar process in the cultural politics of reputation that focuses on discrediting Orwell. Are there principles by which one can assess Orwell's roles as a literary model and even as a cultural hero—and, by implication, those of any writer? Might we begin to formulate an ethics of admiration, so to speak, for our historical figures? This closing meditation addresses these and other questions, all of which are raised by Orwell's special place in Western intellectual life since his death in January 1950.[8]

II

Unlike in the case of my previous two studies of Orwell's heritage, I have chosen in this book to limit my inquiry to Orwell's reception within selected Anglo-American intellectual circles. My reasons are threefold. First, British and American intellectuals have responded with the greatest insight and passion to Orwell's life and work, and their reception has determined the emergence of his reputation and has conditioned the course of his wider influence in popular culture. I have been particularly interested in Orwell's reception among readers in intellectual *circles*,[9] rather than the reception of unaffiliated (or even loosely affiliated) intellectual readers who responded strongly to Orwell's work and decisively shaped his reputation (such as V. S. Pritchett in Britain and Edmund Wilson in the United States). Rather, readers prominent within their intellectual groups— whom I have elsewhere termed *authoritative voices*—are conceptually advantageous for the study of reception. For they are usually so positioned within a group that their personal responses can be interpreted, using information about their reference group affiliations, to represent far more than a private, idiosyncratic response.[10]

But a second concern has also governed my choice of reception scenes, involving a factor particular to Orwell's own case: the *politics* of reception. Orwell was "a political animal," a man who "could not blow his nose without moralizing on conditions in the handkerchief industry," as his friend Cyril Connolly once remarked.[11] It is not surprising, therefore, that Orwell has elicited politically motivated responses from readers—especially from intellectuals who have strongly identified (or disagreed) with him. Indeed, Orwell's politicized heritage is a minor political issue in its own right, and I have been especially interested in the Left/Right battles for his mantle, whether the issues have centered on ideological or cultural politics. As a result, this book illustrates Orwell's politically ambidextrous reception (and the frequent confusions about his life and work) via reception scenes from a range of political perspectives, all of them featuring readers who have claimed (or disclaimed) Orwell as a forerunner or model (or anti-model).

Third, while I have retained my previous books' conception of a "scenic" approach to Orwell's legacy, I am interested not just in the politics of reception but also in the *ethics* of reception. The shift from a politics of reception to an ethics of reception signifies that I am concerned not just with linguistic strategies or with ideology or with the social psychology of reader response, but with the status of claims to (and disavowals of) Orwell's legacy. In my earlier studies of Orwell, I discussed extensively the rhetoric and aesthetics of literary reputation.[12] Here I am concerned with the ethics of admiration and detraction, or what could more broadly be termed *reception ethics*.[13]

III

All this attests to the fact that Orwell has been a notable presence for several generations of readers now. His nondescript pseudonym, drawn from a placid English river, is known throughout the world as a synonym for decency—just as the adjective *Orwellian* is widely perceived to mean "tyrannical," even "totalitarian." This familiarity with Orwell's life and work owes much to the powerful engagement with him by the intellectuals featured in these pages—his literary siblings—and it is through the filter of their lives and literary responses that we value him today as we do.

Whether we admire or reprove Orwell, he is part of our common cultural life. All of us are, in some sense, his intellectual progeny.

PART ONE

Their Orwell, Left and Right

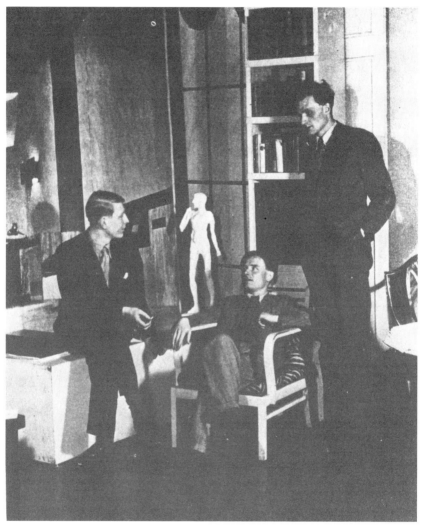

Left to right: W. H. Auden, Christopher Isherwood, and Stephen Spender in the early 1930s. The Huntington Library; used with permission.

CHAPTER ONE

"Not One of Us?"

Orwell and the London Left of the 1930s and '40s

I

Historians and social theorists have written extensively about the modern intellectual's class origins, political allegiances, and social function.[1] Yet, as Charles Kadushin notes, "Despite (or perhaps because of) the many works on intellectuals, there is no adequate sociological theory of intellectuals or intellectual life. . . . Theory-building in this field has been marred by an abundance of opinion and moralization, a dearth of facts, and a plethora of parochial definitions."[2]

Much of the scholarship on the sociology of intellectuals is purely descriptive; and even worse, unlike the case in other subfields of the sociology of occupations, as Robert Brym notes, sociologists have tended to accept the self-descriptions (or "professional ideologies") of intellectuals about their political outlooks at face value.[3] Brym calls for a moratorium on general theories about the correlation between social structure and intellectuals' patterns of mobility, and he instead urges careful study of the relation between partisan affiliation and the intellectual's career trajectory through the changing social structure.[4] Given the observations of Kadushin and Brym about the theoretical imprecision and "intellectual backwardness" of the political sociology of intellectuals,[5] it may prove a modest contribution merely to broach the conceptual issues of the field through the single rich example of a particular intellectual and his intellectual milieu.[6]

George Orwell and the London intelligentsia of the 1930s and 1940s provide an instructive case. The special historical relation of Orwell to the British intellectuals of his day sheds light on the changing situation of the modern Western intellectual. "When the history of intellectuals of the twentieth century is written," William Steinhoff has predicted, "some part of it will be devoted to Orwell's analysis and criticism of his fellow intellectuals."[7] Or, as a disgruntled left-wing journalist derisively remarked of Orwell to the young Alfred Kazin in the wartime London of 1944, "He's not one of us."[8]

The case of Orwell, however, possesses more than merely historical interest, for it represents not just one man's dispute with his fellow literary intellectuals. Rather, it signals the emergent position of the modern writer-intellectual in Britain, responding to two new, related, historical developments in the 1930s: the birth of a radical intelligentsia and the rise in Europe of totalitarianism.

How did English writer-intellectuals react under such conditions? What factors contributed to the rise and decline of widespread intellectual dissidence? What accounts for political rebellion and adaptation occurring variously in political, religious, and aesthetic terms? How do the intellectual's class origins, education, and mature social experience shape his or her political orientation? Does the writer-intellectual have a special political function to fulfill in society?

These broad historical, conceptual, and normative questions cannot, of course, be addressed adequately in a single example. Moreover, to approach them via the filter of the vivid historical personalities and complicated social conditions of the 1930s and 1940s in Britain runs the risk of generalization from skewed or impoverished data. Yet advantages emerge too. The sociologist's restricted case allows for a combination of observational detail and conceptual delimitation seldom found in cultural history, and the case of Orwell, an unusually rich and suggestive one, is particularly well-suited to a study of the political sociology of intellectuals. His appropriateness arises, perhaps paradoxically, from the adverse stance which he took toward his adopted "class" of fellow intellectuals.

By the very fact of his distinctiveness Orwell offers insight into the typicality of his intellectual generation. Because he was never directly affiliated with the left-wing writers of the "Auden generation"—"a generation he was in but never part of," in Stuart Samuels's characterization[9]—he could stand at once inside and outside the Left. He thereby could both participate in and give witness to his generation's experience, reflecting its larger dilemma between political detachment and commitment. "To learn what the world then looked like to an English intellectual," wrote his friend and *Tribune* colleague T. R. Fyvel in *Intellectuals Today* (1968), "one can go to George Orwell, who wrote so explicitly and precisely about this, and one can also see how the issues of the time were reflected in his own career." His diverse engagement with poverty, imperialism, fascism, and socialism established Orwell, in Fyvel's view, as "the characteristic literary figure of the thirties," and Fyvel urged readers "to consider Orwell's historical role as an intellectual of his day."[10]

Indeed, several observers have dubbed the 1930s not the "Auden Decade," but rather the "Orwell Decade"—and not at all to the liking of many left-wing literary historians. Orwell's biographer, D. J. Taylor, calls their criticism "wholly legitimate" and explains:

> The posthumous reputation-brokering has allowed him to dominate the literary 1930s to the exclusion of nearly everyone else. Evelyn Waugh once protested, in an early 1950s review of Stephen Spender's autobiography, that members of the Auden-Isherwood-Spender axis had "ganged up" to capture the decade for themselves. Half a century later, it would be accurate to say that Orwell's admirers have since ganged up to capture it for Orwell, so that this unattached, marginal figure of the prewar era has gradually moved center stage, while a swath of contemporary left-wing literature of the type that he disparaged in *The Road to Wigan Pier* (1937) is largely ignored.[11]

Chapter One takes this observation as a point of departure for addressing the theoretical issues framed by the foregoing questions. Periods of political crisis invariably raise such questions with special directness, whose responses often manifest themselves most clearly in the experience of one centrally involved in the struggle. As his intellectual generation's posthumously proclaimed "conscience" and "voice,"[12] Orwell and his work arguably constitute not only a sociological but also an ethical guide to the contemporary relation of the intellectual and politics.[13]

II

Whereas various continental traditions of intellectuals involved in radical politics stretch as far back as the eighteenth century, Britain alone possessed no dissident left-wing intelligentsia until the 1930s. The "philosophical Radicals" of the 1820s, including James Mill, were parliamentary reformers, and they numbered in any case no more than a coterie of twenty. The nineteenth-century intellectual "Lights of Liberalism"—led by John Stuart Mill, Herbert Spencer, James Bryce, and Henry Sidgwick—were similarly in or close to the corridors of power and fully assimilated into the governing classes by birth and education. Edwardian liberals like L. T. Hobhouse and J. A. Hobson, and Fabian socialists like H. G. Wells and Sidney and Beatrice Webb, likewise invested their progressive hopes in gradualism, social planning, technological advance, and administrative efficiency. With occasional exceptions like Robert Owen, William Morris, and George Bernard Shaw, English intellectuals were traditionally Liberal or Conservative, or frequently apolitical. Historically they have not been models of the "alienated intellectual," Robert Park's "Marginal Man."[14] Indeed, even when an English socialist intelligentsia finally did emerge late in the nineteenth century, its leading members (Shaw, Wells, the Webbs) became Establishment figures, hardly more alienated or distant from the corridors of power than Victorian liberal and conservative intellectuals had been.

The conditions responsible for the traditionally moderate political stance of British intellectuals and their tendency to form part of the ruling consensus rather than a critical opposition or "adversary culture" are numerous and complex. Alan Swingewood cites as significant factors such traditions in English society as

political stability, historical continuity, a gentrified bourgeois culture, the strength of philosophical currents relying on common sense, experience, and practicality (utilitarianism, empiricism), combined with the absence of a broadly based revolutionary socialist movement . . .[15]

These so-called "peculiarities of the English" have facilitated the integration of the British intelligentsia into a society with a smoothness unknown elsewhere in Europe—especially unlike the cases of France and Italy, neither of which possesses an established tradition of cooperative intellectual participation in government and politics.[16] As Lewis Coser once summed up the distinction, the salons led to the French Revolution and the coffeehouses to the 1832 Reform Bill.[17] British intellectuals have typically maintained access to important official channels of communication and power, and have thereby constituted an "intellectual aristocracy," in Noel Annan's phrase, closely bound to the ruling classes and one another by family, school, and professional ties. As Annan explained:

The influence of these families [the Stracheys, Darwins, Huxleys, Stephenses, and others] may partly explain a paradox which has puzzled European and American observers of English life: the paradox of an intelligentsia which appears to conform rather than rebel against the rest of society. The proclivity to criticize, of course, exists; Matthew Arnold flicked Victorian self-confidence with his irony. . . . But the pro-consular tradition and the English habit of working through established institutions and modifying them to meet social needs only when such needs are proven are traits strongly exhibited by the intelligentsia of this country. Here is an aristocracy, secure, established, and, like the rest of English society, accustomed to responsible and judicious utterance and skeptical and iconoclastic speculation.[18]

The main focus of political sociology is the analysis and explanation of partisan affiliation. In their efforts to explain intellectuals' behavior via correlations between social position and political outlook, political sociologists usually identify "malintegration" within the existing social structure as the chief cause of radical protest. Unemployment and underemployment locate intellectuals on the margins of society. Poorly embedded in Establishment institutions, they feel rootless, estranged, and well-disposed to revolutionary appeals.[19] What the social malintegration–political radicalism thesis often ignores, as Brym points out, is whether alienated intellectuals possess "the political resources to change their ire into action"—sufficient numbers, influence on other revolutionary-minded groups, links to communication networks, and high social organization (journals, meeting societies, discussion circles, cooperatives).[20] As we shall see, Britain in the 1930s sustained radical intellectual politics so long as both the social structure failed to absorb intellectuals and their political resources could be maintained. With the arrival of World War II, both conditions for the widespread *political* expression of intellectuals' alienation disappeared.

III

The 1930s witnessed the first society-wide dislocation of British intellectuals. They were cut off from many traditional connections to prestige and power, or their sources of private patronage dried up following graduation from Oxbridge or London. As Fyvel recalled it, British intellectuals "searched, some of them desperately indeed, for ways of becoming integrated in their society."[21] The major cause of marginalization was the worldwide depression. Unemployment in Britain hovered above two million for most of the decade. Hard times forced middle-class graduates to make ends meet as journalists, publishers, schoolmasters, and private tutors. W. H. Auden, C. Day-Lewis, Evelyn Waugh, Rex Warner, Orwell, and hundreds of others took poor-paying jobs in private schools. Other graduates traveled to Europe or, like Malcolm Muggeridge, William Empson, and Orwell, observed how the British Empire operated away from home. They saw conditions no better abroad; capitalism seemed to be failing everywhere. At the same time, the new Soviet state and its romantic promise of equality and prosperity—and its celebration, rather than mere toleration, of intellectuals—struck many young intellectuals as a cultural paradise. Pilgrimages to Moscow became routine for socialists, and glowing return reports from the Webbs and others confirmed the happy rumors.[22] Outrage about underemployment at home and admiration for the Soviet Union soon led to the formation, as Samuels puts it, "of a radical intelligentsia in England—a body of creative people who, as a group, openly criti-

Tosco Fyvel, c. late 1930s, an English Jewish intellectual,
fellow *Tribune* editor of George Orwell, and vocal Zionist.
Fyvel admired Orwell intensely even though they sharply
disagreed about whether to found an independent Jewish
state in Palestine.

cized the existing form of society and who established institutions and intellectual pressure groups to mount a campaign to alter that society."[23]

The criticism actually began in the late 1920s, in the absence of any developed political consciousness, as the college protest of a bourgeois literary elite.
The "Left Poets" at Oxford (Auden, Stephen Spender, Day-Lewis) formed the
heart of a group (including Warner, Louis MacNeice, Hugh Gaitskell, Isaiah Berlin, Christopher Isherwood, Harold Acton, Edward Upward, and A. J. P. Taylor)
known variously as "the gang," "the Happy Few," and "the Lads of the Earth."

They resembled an undergraduate Bloomsbury group. They crammed their publications, such as *Oxford Poetry*, with insiders' gossip and private allusions. Art was for the happy few, namely themselves, not for what they considered the ill-bred masses. They were quite self-consciously members of Oxford's literary minority (the "arties"), contemptuous of the uncultivated, athletic majority (the "hearties"). They aspired to aesthetic priesthood; their bishop was Auden and their vicar T. S. Eliot. Political commitment, social activism, and artistic responsibility were vulgar, alien notions to them.[24]

Around 1930 all this began to change. Auden, Spender, Isherwood, Upward, David Guest, and some others of the Auden "gang" (for example, John Lehmann from Cambridge) traveled to Berlin. The initial attraction was decadence, for Berlin was to the late Weimar Republic what Paris's Left Bank had been to France a few years earlier. But as Spender put it in 1937: "One began by noticing symptoms of decadence, suffering and unemployment; one looked further and saw, beneath the decay of the liberal state, the virulent reaction of the Nazis and the struggle for a new life of the Communists."[25] Although they themselves were usually quite comfortable because of favorable exchange rates, the young bohemians had brushed up against what they had never encountered before: unemployment, physical suffering, poverty, disease.[26]

Most young intellectuals returned to England shortly before Hitler came to power and near the nadir of the depression in Britain in 1933, when unemployment peaked at 2.75 million. Although the German situation, with 6 million unemployed, was far worse than Britain's, the social consciences of the Auden group awakened only on their return home, in the face of the hunger marches of 1932 and 1933. As Spender recalled:

I did not, at first, feel that I could do more than pity [the Germans]. This was partly because, as a foreigner, I felt outside Germany. Only when the crisis spread to Great Britain and other countries did I begin to realize that it was a disease of capitalism throughout the world. Gradually I became convinced that the only cure for unemployment, other than war, was an international society in which the resources of the world were exploited in the interests of all the people of the world.[27]

Thus did the "happy few" become aware of the miseries of the unhappy multitude.

The names Auden, Spender, and Day-Lewis first became publicly linked through their joint appearance in a little anthology, fitly titled *New Signatures* (1932). Although it was primarily a rebellion against esoteric, coterie poetry, it

Left to right: W. H. Auden, C. Day-Lewis, and Stephen Spender in Venice during the
PEN club conference in 1949. Getty Images; used with permission.

also marked the Left Poets' first halting steps toward political consciousness. In
New Country (1933) they explicitly repudiated bourgeois values and called for a
socialist revolution. They were "concerned no longer with a purely aesthetic approach, with finding a new signature, a new moral code, but with discovering
a new country, a new social order."[28] That order was the classless society—but
overlaid with a romantic veneer suffused with fellow-feeling, a self-dramatizing
"Marxism of the heart." "Prepare the way for an English Lenin," cried Michael
Roberts in his introduction to *New Country*. Intellectuals were moving "forward
from liberalism," per the title of Spender's 1936 book. They could "no longer remain aloof from politics," declared Roberts. Radical aesthetics had given way to
radical politics.[29]

Few young intellectuals did remain aloof from politics. Membership in the
Communist Party of Great Britain (CPGB) rose from 1,356 in 1930 to 15,570 in
1938, an increase "due in no small measure to the many middle-class intellectuals who became politically conscious in the 1930s and streamed into the Party
ranks."[30] Per Lenin's conception of the Party as a revolutionary vanguard, intellectuals began to spearhead left-wing activities, raising workers' consciousness by
organizing societies and sponsoring publications. Led by John Strachey, whose
The Coming Struggle for Power (1932) proved one of the most influential books of
the decade, middle-class intellectuals set up in 1934 a section of Writers' Inter-

national, chaired by Day-Lewis and represented by the journal *Left Review*. A British branch of Artists International was formed that same year. Politically minded leftist dramatic groups, like Unity Theatre, Left Theatre, and Group Theatre, sprang up. John Grierson's GPO Film Unit launched a revolutionary movement in documentary film. Founded in May 1936, Victor Gollancz's Left Book Club, boasting 57,000 members by 1938, served as the umbrella group for many of these political and cultural activities. It was as close as Britain got to a popular front.[31]

Still, neither the Left Book Club nor these other activities were really popular. Nor did they ever enjoy strong Labour Party support. "Political radicalism was not popular with the masses," wrote Neal Wood in his history of British communist intellectuals. "The intellectuals on the Left were somewhat isolated on the whole. . . . The country tended to be to the right of the intellectuals, as was the government."[32] Nevertheless, participation in socialist programs gave many intellectuals a sense of fellow camaraderie as "radicals," the feeling of being socially useful, of being "in touch" with one another and with "the people."[33] Social malintegration therefore sparked political radicalism, but the partial result was that intellectuals' sense of shared mission integrated the intelligentsia itself. Of course, the interlinked pattern of alienation, malintegration, and radicalization did not cover all intellectuals, nor were those who were alienated and radicalized uniformly and equally so. Yet as Samuels observes:

> By 1935 few young, sensitive English intellectuals could avoid becoming
> either involved in one of the various intellectual organizations established to
> mobilize an attack on fascism, economic depression, and war, or convinced
> of the necessity of making their intellectual products reflect the social crises
> of the period and serve a genuine social function. Artists became socially
> aware, poets socially conscious, writers more didactic . . .[34]

IV

George Orwell, however, was one of these uncommitted few, still without what he called "a political orientation." "By the end of 1935," he recalled in "Why I Write" (1946), "I had still failed to reach a firm decision."[35] That decision was perhaps further complicated by his reported friendship with devout Anglicans, his casual contact with British socialists and Trotskyists, and his serious flirtations with poetry writing and with modernist aestheticism (e.g., his Joycean stylistic experimentation in *A Clergyman's Daughter*, 1935).[36]

Orwell's indecision about his politics in the mid-1930s furnishes a clue to his

lifelong "outsider" stance toward the London intelligentsia. Superficially his career does possess a comparable shape and sequence to those of other 1930s intellectuals: public school, travel abroad, return to teach, occasional journalism, a
"new signature," contact with the British unemployed, embrace of socialism, and
off to Spain. But that narrative abstract masks and bleaches the very different experience which Orwell actually had from most intellectuals of his generation, at
least after public school, and which set him apart from them. Detailed attention
to the trajectory of his career suggests both the fallacy of mechanically linking
class origins with political affiliation and the necessity of injecting a dynamic,
historical dimension into an inquiry on the conditions for intellectuals' political
radicalization.

How and why did Orwell differ from the members of the Auden group and the
majority of other 1930s intellectuals? Three factors stand out, all of them rein-
forcing his antagonism toward English "clubbishness" and shaping his evolving
"outsider" stance toward the London intelligentsia.

First, although Orwell was from the middle class, his family was poorer than
most of those which produced public school boys, from whose ranks the leading intellectuals of his generation emerged. He evidently retained this acute consciousness of his relative poverty throughout his adult years, as the bitterness and
anguish of "Such, Such Were the Joys" suggests.[37]

Second, Orwell was slightly older than the decade's radicals. Although just a
year senior to Day-Lewis, he was four years older than Auden and MacNeice and
fully six years older than Spender. This age difference may account in part for
Orwell's much stronger attachment to pre–World War I England and Edwardian memories. If Cyril Connolly's recollections are accurate, the man born Eric
Blair—who later adopted the pen name George Orwell—had already read much
of Butler, Wells, and Shaw by the time of his entry to Eton (1916), and seems to
have possessed an extraordinarily mature (and fatalistic) outlook on the ultimate
consequences of World War I for the Empire.[38] It is interesting too that in *Coming Up for Air* (1939) Orwell casts George Bowling, the most autobiographical of
Orwell's heroes and a thinly disguised mouthpiece for many of the author's own
views, exactly one decade older than himself. Eric Blair at thirteen evidently
had the political sophistication of Bowling at twenty-three. (Orwell, according to
Richard Rees, felt guilty throughout his adulthood for being too young to serve
in the war—and appropriately enough, Bowling gets wounded in 1916 on a French
battlefield.)[39] It may have been that Blair-Orwell was just over the generational
divide which permitted a passionate identification with the "eternal summer" of
Edwardian England represented by Bowling's long lazy days at the Mill Farm
fishing pond.

A third difference was the crucial one: Blair's Burma police service. His

Burma years put him on a track which was to divide him permanently and irrevocably from his coevals, even after his return home. Virtually all of the leading
intellectuals of the 1930s and 1940s had gone up to Oxford or Cambridge. Very
few intellectuals did not go to some university.[40] At the time that Oxford's literary
"Lads of the Earth" encircled Auden in 1928, Orwell was already back from five
grueling years in Burma—where, as John Wain once remarked, five years would
seem like fifteen in a young Etonian's development.[41] Indeed, Blair had missed
the relatively prosperous 1920s and the dramatic political events that would give
rise to 1930s radicalism: Lloyd George's fall from grace in 1922; the rise to power
in 1923 of the first, short-lived Labour government; and the May 1926 General
Strike, prompted by proposed reductions in the miners' wages. Numerous upper-
and middle-class families viewed the strike as a possible syndicalist revolution in
the making. With their support—and that of hundreds of undergraduates—Stan-
ley Baldwin's Conservative government put down the strike. The Auden group
watched from a distance and treated the whole affair as springtime amusement.
Quite probably Orwell met some of these same miners exactly a decade later at
Wigan.

Blair had also missed the heyday of the literary revolution. By the early 1920s
Eliot's *Waste Land* (1922) and Joyce's *Ulysses* (1922), and also the doctrines of
the publicists of modernism (e.g., Pound, Hulme, Ford Madox Ford), had begun to filter down to the Oxbridge undergraduates. When Blair returned from
Paris at Christmas 1929, having spent little more than six months in England
during the previous seven years, many of his peers were already well established in literary London, and the new Auden era of committed political art was
dawning.[42]

This personal history may suggest that Orwell was always one step behind his
generation and therefore forever playing intellectual "catch-up" in the 1930s. The
political, and even the literary, evidence is copious. For instance, by choice and
circumstance, Orwell never felt completely at home with the modernists and the
"committed" writers of the 30s: the Victorian and Edwardian avant-garde of his
boyhood (Dickens, Charles Reade, Butler, Gissing, Wells) remained his favorite
novelists. Thus, he was still reading the advanced writers of two decades earlier,
went to Paris to live like a bohemian when the "poet-in-the-garret" vogue about
Paris was ending, and saw lower-class life from the gutter up when the university
youths were editing manifestos and publishing books.

Yet this way of explaining Orwell's development—as if he experienced a literary-political lag vis-à-vis his generation as a result of having gone to Burma
rather than university—frames a comparison which, once again, rests on a superficial appearance of mere belatedness to his contemporaries. But it is not just that
his experience was *later;* his experience was *different* from theirs, and he learned

different things from it. He did, it is true, come to fashions when they were no longer fashionable. For example, like some of his contemporaries, he reached political consciousness abroad. But whereas they arrived en bloc as a politicized coterie, he arrived alone, and his stance, unlike theirs, was never simply that of a spectator. Orwell *lived* with the tramps and miners; he *fought* at the Aragon front (significantly, with the POUM dissident Marxist militia rather than the Stalinist-controlled International Brigades), not merely visited it like Auden and Spender (or like the numerous British delegates to the 1937 International Conference of Writers Against War and Fascism in Valencia). Orwell engaged so deeply in the events of the decade that he could digest and reflect on them only some-what later—approximately when the intellectual spectators, who had observed events at a distance, were no longer caught up in them. But this participant-witness stance, as an outsider able to feelingly describe what he has seen "from the inside,"[43] gave Orwell valuable psychological distance (and subsequently, high credibility and immense authority) which most intellectuals of his genera-tion did not possess.[44] When Orwell made a decision, as he did in 1936–1937 to embrace democratic socialism, it was a firm and enduring one.

The fact is, as Samuels remarks in a passage already quoted, Orwell belonged . to "a generation he was in but never part of"; he stood outside "a movement he toyed with but never joined."[45] He could stand outside precisely because, in the most literal sense, he was never part of "the Auden generation"—nor of any other. His Burma years had placed him among working-class men slightly older than himself, many of whom had served in World War I; and even after Burma and Paris in the mid-1930s in Hampstead, he associated not with his coevals but mainly with provincial university graduates and other bohemians (e.g., Rayner Heppenstall, Michael Sayers) eight to ten years younger than himself. Some of them looked upon thirty-two-year-old Eric Blair, in Heppenstall's phrase, as "a nice old thing, a kindly eccentric"—"ill-read," middlebrow, without a university degree, and always going on insufferably about Butler, the *Magnet*, and comic postcards.[46]

Thus Orwell found himself always between and outside generations, not just political groups.[47] That, too, is why his mature experience was so "different" from that of the Auden group, and it is revealing that Hynes opens and closes *The Auden Generation* with quotations from Orwell's oeuvre.[48] Orwell possessed nei-ther the generational consciousness of "the Auden generation," which is acquired only by shared participation in psychologically decisive events, nor that of the younger and older generational groups in Hampstead and Burma with which he associated. Yet this separation from his contemporaries, especially in the case of his contact with the provincial graduates, probably helped form Orwell's quix-otic, plain-speaking character: he could be less inhibited with such youthful, unthreatening, still unestablished fellow bohemians, caring little that they disagreed with or mocked him. Generational discontinuity thus nourished Orwell's natural antinomianism, inadvertently furnishing him with a setting in which he could do his own thinking, draw on his own experience, and work out his own positions without the pressure to bend to the institutional and intellectual authority of his already successful contemporaries.[49] As Bernard Crick observes:

> His time-out in Burma had made him older than most of the young writers still leading this kind of "floating life"; but it also gave him an emotional detachment from them and immunized him from fashion. (*GO*, 177–178)

Indeed, the singularity of Orwell's early manhood, marked by police work in Burma rather than attendance at Oxbridge, further helps explain the specifics of the distinctive arc of his career in the late 1930s and early 1940s: his exceptional responses to the course of the Spanish Civil War, to the revelations about Stalin's crimes, and to the changing CPGB line. What may have seemed Orwell's non-university "untrained mind," as Crick notes, turned out to be a fiercely independent radical's *untamed* mind.[50]

Typically, Orwell arrived at the Spanish war late, after the fighting had been on for nearly half a year (December 1936) and just as some leading British Marxist intellectuals (e.g., Ralph Fox, David Guest) were killed in action. The Loyalists' prospects were already dimming by the time Orwell was defending Barcelona in May 1937, and most intellectuals in 1937–38 were quickly growing disillusioned with Stalinism and Left politics. Precisely at this moment, in the face of Franco's looming triumph and the Stalinists' suppression of POUM and other non-communist militias, Orwell was wholeheartedly committing himself to socialism and penning his eloquent *Homage to Catalonia* (1938). "I have seen wonderful things," he wrote Cyril Connolly from his Barcelona sickbed in June 1937, after having narrowly escaped death from a throat wound, "& at last really believe in socialism, which I never did before" (*CEJL*, 1:269). Very few other returning leftists felt the same. And for the intellectuals who stayed home, their skin-deep commitment to socialism was waning, largely as a result of an avalanche of evidence no longer deniable about Stalin's betrayal of the Revolution during the 1930s: the Kirov murder, the brutal extermination of the kulaks, the deliberate scheme of mass famine in the Ukraine, the labor camps, the wholesale purges of rival Party members, the show trials of fellow Old Bolsheviks, the ferocious repression of all dissent. Just at the time when most Left intellectuals were beginning to doubt the Marxist pieties, Orwell had met his Italian militiaman in Catalonia and found his communitarian vision.

For Orwell had never been attached to Marxism, Stalin, or Russia, unlike most

1930s radicals, and so he (unlike the Auden group, the Webbs, Kingsley Martin and the *New Statesman*, and thousands of other CPGB members and fellow-travelers) had nothing to lose by branding "the Soviet myth"—"the belief that Russia is a socialist country"—for what it was. The USSR, he declared, "embodied the corruption of the original idea of Socialism" (*CEJL*, 3:404–405). While many British leftists became defensive about the transformation of Bolshevism into "oligarchical collectivism," Orwell only became more confirmed in his negative judgment of Stalinism, which he claimed to have arrived at as early as 1931—long before the purges and show trials, the Spanish war, and the 1939 Ribbentrop-Molotov pact.

To CPGB members like Day-Lewis and Spender, Russia was "the god that failed." Not for Orwell. For he had already experienced his period of disillusionment, much earlier in Burma. He had seen "the dirty work of Empire at close quarters"—and he had hated and finally rejected it (*CEJL*, 1:236). His attempts to expunge his guilt and his search for social reintegration followed in Paris, London, and Spain. By the time his fellow intellectuals were touting the organized efficiency of the Soviet state, Orwell's Burma years had confirmed and deepened his "natural hatred of authority" (*CEJL*, 1:4). This early experience—his ordeal in Burma and his subsequent vocational and political crises in the 1920s and early 1930s—was probably no less traumatic than his contemporaries' agonized reappraisal of Stalinism and communism a decade later. It did, however, act as an ideological vaccine: he became no Stalinist dupe. Thus, what Orwell once described as a waste of five years in a tropical swamp actually may have inoculated him against leader worship and literary cliques, and thereby saved him from the more serious political errors of his generation, particularly "the stupid cult of Russia" (*RWP*, 216). He had "chucked" Burma; many of his contemporaries would not do the same with Stalin and the CPGB until years later. In this respect Orwell was not only behind but also ahead of his generation, as well as between and outside it.[51]

When his intellectual contemporaries finally did repudiate communism, as Orwell pointed out in "Inside the Whale," the "something to believe in" which they embraced was not a political party line but rather a religious orthodoxy or aesthetic doctrine (*CEJL*, 1:515). Many intellectuals in the 1930s and 1940s discovered the Anglican or Catholic Church; others opted out of politics and rededicated themselves to Art. Cyril Connolly's editorial policy in the inaugural issue of *Horizon* (March 1940) ushered in the latter aspect of the new mood of the 1940s: "Our standards are aesthetic, and our politics are in abeyance." Or as Connolly put it two years later in *The Unquiet Grave:* "The true function of a writer is to produce a masterpiece . . . no other task is of any importance."[52]

The turn toward Art in 1940 was, however, sharply different from the case of

Orwell at the BBC, recording one of his *Voice* magazine programs. *Left to right, stand-ing:* Orwell, Nancy Parratt (secretary), and William Empson. *Sitting:* Venu Chitale, J. M. Tambimuttu, T. S. Eliot, Una Marson, Mulk Raj Anand, Christopher Pemberton, and Narayana Menon. *Voice,* the monthly radio magazine program in the Eastern Service of the BBC, was first broadcast in 1942.

the 1920s: whereas the undergraduates of the 1920s rebelled via Art, young and maturing intellectuals of the 1940s escaped into it. Whereas political detachment was the posture of the 1920s and commitment that of the 1930s, disenchantment was the attitude of the 1940s. One notes here that radicalism and conservatism can take many forms. Religious or aesthetic radicalism may not only accommo-date but also often entail political quietism. What determined the outbreak of radicalism in a specifically political form in the 1930s was in part British intel-lectuals' recent rejection of other possible manifestations: God was already dead and Art had failed as Hulmean "spilt religion." In the middle of a depression and within a revolution eastward already succeeding, Marxism and Russia offered in-tellectuals of the day a model and a plan of action.

By the decade's close, however, many leading London Left intellectuals were politically deradicalized. The advent of World War II catalyzed the process by giving them something productive to do *as intellectuals*—in the BBC, the Minis-

try of Information, the War Office selection boards, military intelligence—and
thereby reintegrating them into society.[53] "Probably in no belligerent country
had the intelligentsia volunteered so wholeheartedly as in England to serve the
State at war," Fyvel later observed. "The meaningful social integration which had
been talked about in the Thirties was suddenly easier."[54] The English tradition
of intellectuals' cooperative participation in government and official politics—or
what one critic has termed the venerable British practice of "massive cooptation
of intellectuals by the State"[55]—had reasserted itself. It would continue largely
undisturbed—through the war years, the Labour government under Clement
Attlee, and the consensus politics of "Butskellism"—until the Suez crisis and the
birth of the New Left in 1956–1957.[56]

Because Orwell was so alienated from and malintegrated within the London
Left intelligentsia, however, he was never quite so well socially reintegrated as
a BBC broadcaster in the early 1940s, either. The ideological moderation characteristic of most other wartime Left intellectuals began at a time when Orwell
was at his most revolutionary and optimistic about the possibilities for an English socialist revolution (1939–1941). In *The Lion and the Unicorn* (1941), he argued that the war would transform Britain into a democratic socialist nation. It
was not his hope alone, but few others held such a rosy view, and his own faith
soon dimmed.[57] Although he enjoyed much of the social contact of his BBC work,
he formally resumed his stance as intellectual outsider and radical iconoclast in
1943, eagerly accepting the literary editorship of *Tribune*, Aneunin Bevin's still
struggling dissident Left paper.

V

This brief sketch of the interrelations among the Left intelligentsia, British politics in the 1930s, and Orwell's development highlights important theoretical issues
and inadequacies in the accepted sociology of intellectuals. For the intellectual
is that difficult creature, neither worker nor owner. He is, as it were, ideologically
ambidextrous according to the literature of the sociology of occupations, which
argues variously that the intellectual invariably serves the elite, allies with the
workers, constitutes a separate class, and is essentially "classless."[58]

Thus, functionalists (S. N. Eisenstadt, Daniel Bell) have portrayed intellectuals as gradually becoming co-opted into the service of the presiding bureaucracy.
They become what the neo-Marxist C. Wright Mills in *White Collar* (1951) termed
"Brains, INC." and experience embourgeoisement. Classical Marxist sociology
has also cast the intellectual within the middle class as a petit bourgeois, a tag
once much applied by Stalinist critics of Orwell and generating more heat than
light. Conversely, neo-Marxists (Bettina Aptheker, Alain Touraine), influenced

by New Left social theory, have taken the opposing view that the intellectual's institutional incorporation effectively "proletarianizes" him, making him a wage earner. The necessity for teams to pursue sophisticated scientific projects, the modern corporation's demand for the expertise of a wide range of specialist consultants, and the existence of large bureaucratic research staffs alienate intellectuals from the fruits of their labor. They become radicalized "Brain Workers." Classical and recent elite theorists (Robert Michel, Alvin Gouldner) have held that intellectuals constitute a class in their own right, a "New Class." In developing countries they often form the political elite; under advanced capitalism intellectuals become a credentialed professional class deriving income and status from their "cultural capital" (technical and language skills). Finally, in his *Ideology and Utopia* (1929), the first influential discussion of intellectuals via the sociology of knowledge, Karl Mannheim characterized them famously as "a relatively classless stratum which is not too firmly situated in the social order." Mannheim held that intellectuals constitute a unique, socially "rootless" class of their own whose spiritual preoccupations enable them to transcend ordinary, material class interests. Intellectuals emerge from various classes, and their education, rather than their class origins, decisively shapes their development and unites them in political outlook. Their education makes it possible for them to place "ideals before interests," in Martin Malia's phrase, to see political issues sensitively and with an open mind. Intellectuals thus *choose* their partisan affiliations; their class background is a secondary influence.[59]

The case of Orwell and his contemporaries makes clear how and where these theories fall short as heuristic tools for understanding the relationship between interwar politics and the British intellectual. The old Marxist notion of class origins as the lifelong determinant of political allegiance is obviously insufficient. Although Orwell had a similar middle-class birth and rearing to that of most '30s intellectuals, his course in the educational system and his subsequent occupational experience led him to adopt an outsider stance toward the intelligentsia at large—for example, his early anti-Stalinism and brief active membership in the anti-war Independent Labour Party (1938–1939).

Nor are intellectuals necessarily "embourgeoisified"—or radicalized—by government or official institutional employment. For many intellectuals in the 1930s who were formerly dislocated from English society, wartime service brought reintegration and a renewed feeling of usefulness, identity, and power. For Orwell, however, the war years first brightened and then clouded his socialist hopes, and he sought by 1943 to escape integration and London for independent work and greater privacy (e.g., his purchase in 1944–1945 of a home on Jura in the Scottish Hebrides). The divergence of Orwell from the patterned responses of his generation makes it imperative to approach the multivalent relationships among class, education, occupation, and partisan affiliation in dynamic, concrete, and interpersonal terms, rather than simply according to theoretical paradigms: the conditions of political allegiances are not reducible to a single factor or invariable structural pattern.

Yet this does not mean that the intellectual constitutes a separate class or is socially unanchored, as the elite theorists and Mannheim, respectively, have argued. Rather, as Brym notes, and as the case of Orwell's distinctive career exemplifies, it is to intellectuals' *shifting* patterns or *rootedness* that attention must be paid, to the dynamics of political affiliation and disaffiliation.[60] The case of Orwell points up, in the first place, the significance of how *evolving* intellectual attachments to *other* mass agents (the British worker, the British war machine) and "generational consciousness" condition partisan affiliation. The intellectual is not "relatively classless" and "rootless" but rather variously and complexly rooted in the spongy, ever-malleable soil of social and historical relations. His political behavior can therefore only be understood by appreciating the institutional web and stages of his complicated mobility pattern within and among classes and groups—that is, by scrutinizing the course of his class origins, education, and employment and career experience. As Brym, following Gramsci, notes, partisan allegiance is not noncausal but radically contingent:

> . . . intellectuals' partisan loyalties [are not] mere mechanical and static responses to their current class and other group locations. . . . In order to explain intellectuals' partisan affiliations one must trace their paths of social mobility, from their origins to their social destinations, as these are shaped by the capacity of classes and other groups to expand the institutional milieu through which they pass in the course of their careers. . . . [T]he determination of intellectuals' ideological outlooks is really a problem of multivariate causation. That is to say, social origins, school, and economic and political opportunities are independent causes of political allegiance, and one variable may reinforce or, at the other extreme, cancel out the effects of another.[61]

Thus, unlike Orwell, British intellectuals in the 1930s were radicalized during or after their university years; their disenchantment with communism late in the decade and absorption into the literary Establishment and the war bureaucracy produced political moderates. On the other hand, Orwell's Burma service, his "belated" bohemianism, and the Wigan Pier and Spain trips radicalized him and effectively "canceled out" the integrative potential of his BBC work. The political orientations and actions of intellectuals evolve according to their career mobility paths. No single general factor conditions or freezes their partisan affiliations.

Moreover, contrary to what Gouldner and Mannheim imply, the example of

Orwell makes clear that "*the* intelligentsia" is not monolithic. Nor does education lead to uniform intellectual-political outlooks, as the postwar decline of the Left's dominance of intellectual life and the rise of strong conservative and neoconservative intellectual movements throughout the West in the 1970s and 1980s demonstrate. Despite our casual use of the word *intelligentsia* in the singular, intellectuals constitute a multiform, heterogeneous stratum whose members' diverse ideologies are linked to various mass institutional groups and classes (business, labor, working-class movements, etc.). Intellectuals do not constitute an ideological bloc, and even in the 1930s in Britain the degree and intensity of their radicalism was by no means uniform.

Third and finally, what this chapter suggests about the frenzied embrace of communism by European intellectuals throughout the West in the 1930s also problematizes Mannheim's thesis that intellectuals grandly "choose" their political allegiances, dispassionately and with reasoned calculation, as if immune to the historical pressures acting upon lesser men. Intellectuals do *in part* choose their loyalties, as do other historical actors, but their choices are enabled and constrained by their historical situation. The personal and group histories of intellectuals are bound up in social history, just the same as that of other individuals and groups. Hence the need to enrich the political sociology of intellectuals within the empirical concreteness of intellectual history: one must approach the study of their political allegiances in historical and social context, for intellectuals' ideas are developed in an engagement within events, and that can be understood only via an attempt to recover that engagement.[62]

VI

Orwell's independent stance toward the Left intelligentsia of his generation furnishes one man's answer by word and deed to a normative issue in the sociology of intellectuals. Indeed it is a topic with an even longer history of controversy than the previous historical and conceptual ones: Does the intellectual have a "proper" social function? What should be his special role, if any, in the modern age of ubiquitous ideology and totalitarian politics?[63] The adversaries alternately define these questions in terms of personal integrity (Julien Benda, Ortega y Gasset, Allen Tate) and social responsibility (Trotsky, Sartre).[64]

The locus classicus of the traditionalist position advocating intellectual disengagement from politics is Benda's *La trahison des clercs* (1927). Writing in the aftermath of World War I, Benda saw the danger of the intellectual's Hegelian tendency to spiritualize history and political leaders, to "deny God and then shift Him to man and his political work."[65] Instead, Benda argued that the intellectual, the rightful heir of the medieval clerk, betrayed his vocation and legacy if he abandoned the universal and attached himself to the particular and practical. In opposition to Benda's view has been the Marxist-existentialist "responsible art- ist" position. Radicals and existentialists have argued that the rise of totalitari- anism ushered in a new age of pervasive ideology, in which all cultural activity is politicized and therefore precludes the luxury of detachment. The intellectual "objectively" supports injustice and tyranny by political disengagement. He must be willing to "change" the world, not just "interpret" it—to risk getting "dirty hands," per the title of one of Sartre's plays.

Orwell stands firmly in the latter tradition, but in a characteristically unortho- dox way. His pragmatic stance signals a reluctant commitment that is spiritual in its defiant insistence on a higher, objective, this-worldly truth. In "Writers and Leviathan" (1948) he gave his ambivalent answer to the question of the intel- lectual's "proper" social function. Acknowledging the "invasion of literature by politics," Orwell insisted on "the need to take sides politically" in "an age of State control."[66] The totalitarian leviathan had to be confronted and resisted. "Keep- ing out of politics" was not possible, Orwell said. One possibility presented itself: the split self. Orwell urged *engagement*, but only on the condition that the writer- citizen divide himself in two—and that the "literary" self remain untainted:

> . . . we should draw a sharper distinction than we do at present between our political and literary loyalties, and should recognize that a willingness to do certain distasteful but necessary things does not carry with it any obligation to swallow the beliefs that usually go within them. When a writer engages in politics, he should do so as a citizen, as a human being, but not as a writer. I do not think that he has the right, merely on the score of his sensibilities, to shirk the ordinary dirty work of politics. Just as much as anyone else, he should be prepared to deliver lectures in draughty halls, to chalk pavements, to canvass voters, to distribute leaflets, even to fight in civil wars if it seems necessary. But whatever else he does in the service of his party, he should never write for it. He should make it clear that his writing is a thing apart. (*CEJL*, 4:412)

To get one's hands dirty yet keep one's spirit clean: this was Orwell's pained compromise. He recognized that his stance amounted to an "orthodoxy" like any other, insofar as it entailed "unresolved contradictions" (*CEJL*, 4:411). He was not blind to the tensions in his position:

> To suggest that a creative writer, in a time of conflict, must split himself into two compartments, may seem defeatist or frivolous: yet in practice I do not see what else he can do. To lock yourself up in an ivory tower is impossible

and undesirable. To yield subjectively, not merely to a party machine, but even to a group ideology, is to destroy yourself as a writer. (*CEJL*, 4:413)

Caught between the ivory tower and the party machine, "between the priest and the commissar," as Orwell put it in a 1936 poem, one had to reject both (*CEJL*, 1:5). Politics was merely another aspect of the supreme dilemma which he had first identified at St. Cyprian's: "The good and the possible never seemed to coincide" (*CEJL*, 4:360). Politics was always a choice of lesser evils, "and there are some situations from which one can only escape by acting like a devil or a lunatic" (*CEJL*, 4:413). These escape routes, which are associated with the aestheticism of a Dali and the derangement of a Pound, respectively, Orwell himself would never take. The quandary of commitment versus detachment was *the* torturous predicament of the modern intellectual as citizen-artist, and it could be neither evaded nor reconciled. Orwell rightly saw that the writer faced the general problem in a particularly acute way:

If you have to take part . . . and I think you do . . . then you also have to keep a part of yourself inviolate. For most people the problem does not arise in the same form, because their lives are split already. They are truly alive only in their leisure hours, and there is no emotional connection between their work and their political activities. Nor are they generally asked, in the name of political loyalty, to debase themselves as workers. The artist, and especially the writer, is asked just that—in fact, it is the only thing that politicians ever ask of him. (*CEJL*, 4:413–414)

Orwell finally, in effect, argued that the writer's spiritual self, the noble Don Quixote inside him, could and must act independently of the fat little Sancho Panza within:

If [the intellectual] refuses [to compromise himself], that does not mean that he is condemned to inactivity. One half of him, which in a sense is the whole of him, can act as resolutely, even as violently if need be, as anyone else. But his writings, in so far as they have any value, will always be the product of the saner self that stands aside, records the things that are done and admits their necessity, but refuses to be deceived as to their true nature.[67]

To love truth more than power: that was Orwell's injunction to his fellow intellectuals. The special function of the intellectual in a totalitarian age was to bear witness to historical and political Truth—the "record" as objective reality and social fact. Orwell's allegiance to "truth" was the screeching brake to his political commitment; it guided and limited his ideological sympathies and political involvements, and beyond or outside that limit he would not go.

Orwell's key example of the intellectuals' collective self-betrayal of their trust was, of course, the issue of Stalinism: "The sin of nearly all left-wingers since 1933 is that they have wanted to be anti-fascist without being anti-totalitarian" (*CEJL*, 3:125).

His harsh criticism of Stalinism derived, not from any reflexive anti-communism, but from his concern with truth-telling, freedom, and justice. After Spain, Orwell saw his "truth" being most threatened by the continuing Stalinist bent of the British Left. In his journalism after his return from Spain, he campaigned energetically to publicize what he learned from his experience of POUM's suppression in Barcelona, and he felt ostracized because he was challenging a party line. That feeling endured and deepened. In 1944 Orwell told his friend John Middleton Murry, a wartime pacifist:

> I consider that willingness to criticize Russia and Stalin is *the* test of intellectual honesty. It is the only thing that from a literary intellectual's point of view that is really dangerous. . . . The thing that needs courage is to attack Russia, the only thing that the greater part of the British intelligentsia now believe in. . . . But to be anti-Russian makes enemies, whereas the other [criticism of British imperialism] doesn't—i.e., not such enemies as people like us would care about. (*CEJL*, 3:203)

Indeed, Orwell made it clear in a 1946 exchange with communist Randall Swingler that he considered calculated appeals to emerging anti-communist intellectual orthodoxy just as corrupt as a reflexive pro-communism. His reply to Swingler seems almost prescient in light of the rise of McCarthyism in 1950:

> In five years it may be as dangerous to praise Stalin as it was to attack him two years ago. But I should not regard this as an advance. Nothing is gained by teaching a parrot a new word. What is needed is the right to print what one believes to be true, without having to fear bullying or blackmail from any side.[68]

VII

However satisfactory Orwell's attempt to negotiate between the Scylla and Charybdis of commitment and detachment, contemporary advocates of both traditional positions—the intellectual as activist and as *clerc*—have hailed Orwell for his praxis, if not for his theory. To Noam Chomsky, Orwell is no dispassionate critic but the model of "the responsible intellectual," whose documentary "honesty, decency, and concern with the facts" in *Homage to Catalonia* signified his exemplary commitment to democratic socialism.[69] To John Wain, Orwell the truth-teller was the intelligentsia's relentless critic, whose role was to "keep their consciences alive": "As for his relevance, who can feel that the situation that faces free men has changed much from what it was in the '30s and '40s. The thing to be feared is still a *trahison des clercs:* freedom still needs to be defended against those whom Nature most favours, whom she showers with advantages."[70]

As Wain notes, to argue, as some New Left critics have done, that Orwell, given his pragmatic ethos and distaste for theory, was no intellectual whatsoever, is to misconceive the nature of his intellectuality and of his dispute with his fellow radical intellectuals. For Orwell indicted precisely their cowardly flight into Abstraction, their "pea-and-thimble trick with those mysterious entities, thesis, antithesis, and synthesis . . ." (*RWP*, 177). He was indeed their harshest critic; he held them to the same ruthlessly severe standards that he set for himself.[71] As the intelligentsia's scourge, particularly toward his own side, he may thereby seem "the supreme example of the intellectual who hated intellectuals."[72]

But this elides the point; in fact, Orwell hated not intellectuals but rather their readiness to do dirt on the intellect and betray their spiritual vocation: the defense of truth, liberty, *and* social justice. Orwell was no intellectual-baiter. He mercilessly criticized the intelligentsia's literary cliques "just because I do take the function of the intelligentsia seriously."

To keep civilization's conscience alive, thought Orwell, was the intelligentsia's function, and his own self-appointed task did indeed become to keep the consciences of the intellectuals themselves alive. He castigated their equivocations about Stalinist Russia and their prolix jargon "not because they are intellectuals but because they [are] not . . . true intellectuals." True intellectuals thought and spoke clearly, independently, and courageously. Clique members took their ideas and language prefabricated.[73]

By this standard, Orwell was indeed a "true" intellectual. Furthermore, his criticism was almost always directed at social*ists,* not social*ism:* he railed at socialists because he wanted socialist intellectuals to be worthy of socialism. A "conscience of the Left" *does* criticize from within; and though Orwell may sometimes have been the guilty or excessively scrupulous "wintry conscience of his generation," he flayed the Left intelligentsia in order to fortify it, not to weaken or abandon it.[74] In this respect his distinctive career not only illumines the complex conditions underlying the formation and fluctuations of intellectual rebellion, adaptation, and radicalization. It also serves, as so many admirers of George Orwell have testified, as one example of how a person of conscience may live the intellectual life.

John Wain, mid-1950s.

CHAPTER TWO

"A Moral Genius"

Orwell and the Movement Writers of the 1950s

Although Orwell's significance for understanding the London Left of the interwar and wartime era is well-known, it is also true that no British writer has had a greater impact on the Anglo-American generation which came of age in the decade following World War II than George Orwell. His influence was deeply felt by intellectuals from his own and the next generation of all political stripes, including the Marxist Left (Raymond Williams, E. P. Thompson), the anarchist Left (George Woodcock, Nicolas Walter), the American liberal-Left (Irving Howe), American neoconservatives (Norman Podhoretz), and the Anglo-American Catholic Right (Christopher Hollis, Russell Kirk).[1]

Perhaps Orwell's broadest imprint, however, was stamped upon the only *literary* group which has ever regarded him as a model: the Movement writers of the 1950s. Unlike the above-mentioned groups, which have consisted almost entirely of political intellectuals rather than writers—and whose members have responded to him as a political critic first and a writer second—some of the Movement writers saw Orwell not just as a political intellectual but also as the man of letters and/or literary stylist whom they aspired to be.

The Movement writers were primarily an alliance of poet-critics. The "official" members numbered nine poets and novelists; a few other writers and critics loomed on the periphery. Their acknowledged genius, if not leading publicist, was Philip Larkin (who later was offered the post of Britain's poet laureate, but refused it). Orwell's plain voice influenced the tone and attitude of Larkin's poetry and those of several other Movement poets, especially Robert Conquest and D. J. Enright.[2] But Orwell shone as an even brighter presence among the poet-novelists, particularly John Wain (1925–1994) and Kingsley Amis (1922–1996), both of whom I interviewed about their lifelong preoccupation with Orwell. Both Wain and Amis openly acknowledged that Orwell's example deeply influenced them as prose writers—and that their early fictional anti-heroes were direct descendants of Gordon Comstock in *Keep the Aspidistra Flying* (1936) and George Bowling in *Coming Up for Air* (1939).

For Wain above all, Orwell was a literary-intellectual model, "a moral hero."[3] Wain's admiration for Orwell—unlike Amis's—never wavered; he cherished, and mused on, the unfulfilled tributes to him in the 1950s as "Orwell's natural successor." Ever afterward he continued to hold fast to "the rope that . . . connect[s] me directly with you," however frayed his Orwell connection sometimes seemed to unsympathetic observers and however rough-and-tumble his tug-of-war with other political intellectuals for Orwell's mantle sometimes became.[4] Into the 1990s, Orwell remained a constant presence in Wain's life, though his history of impassioned response modulated with changes in his personal life and the literary-political scene.

This chapter centers on Wain's reception of Orwell, periodically comparing it to Amis's response and placing them in the contexts of both the Movement's history and larger political currents. Wain's and the Movement writers' image of Orwell developed against a wide panorama of cultural history, evolving in four stages. This reception history alters focus through the Movement's ascendancy in the mid-1950s, through its breakup in the late 1950s and its members' growing fear of totalitarianism in the early 1960s, through the years of the New Left and Vietnam War, and finally through the Reagan-Thatcher era of renewed East-West hostility. Like Amis and most other Movement writers, Wain in the 1960s and 1970s adopted Toryism ("Experience is a Tory," Amis once quipped)[5] and a fierce anti-Communism—and, in turn, projected a sharply ideological, indeed curmudgeonly, conservative image of Orwell. In searching for the Orwell in himself, that is, Wain came to spotlight the John Wain that he perceived in George Orwell. He even went so far in 1983, with the political showdown that would lead to the longest miners' strike in British history looming, as to try to explain in an open letter to "Dear George Orwell" why Orwell's sympathetic view of the miners (recounted in *The Road to Wigan Pier*) was obsolete and why Wain's harder line toward trade unionism was necessary.[6] Wain's reception history of Orwell thus constitutes not only a barometer of the fluctuations in the postwar British cultural climate and a glimpse into the ideology and aspirations of an important group in British literary history. It also furnishes insight into the mentality of a postwar generation who have agonized over their status as successors to the 1930s radicals, as latecomers deprived of "good brave causes"—and who have not infrequently justified their rightward turns by pointing to the example of the author of the quietist "Inside the Whale" and the anti-totalitarian *Nineteen Eighty-Four*. Ultimately Wain's response also raises larger conceptual questions—pursued herein only suggestively—about the dynamics of literary response, the nature of author-reader relationships, the formation of readers' identities, the construction of intellectual genealogies, and the sociology of artistic reputation.

I

The Movement belongs to both the history of publicity and the history of poetry. The group's rise to prominence owed partly to the BBC-radio Third Programme broadcasts made by twenty-eight-year-old Wain in 1953 ("First Reading"), in which he aired published Movement poems and works-in-progress, and also to favorable promotions by sympathetic literary journalists at the *Spectator* (e.g., Anthony Hartley, a fringe member of the group). Charter documents include Wain's *Hurry on Down* (1953), Amis's *Lucky Jim* (1954), and the Movement anthologies *Poets of the 1950s* (1955, edited by Enright) and *New Lines* (1956, edited by Conquest). Officially launched in March 1954 when the literary editor of the *Spectator*, J. D. Scott, first tagged several of the writers with the label, the Movement was a tight alliance of old Oxford friends (Larkin, Amis, Wain) and of postgraduate acquaintances of similar age from London literary circles in the early 1950s.[7]

The Movement fitted and formed the temper of postwar reconstruction. In the aftermath of a global war and in the shadow of the Bomb, Wain has recalled, the Movement writers felt "the impulse to *build*." Writing "regular and disciplined verse forms" seemed to them a stay against postwar exhaustion and ennui; it was a small effort "to make something amid the ruins."[8] Orwell's limpid style and pragmatic ethos served as blueprint and cornerstone; his empirical, workaday sensibility undergirded the Movement's call to reassert order, tradition, and restraint.[9] His example and the Movement's priorities seemed to match the decade's, an Arnoldian epoch of concentration, or more exactly "consolidation," rather than expansion.[10] In revolt against the obscurantism of Eliot's followers, the agitprop verse of the 1930s, the apocalyptic mysticism of some wartime pacifists, and the neo-Romanticism of Dylan Thomas, the Movement poets exalted (in Wain's words) "the return to a more level tone, the disappearance of panache and prophetic pomp, . . . the submission to a new discipline of form, the refusal to make large gestures."[11] Formal strictness, clear expression, concrete imagery, and a controlled voice summed up the Movement credo. The Movement writers maintained that poetry was a form of public communication, not an occasion for display of personality or ideological solidarity. Given their emphasis on reason, ordinary language, familiar allusions, everyday feelings, accessibility, and the wider audience, it is hardly surprising that they came to admire Orwell's lucid, straightforward prose and demonstrable appeal to the general reading public.

During the opening phase of his reception (c. 1950–1956), Orwell stood be-

Robert Conquest, 1966. Courtesy of Robert Conquest.

fore the Movement writers explicitly as a literary-intellectual figure. Most highly
valued were Orwell's realistic novels and essays, three new collections of which
appeared during this period (1950, 1953, 1956). Orwell was not a great novelist or
artist, the Movement writers agreed. But he was practically the only twentieth-
century Englishman to whom the Movement novelists could turn for examples
of "the compromising hero," as Blake Morrison has observed.[12] The picaresque
anti-heroes in Wain's *Hurry on Down*, or Amis's *Lucky Jim* and *That Uncertain
Feeling* (1956)—so ambivalent toward issues of class and inequality, social "compromise" and "adjustment," bourgeois "conventionality," and political involvement—closely echo the confused, alienated Gordon Comstock of *Keep the Aspidistra Flying*. Moreover, as a critic, Wain insisted in 1954, Orwell was "as good as any

in English literature."[13] Wain argued that the permanent value of Orwell's work lay in his criticism; indeed, he speculated that a piece like "Lear, Tolstoy and the Fool" would ultimately gain more readers than *Animal Farm*.[14]

The Movement was attracted not merely to Orwell's prose technique but also to his literary persona. "Literary integrity" and "moral uprightness" go "hand in hand," Wain argued, casually accepting that *le style c'est l'homme*.

> It was Orwell's aim to forge a style in which it would be *impossible* to tell lies. . . . That bareness, that clarity, that directness, that fertility in images drawn from everyday life could only be achieved by two means: first, constant vigilance and imitation of the best models; second, by being that kind of person. In reading a page of Orwell one knows instinctively, even without knowing anything about his personal story, that here was a man who would be prepared to give his life for what he believed in. There is no short cut; a pusillanimous man cannot write a forthright prose; if he tries, he will sink into heartiness and that is all.[15]

That closing verdict could apply as self-criticism; even in the 1950s, and more so in his later years, Wain's prose sometimes degenerated into "Jolly Jack" bluffness or mannered bluntness.[16] But no Movement writer contested Wain's high assessment of Orwell's character. Indeed, already by 1954, J. D. Scott noted in the *Spectator* that "admiration for . . . Orwell above all" represented a "sign by which you may recognize the Movement."[17] Conquest's memorial poem ("George Orwell") is a eulogy to a "moral genius":

> Moral and mental glaciers melting slightly
> Betray the influence of his warm intent.
> Because he taught us what the actual meant
> The vicious winter grips its prey less tightly.
>
> We die of words. For touchstones he restored
> The real person, real event or thing;
> —And thus we see not war but suffering
> As the conjunction to be most abhorred.
> He shared with a great world, for greater ends,
> That honesty, a curious cunning virtue
> You share with just the few who won't desert you,
> A dozen writers, half-a-dozen friends.[18]

In his introduction to *New Lines*, Conquest added:

> One might, without stretching matters too far, say that George Orwell with
> his principle of real rather than ideological integrity, exerted, even though
> indirectly, one of the major influences on modern poetry.[19]

The Movement writers therefore embraced not only Orwell's "pure" prose style
but also his "authentic" style of life. They strongly identified with their image of
"the man within the writings," with Orwell's trustworthy, "decent" voice in his
essays and documentaries. Wain's recollections, sometimes directly addressed to
Orwell, possess group significance:

> I had no political opinions, except a vague general sympathy with the social
> revolution that started in England in 1945. . . . As I gradually came to have
> some notion of politics, both domestic and international, it was two books
> of yours, *The Road to Wigan Pier* and *Homage to Catalonia*, that opened my
> eyes most. . . . I knew I was hearing the voice of a decent, unselfish man,
> ready to make sacrifices for others, while at the same time enjoying his own
> life and getting on with it; and also the voice of a writer, which I hoped to be.
>   I was twenty-five when you died, and I shall never forget the shock,
> the sense of a profound *personal* disappointment, with which I heard the
> news. There were to be no more books and articles by George Orwell! I felt
> robbed. . . .[20]

"It had been absolutely uncanny," Wain said elsewhere. "They were like a series
of books that had been written expressly for me."[21]

The other Movement writers were in "vague general sympathy" with the Labour Party, too. Yet all of them were "neutralists" who scoffed at politics. This
stance certainly owed something to Orwell's disillusionment with left-wing utopianism, particularly his caustic deprecation of political "idealism" in "Inside
the Whale." Blake Morrison has aptly termed him a "maturing influence" on the
Movement writers.[22] Their nonpolitical attitudes, however, were also part of the
larger current of "end of ideology" and "consensus" politics ("Butskellism")
prevalent in the mid-1950s among a generation of Cold War liberals proud of
the recent successes of welfare-state capitalism. Kingsley Amis probably exaggerated the direct effect of Orwell's anti-ideology stance on British intellectuals,
insofar as he suggested it was a primary, exclusive influence. His observations
leave no doubt, however, as to Orwell's privileged place in the Movement canon
by August 1956:

Any intellectuals who may submit to have a list of their heroes wrung from them are likely to put him in the first two or three whatever their age (within reason), whatever their other preferences, and—more oddly at first—whatever their political affiliations. And if they have none, incidentally, this is as much Orwell's doing as anyone else's.[23]

Anti-wet, anti-phony, undeceived, uncommitted: the Movement's politics was an anti-politics, and Orwell served as a sort of *negative* political model. "It is for us to keep Orwell's example constantly before us," urged Wain in 1954.[24] The focus on Orwell's intellectual and moral purity allowed the Movement writers to indulge their own tendencies to equate acumen and virtue with political inactivity, so that to follow "Orwell's example" entailed detachment, even cynicism, toward politics. Overlooking the historical conditions that generated Orwell's pessimism in the dark war year of 1940, when "Inside the Whale" was written, the Movement writers identified his politics with the "sophisticated" withdrawal of the figure whom he criticized, Henry Miller, for whom all political affiliations were foolish.[25]

The Suez crisis and the ruthless Soviet suppression of the Hungarian uprising in October–November 1956 transformed the meaning of "Orwell's example" to the Movement writers overnight. British intellectual opinion now regarded political indifference as passive, not sophisticated. As public debate heated up over British foreign policy, the Movement writers were widely criticized for their detachment. And some of them, in turn, blamed Orwell. The shift in attitude is most apparent in Amis's Fabian pamphlet, *Socialism and the Intellectuals* (1957), written in November 1956. Amis's earlier judgment of that August as to Orwell's quietist influence is repeated, but this time its baneful consequences are noted:

Of all the writers who appeal to the post-war intelligentsia, he is far and away the most potent. . . . No modern writer has his air of passionately believing what he has to say and of being passionately determined to say it as forcefully and simply as possible. Most passionately he believed that left-wing politics are a trap for what I have called the political romantic; so passionately, indeed, that the trap becomes a trap and nothing else. Orwell's insistence that the political *can* be dirty and dishonest and treacherous, that it *often* is, betrays him into implying that it *must* be and *always* is. . . . He was the man above all others who was qualified to become the candid friend the Labour Party needed so much in the years after 1945. But what he did was to become a right-wing propagandist by negation, or at any rate a supremely powerful—

though unconscious—advocate of political quietism. . . . [He] completed his long-impending development into a hysterical neurotic with a monomania about the depravity of British intellectuals.[26]

The man whom Amis saw as an "intellectuals' hero" in the summer had become a "hysterical" intellectual-basher by autumn; the man of tough-minded common sense had turned into a political romantic.[27]

The deflation reflected not only the turmoil in Amis over the events of 1956. It also betokened a change of heart toward Orwell by the postwar generation, though many admirers soon began focusing on Orwell as the author of *Wigan Pier* and *Homage to Catalonia*—rather than "Inside the Whale"—and so began valuing him precisely for his stirring activism.

No longer were the Movement writers being depicted in the literary press as generational spokesmen after Suez. Young Britons were now described as "angry," and though Wain and Amis were portrayed in the press as Angry Young Men (a catch phrase belonging almost entirely to the history of publicity), fictional heroes like Charles Lumley in *Hurry on Down* and Jim Dixon in *Lucky Jim* actually exhibited no more than irritation and frustration, not outrage.[28] The critical success of *New Lines* in 1956 had marked the arrival of the Movement; already by 1957, Wain was speaking in the past tense, announcing that "there was a 'movement' and it did cohere. Then, as always, each moved away on his own path."[29] Suez and Hungary hastened the dispersal, as the consensus shared by the Movement unraveled, with most members (unlike the rest of their generation) remaining neutralist about British neo-imperialism in Suez, and some speaking out against the Soviet invasion.[30] Eden's disastrous, widely condemned decision to send troops to Egypt had undermined Britain's moral authority and exposed its loss of power in the postwar world, developments on which the Movement writers looked with mixed feelings; and Hungary had made clear the price of "peaceful co-existence." October 1956 thus rendered the Movement's quizzical anti-politics stance widely suspect as irresponsible attitudinizing. The age of noncommitment had ended. Anger replaced languor as the de rigueur emotion of the hour.

The 1957 manifesto *Declaration*, to which Wain (along with several other "Angries") contributed, captured the new mood in a word. British intellectuals moved, in E. P. Thompson's phrase, "outside the whale."[31] Some New Left spokesmen, including Thompson and later Raymond Williams, echoed Amis in blaming Orwell. "We can write Berlin, Algiers, Aden, Watts, Prague in the margins of Orwell's passivity," wrote Williams. "What in Orwell was a last, desperate throw became for many others, absurdly, a way of life."[32] This negative assessment of Orwell was one of the few topics on which Amis and his New Left coevals agreed.

II

In no way did such agreement signify, however, a consensus by their generation. Rather, many young intellectuals, caught between the inclination to adapt and the impulse to rebel, felt both an anxiety of influence and the inspiration of the heroic toward Orwell. Indeed, some young writers began calling attention precisely to Orwell's "generously angry" side, giving rise to a more feisty and political, less noble and "pure," public image. This new emphasis is broadly discernible in the work of Wain and certain Movement-affiliated writers (Hartley) and a few of the Angry Young Men (John Osborne, John Braine, Alan Sillitoe), and it represents an equally strong current within the second stage of Orwell's reception (c. 1957–1963) by postwar British writers. "Personally, I always think of him as he thought of Dickens: . . . the face of a man who is *generously angry,*" wrote Hartley. Taking issue with Amis's and Thompson's harsh judgments, Hartley insisted that the author of *Wigan Pier* was "far and away the most powerful advocate of a fair deal for the British working classes," and that the apathy of postwar intellectuals arose not from reading Orwell but "because of what they read in the newspapers." Events, not Orwell, caused their political disillusionment. "If, as is fashionable to say, he was not a Socialist," concluded Hartley, "so much the worse for Socialism." And yet, even while noting gratefully that "the no-nonsense air of a generation came from Orwell," Hartley admitted that the limitations in vision and aspiration implied by that attitude had entailed "jettisoning some valuable cargo": "Something, I feel, was lost by my generation. Perhaps we played [it] too safe, were too concerned not to be criticized for romantic or sentimental nostalgia. Perhaps the something was youth."[33] A flexible, down-to-earth habitude had ossified into the earthbound doctrine of a generation.

The fiction and drama by the postwar generation in the post-Suez years also contributed indirectly to the "angry" and "quietist" (or "neurotic") images of Orwell. Joe Lampton in Braine's *Room at the Top* (1957) and Arthur Seaton in Sillitoe's *Saturday Night and Sunday Morning* (1958) were widely recognized antiphony cousins to Gordon Comstock—who is usually taken (far too casually) as a thinly autobiographical Orwell—all three of them choleric, poor provincial boys alternately defiant and craven toward "the money god" and "bourgeois" family values. ("This Angry Young Man of the Thirties . . ." blazoned the cover of the 1962 Signet edition of *Keep the Aspidistra Flying*.) Orwell is clearly the Angry Young Man of the Thirties towering behind Osborne's *Look Back in Anger,* key scenes of which echo "Inside the Whale," "Reflections on Gandhi," and *The Lion and the Unicorn*.[34] Indeed, the play reflected and reinforced the split in Orwell's post-Suez reputation: Was he an erstwhile Jimmy Porter? Or did the heroic father whom young Jimmy watched die on his return home from the Spanish Civil War evoke Orwell (who had almost died of a throat wound in Catalonia)?

Wain remained Orwell's biggest champion—and Orwell remained, of Wain's and the Movement's onetime masters from the older generation, Wain's single abiding enthusiasm.[35] Implicitly challenging the revisionism by Amis and other contemporaries (e.g., Anthony West's psychoanalytic reading of "Such, Such Were the Joys")[36] who began revaluing Orwell downward after 1956, Wain declared in a 1957 essay ("Orwell in Perspective") that Orwell was being "grotesquely misjudged." Preoccupied with his life rather than his work, critics were devoting excessive attention to his "idiosyncrasies," charged Wain.[37] Ironically, of course, the keen critical interest in Orwell's life was partly due to Wain's preoccupation with the Orwell persona just a few years earlier.

Rather than discuss Orwell's impact on his generation or on the 1950s, Wain sought, as it were, to "update" Orwell in the new activist climate and to furnish a critical approach to his work, which would properly value his achievement. Wain's previous characterization of Orwell as "critic" was inadequate, he now realized. Nor would "novelist" or "essayist" do. An entirely new perspective was needed, a category which would foreground the engagé Orwell and do justice to his literary strengths. If one stepped back and considered Orwell's work collectively and from a wide historical angle, argued Wain in "Orwell in Perspective," his oeuvre falls within the tradition of "the polemic."

> He was a novelist who never wrote a satisfactory novel, a literary critic who never bothered to learn his trade properly, a social historian whose history was full of gaps. Yet he matters. For as polemic his work is never anything less than magnificent; and the virtues which the polemic demands— urgency, incisiveness, clarity and humour—he possessed in exactly the right combination.[38]

Partly in reaction to the rise of the British New Left in the late 1950s and a harrowing one-month visit to the Soviet Union in 1960 (both satirized in *The Young Visitors*, 1965),[39] Wain himself was becoming more politically active. Wain's catalog of "virtues which the polemic demands" constituted a personal inventory: a polemical Orwell was precisely the new model whom *he* needed. And so Wain again remolded Orwell as he assimilated him, bending him into the figure whom he now required—less a lonely figure of intellectual integrity and more a committed pamphleteer, though one of anti-radical convictions. (That both Osborne and Wain could admire and use "the rebel Orwell" from opposite ends of the ideological spectrum suggests how politically ambidextrous and culturally fashionable the category turned out to be in the 1950s—as well as how protean Orwell's reputation was becoming.)

Russia was Wain's Catalonia. "In retrospect these four weeks have expanded steadily until they now seem the equivalent of four years," Wain wrote on his return home. Having "fallen for a lot of the stuff I'd read about the thaw" during the de-Stalinization period under Khrushchev, Wain was "shocked" to "encounter a real, fully fledged totalitarian society." The experience contrasted sharply with an enjoyable visit to America in 1959: it was almost as if the drama of the Cold War were being enacted in his life. His Soviet trip "depressed me almost suicidally" and "taught me to revalue all my political experience. . . . It taught me what totalitarianism, even with its mild face, . . . is like. . . . Quite simply, it altered my entire view of the world." [40]

Putting Orwell "in perspective" thus soon became not just a critical stratagem but a personal necessity. As Wain gradually developed into a romantic Conservative in the mold of Samuel Johnson, he came in turn to see Orwell not merely as a dissident socialist but as anti-revolutionary altogether. Pointed reference to Orwell's contempt for "progressives"—the word usually enclosed within arch quotation marks—soon became standard practice in Wain's criticism. By 1961 Wain was profiling what Conor Cruise O'Brien later called Orwell's "Tory growl." [41] Highlighting Orwell's romanticism, patriotism, and nostalgia, Wain stressed "the hatred felt for him by 'progressives' with their money on the future and their heads full of Revolution." [42]

Ignoring his 1957 plea that critics avoid psychologizing Orwell, Wain also returned in his 1961 essay ("Here Lies Lower Binfield") to the subject of his enduring fascination: his model's character, now approached in light of Wain's own newly felt romanticism, patriotism, and nostalgia, attributes which Wain projected as the whole of Orwell's personality and work. *Coming Up for Air*, Wain argued, was Orwell's "central book," and "his most important character creation" was George Bowling. "If all his books disappeared without a trace," said Wain, "we should be able to tell, from this one, what kind of writer he was, what his major themes were, and how he treated them." [43] *Coming Up* represented the clearest instance of Orwell's unconscious literary strategy for expressing fully his love of nature, his "Englishness," and his sentimental faith in the common man, said Wain. There was indeed a "thin man" inside George Bowling, struggling to get out: his name was George Orwell. *Coming Up* disclosed the dynamics of Orwell's imaginative life as a series of substitutions: Blair needed Orwell to speak in his

own voice about politics; Orwell needed Bowling to speak about personal matters.[44] Bowling thus growled the Tory truths, Wain implied, which Blair-Orwell
could seldom speak.

                                        III

By the mid-1960s a new "Movement" had arisen. The radicalization of the British New Left after 1962 gave birth to the student movement and counterculture.
Several former Movement writers turned further right in response (Wain, Amis,
·Larkin, Conquest, Donald Davie), and they suddenly found themselves united
in ideological solidarity much as they had been joined on literary grounds a decade before. By 1970 they had become defenders rather than critics of the status
quo, unabashedly conservative domestically, pro-American internationally. The
avant-garde had become a rearguard.

Orwell's Tory growl thundered in this third phase of the Movement writers' response to him (c. 1964–1974). The rumbles sounded loudest in the work of Amis
and Wain. Their attention shifted away from Orwell's essays and early fiction and
toward *Homage to Catalonia* and *Nineteen Eighty-Four*. The image of Orwell the
anti-"progressive" skeptic thereby gave way to an explicitly anti-Communist figure. In 1956 Amis had called Orwell "one of those writers you can never get away
from because no view of him can ever be final."[45] Amis's use of the second person probably indicated his own urge to evade Orwell's influence; but by the early
1960s his politics and his fluctuating view of Orwell were stabilizing and converging. "Hungary turned me into a violent anti-Communist," he admitted; indeed,
Hungary was Amis's Catalonia.[46] A "callow Marxist" during 1940–1942 in his
early twenties, an undergraduate editor of Oxford's left-wing *University Labour
Club Bulletin*, and an ambivalent supporter of the Labour Party throughout the
1950s, Amis confessed that by 1960 his tempestuous relationship with Labour
and socialism "had reached the name-calling and walking-out stage."[47] By the
mid-1960s Amis had parted from the Left and embraced Wain's anti-totalitarian
"perspective" on Orwell. The mark of the late Orwell is clear in *The Anti-Death
League* (1966), a militaristic, apocalyptic, nightmarish world much like Oceania.
Amis's own political maturation, he later recalled, gave him more sympathy for
the trajectory of Orwell's development in the 1940s.

I had once thought Orwell a man of utter integrity—the one intellectual from
the older generation who had not compromised himself. Later I came to mod-
ify that view, but also to realize that part of growing up is that you can still
have a hero whom you know to be impure, whom you can value for what he
got right and not condemn for what he got wrong.[48]

Amis became aware of the odd doubleness, as it were, of Orwell's public persona, which allowed different generations—both angry young men and their chastened elders—to identify with distinctive aspects of him. "Orwell" as a model was not a "trap," as Amis had once thought, but a mirror of his past and a lamp for his future. The figure of Orwell as "young man's hero" possessed the appeal of an idealist; one could identify with his romantic dreaming, his passionate defiance, and his apparent purity. Conversely, the figure of Orwell as "mature man's hero" spoke to the worldly-wise; one could admire his skepticism toward, even his cynicism about, utopian high-mindedness.[49] Orwell had once been the hero of Amis's youth; now the mature Amis recognized the value of his hero's realistic side and even of his flaws, no longer feeling any need to "get away from" Orwell.

In fact it was just the reverse. As Amis's own skepticism in the late 1960s led him to adopt a combative traditionalism hostile to all innovation, his self-image developed into that of an intellectual rebel not unlike Orwell. The difference was that Amis became a curmudgeonly Establishment defender possessed of none of Orwell's feelings of duty toward or compulsion about remaining within the Left-liberal fold. One friend in the 1960s, noting the perverse pleasure which Amis seemed to derive from his numerous unpopular positions, acutely observed that "it seemed as if he could have no orthodoxy except an unrespectable one like Toryism"—almost as if Amis were trying to outdo Orwell as a fashion-hating rebel.[50] Indeed, as Amis finally "broke off my lingering love affair with the Left" and voted Conservative for the first time in 1966, he became almost reactionary in his cultural politics.[51] In his fiction and criticism he attacked new idioms "corrupting" the English language, deprecated rock and modern jazz in preference to early jazz, dismissed free verse and "pop" poetry in favor of metrical laws and regular forms, inveighed against "totalitarian" ideas (prompted by "trendy Left-ies") threatening "humane" (conservative) values, opposed university expansion ("MORE WILL MEAN WORSE," went his much-quoted slogan)[52] in defense of educational "standards" and elitism, and castigated communitarian schemes in support of individualism and free enterprise.[53] Occasionally he implied, indulging in the "If Orwell Were Alive Today" speculations of the period, that Orwell might have done the same.

One sign of Orwell's importance for Amis at this time came in his opening salvo as regular columnist for the *Daily Express* (19 March 1969). Promising to "sound off" against "left-wing idiocy," Amis portrayed Orwell as his predecessor, gratefully characterizing him as "a thorn in the side of the left."[54] By this time Amis had also become an outspoken supporter of the American presence in Vietnam—he and Wain were practically the only leading British intellectuals to do so—a position for which he was pilloried on both sides of the Atlantic.[55] Inevitably he mused on where Orwell would have stood on Vietnam, though he was

Kingsley Amis, 1970, ever ready to "sound off" against "left-wing idiocy" and to champion Orwell, "a thorn in the side of the Left." Courtesy of Martin Amis.

no more certain than some radical critics—most notably Mary McCarthy—as to the answer.[56] Would Orwell, always the iconoclastic enemy of Left faddism, have had the grit to stand alone—outside the Left—as Kingsley Amis did? Amis had his doubts:

> Which way would he have gone? He would have had a horrible time. Certainly I think that he would have wanted to have supported the American side, which meant supporting the fight against Communist aggression. Whether he would have done so or not—I don't know. I don't know whether he would have had the courage.[57]

Wain, though less vocal about the war, similarly "thank[ed] my stars" that "the Americans refuse to retreat before Communist bluster" and instead "stand firm

John Wain, 1960s, then touted (in his own words) as "Orwell's natural successor."
National Portrait Gallery; used with permission.

against Soviet and Chinese threats."[58] Significantly, Wain also revised his judgment about Orwell's "most important book" for "understand[ing] [his] mind":
the clear-sighted anti-Communist *Homage to Catalonia,* not *Coming Up for Air,*
now received Wain's vote.[59] To Wain, the 1960s were a replay of the 1930s. The
age of the hypocritical "right Left people" had returned, and Orwell's pointed,
conscience-pricking jibes at Left ideologues enjoyed a renewed relevance:

[I]t is once more the fashion to decry Orwell, as it was in the Thirties. Now
as then, his truth-telling is dismissed as perverse, and his warnings are
shrugged off by what he called the huge tribe known as 'the right left people.'
Now as then, the most vicious digs at Orwell come from men whose basic
intellectual position is totalitarian, the sort of people who are always ready
to point out the flaws in an untidy democracy, but see nothing disturbing
in the dreadful tidiness of, say, a classroom of North Vietnamese children
squawking in unison: "No one loves Uncle Ho more than the children." We
are plagued with these people now, as we were in the Thirties, and for much
the same reasons.

It is a testimony to the continuing vitality of Orwell's work that
totalitarian-minded critics hate him so much. They hate him because he
is a thorn in their sides. May he stay there forever.[60]

Wain's new image of Orwell was that of a salty political "conscience," a figure
fusing Wain's previous portraits of the intellectual paragon and brilliant polemicist. Orwell's Johnsonian service to his fellow intellectuals, said Wain, had been
to clear their slogan-sogged minds of radical cant, to "keep their consciences
alive."[61] Writing in December 1968, just one month after the biggest anti-war
demonstration in London, Wain nominated himself for a similar task to his own
generation of intellectuals—for the long-vacant office of Orwell's "successor":

> I know that when I hear the pronouncements made by various influential
> people in the England of the '60s, I long for Orwell back again. But, since
> we can't have him, it is good to be able to use his work for its purpose: as an
> example, an incitement, and a justification. . . .
>
> [W]ho can feel that the situation that faces us has changed much from
> what it was in the '30s and '40s . . . ? The thing to be feared is still a *trahi-
> son des clercs:* freedom still needs to be defended against those whom she
> most favours, whom she showers with advantages. At whatever point we are
> engaged in the never-ending battle against cant, whether we are trying to
> reckon up the myriad ways in which Western writers can get a good price for
> their integrity behind the Iron Curtain, or sorting out the multiple confu-
> sions in the latest pronouncement from someone like [Daniel] Cohn-Bendit,
> . . . it is Orwell who provides us with the best model of how to do it, and the
> most generous and communicable vision of why it should be done.[62]

IV

The decade-long "countdown to 1984" raised the "If Orwell Were Alive Today"
speculations to a fever pitch. The Soviet occupation of Afghanistan, the Iranian
hostage crisis, the politicized 1980 and 1984 Olympics, the imposition of martial
law in Poland and the Philippines, the Soviet shooting down of Korean Air flight
007, the controversial U.S. military involvements abroad (in Lebanon, El Salva-
dor, Grenada, and Nicaragua), the Falkland Islands invasion, the birth of the Social Democratic Party: so enveloping was Orwell's ever-lengthening shadow that
there were hardly any major international events between the late 1970s and early
1980s that did not tempt some intellectual or journalist to wonder aloud about
Orwell redivivus all over again.[63]

Neither Amis nor Wain hesitated to weigh in with his own predictions. Amis believed that Orwell would have spoken out against *Sandinismo* just as he had attacked Communism in 1930s Spain. Likewise, he suggested, the liberal-minded, patriotic Orwell would have supported the Thatcher government's Falkland Islands mission as a just defense against Argentinian aggression and of the Islanders' rights to self-determination.[64]

Having already moved in the late 1960s to take Orwell's place as a rebel against (but outside) the Left, Amis came in the 1970s and 1980s to assume, though now as a self-declared "man of the Right," another role often ascribed to Orwell: that of the dire anti-totalitarian prophet.[65] Amis's *Alteration* (1977) depicted a horrific theocratic, Nazi-like state; and *Russian Hide-and-Seek* (1980) portrayed a bleak, left-wing Stalinist-type totalitarian Britain. Thus Amis and Wain—among the leading men of letters of their generation and two of the major voices within the British intellectual Right—wound up filling, as it were, distinct places in English cultural life once occupied by the socialist Orwell, adjusting them to fit their conservative politics. The more truculent, insouciant Amis chose to become a wide-ranging cultural commentator, an aggressively provocative opponent of radical chic, and an almost gleeful sounder of apocalyptic alarms; the more earnest, sometimes moralistic Wain settled into his narrower, self-ordained role as the clerisy's "conscience."

But the elder Wain seemed to accept that along with the office comes the charge, as his younger self had put it, "to keep Orwell's example constantly before us." And so Wain followed Orwell's radiant example as he contentedly walked in Orwell's shadow—though also freely jerking "the rope that connects me directly with you" far right to suit his aims, often dragging Orwell along rather than dutifully trailing behind.

Indeed Wain's "Dear George Orwell" letter, published in the *American Scholar,* then edited by neoconservative Joseph Epstein, provides a signal instance. In the 1983 letter, Wain discussed the contemporary British domestic scene with his absent correspondent, tilting at Orwell's shadow as he boxed rival claimants for "St. George's" halo.[66] Wain argued that Orwell would have opposed anti-Zionism, Scottish and Welsh nationalists, noisy pubs, the "Peace Movement" ("Personally I would not use the word 'peace' if what I really meant was 'surrender,'" Wain observed), and the "anti-democratic Left." The Communists "hated you because you saw through them and said so" and "they still hate you," Wain told Orwell, but some current radicals employ devious tactics "to undermine your influence from within, claiming to admire you but actually working to destroy your credibility."[67] Less blatantly than *Commentary* editor Norman Podhoretz, but no less certainly, Wain suggested that, if Orwell were alive today, he would be standing with the Anglo-American neoconservatives and against the Left.[68] Re-emphasizing the significance of *Homage to Catalonia*, Wain denied that Orwell's radical "admirers and inheritors" (e.g., Raymond Williams or Bernard Crick) belonged in any tradition that included him (thereby making no distinction between the Marxist and democratic Left), only to sign himself, "Your admirer early and late":

> The[ir] technique is to represent you as a founding father of the present-day Left—so that it is perfectly fitting to keep your grave tended and even to lay flowers on it—but as someone who has been left behind by the developing situation and can't any longer be taken seriously. When done skillfully, this is a highly effective technique, and some of your most untiring enemies have managed to muddy the waters so successfully that they are habitually named as your admirers and inheritors. I can only offer one piece of practical advice to people who might wonder whether they are being conned or not. The mark of all such anti-Orwell smear jobs is that they underplay *Homage to Catalonia*.[69]

No issue, however, exercised Wain more than the 1984–1985 miners' strike, led by the self-declared Communist Arthur Scargill and already on the horizon when Wain's letter appeared. Wain, who had grown up among miners in Stoke-on-Trent, reserved his hottest fire for Scargill and appealed to the author of *The Road to Wigan Pier* to bless his hard-line position.

> The new breed of trade union leader is not like the ones you saw in action and heard speak at meetings. . . . As I write, the National Union of Mineworkers has got itself under the leadership of a man [Scargill] who spouts Marxist cliches as copiously as Fidel Castro; he has already announced [that] . . . the strike weapon will be used not as means for getting the miner a fair day's work . . . but as a political battering ram in the service of the anti-democratic Left. Now, what would you, George Orwell, make of this? Would you say, "The miners forever—the common man right or wrong?" But then, who, nowadays, is the common man? Isn't it the case that highly organized key workers, in a position to bring the economy to a standstill and wreck everybody's hopes, form an aristocracy, in the sense of power handed on from generation to generation and unanswerable to the moral authority of a democratic state?[70]

Wain's use of direct address bared his feeling of closeness to Orwell. However fair or correct Wain's stands, Orwell's place as a guiding star in his life impelled him to explain his positions to his model less by arguing them in their own terms than by framing them so that they fit Orwell's pronouncements on related, and sometimes anachronistic, subjects. As he settled into middle age, readily "disclaim[ing]" the title "Orwell's natural successor" as "too big for me,"[71] Wain wondered aloud in this fourth stage of his reception history (c. 1975–1994) about his relationship with Orwell, being more self-conscious than earlier about its tensions and yet unequivocal in his allegiance. In an interview he mused on "Wain's Orwell" then and now:

> In my youth I was a great propagandist for Orwell. I was always pushing him on people, quoting him at people—I was always saying, "As George Orwell remarked. . . ." I wanted to bang the drum for Orwell—which no doubt led some people to think that I was trying to be the next Orwell. . . .
>
> He's always somebody I've enjoyed keeping company with. I'm very fond of the man in the writings, and I think I would have been fond of the man himself—although I don't feel any confidence that Orwell would have liked me. Still, to me he's an endearing, funny figure. You can't really love someone you can't laugh at, and sometimes I have a good laugh about him. But I think that, in his political opinions, he was absolutely right. He rings absolutely right.[72]

Love is not too strong a word for the fealty which John Wain showed since his twenties toward George Orwell. If Wain's admiration "early and late" was sometimes uncritical and self-serving, it nevertheless seems genuine. Indeed, Wain's reception history of Orwell represents an unusually deep and open instance of reader identification with an author, suggesting how readers turn writers into luminous heroic presences to whom they can look for direction in their lives.[73] As Ernest Becker explains it, the fascination of the perceiver for the admired is an attempt to "address our performance of heroics" to another single human being. We "beatify" an Other so that we can know whether our performance is good enough. Our model will guide us, and if our performance is inadequate, we can look to him or her alone and change. Unlike Freud, Becker sees this as natural, healthy projection, a reaching out for plenitude, and he terms this localized, intense charge of affect *transference heroics*. Most of the time we construct composite models, with a mixture of different (and sometimes conflicting) features of persons constituting our image of the heroic, of our ideal selves. And typically we choose living models. But between a willing admirer like Wain and a strong literary personality and autobiographical writer like Orwell, the identification can be sweeping, passionate, and enduring. It may also be that the great dead author, particularly for those readers who are themselves writers, is most amenable to idealization as a secure model. For he is incapable of compromising himself by further action. And he possesses a living voice which represents him before his readers always at his best. The man is dead, but the magnificent work—and the man within the work—cannot die.[74]

As we have already seen, of course, Wain is not the only reader to have exalted Orwell into a radiant figure in his life. Nor is Orwell the only writer who engaged Wain's emotions as an inspirational model. As he moved rightward, Wain began comparing Orwell with the Tory Samuel Johnson—another cherished, curmudgeonly "moral hero" of Wain's, and in some ways a more comfortable political model—thereby recasting Orwell in his own image through Johnson's.[75] In such ways do readers struggle to resolve problems of identity and authors acquire reputations. "The rope that connects me directly with you" has many intricately woven strands, inevitably yanked and twisted and reeled in as readers' needs and aspirations require and as authors' personae and writings invite. A reader's history of response to an author is not merely a literary but also a complex autobiographical and cultural act. As John Wain's and the Movement writers' variegated reception history of George Orwell attests, the fabric of reputations is dyed the color of our lives.

Irving Howe at Stanford University, c. 1962, when he was editing *1984: Text, Sources, Criticism* (1963). Courtesy of Nicholas Howe.

CHAPTER THREE

"London Letter" from a Family Cousin

The New York Intellectuals' Adoption of Orwell

I

The first two chapters focused exclusively on Orwell's British reputation. Now we will turn to Orwell's American reception, attending to the emergence of his reputation in literary New York by the so-called New York Intellectuals. No other group's reception of Orwell has borne so decisively on the growth and shape of his American and even his international reputation, and for this reason we seek here to contextualize the group's reception history of Orwell within its rich and complicated intellectual history.

We are chiefly concerned here with the posthumous response to Orwell within the circle of writers associated with three New York magazines: *Partisan Review* (*PR*), which published Orwell's "London Letter" (1941–1946) and was widely regarded as the premier literary-intellectual quarterly in midcentury America; *politics*, a radical magazine of the 1940s edited by former *PR* editor Dwight Macdonald; and *Dissent*, co-founded in the 1950s by Irving Howe and Lewis Coser.

This chapter focuses chiefly on Orwell's reception by the New York writer who was probably his biggest admirer: Irving Howe. A vocal radical humanist and the most influential American socialist intellectual of his generation, Howe (1920–1993) was the most prominent member of the second generation of New York Intellectuals, the chiefly Jewish secular group associated with *PR*. Howe was also a distinguished literary critic who wrote or edited works on Sherwood Anderson, William Faulkner, Thomas Hardy, Yiddish fiction and poetry, and numerous other authors and literary topics; his most influential critical study was *Politics and the Novel* (1957). Howe's most successful works of nonfiction were *World of Our Fathers: The Journey of the Eastern European Jews to America and the Life They Found and Made* (1976), which became a bestseller and received the National Book Award, and his intellectual autobiography, *A Margin of Hope* (1982).

As we shall see, Howe engaged Orwell's work seriously and repeatedly: he edited two books about Orwell, wrote several essays and reviews of his work, publicly proclaimed Orwell as his "literary model" and "intellectual hero," and ultimately became the American intellectual most closely identified with Orwell's democratic socialist heritage.

II

George Orwell was a major influence and near-constant presence in Irving Howe's intellectual life for almost a half century. But Howe's relationship to Orwell deepened over time and was strongly conditioned by Howe's ideological evolution and by contemporary political and social events. His history of reception of Orwell can be roughly divided into four phases.

Howe first met Orwell in 1941 through his quarterly "London Letter" in *PR*'s pages. As the United States entered the Second World War in December 1941, the twenty-one-year-old Howe was a fierce anti-war Trotskyist and the editor of the Trotskyist paper *Labor Action*. He was also a contributor to *New International*, the theoretical organ of Max Shachtman's Trotskyist sect known as the Workers Party (WP)[1] in whose pages Howe castigated Orwell for his "uniformly pro-imperialist letters" from England. Howe was particularly incensed by Orwell's "preposterous statement—fit for the garbage pails" that "to be anti-war in England today, is to be pro-Hitler." Orwell's wartime support for the Allies and his statement that pacifism was "objectively pro-fascist" outraged the young Howe.[2]

In the course of his wartime service in Alaska (1942–1946), however, Howe began drifting away from Trotskyism. Demobilized and back in New York in January 1946, Howe lived on the G.I. Bill and resumed both editing *Labor Action* and writing for *New International* gratis. He also continued to promote the pre-war Trotskyist line, vowing both to "destroy . . . the illusion that Stalinism or Social Democracy can bring Socialism" and to "build . . . a revolutionary party which can."[3]

But the old fire of sectarian conviction was dying. In July 1946, he contacted Dwight Macdonald, an older ex-Trotskyist and ex-Shachtmanite.[4] Howe asked if he might work for Macdonald's independent (and largely one-man) magazine, *politics*, which Macdonald had founded less than a year after resigning his editorial position at *PR* in July 1943. Soon Howe was hired as an editorial assistant, where he patched up subliterary submissions and contributed (under the pseudonym Theodore Dryden) a regular feature.[5] The affiliation with *politics* and Macdonald, a superb literary stylist who had by mid-1946 embraced pacifism and

The editorial board of *Partisan Review*, 1940. *Sitting:* F. W. Dupee and William Phillips. *Standing (from left):* G. L. K. Morris, Philip Rahv, and Dwight Macdonald. Courtesy of Nick Macdonald.

anarchism (trumpeted in 1945 through his personalist manifesto, "The Root Is Man"), did not please his orthodox Trotskyist colleagues in the Workers Party.[6] But they allowed that Howe could continue to assist at the "deviationist" *politics* so long as he avoided "editorial collaboration."[7] Nonetheless, as they no doubt feared, Howe's close connection with Macdonald and other *politics* contributors (C. Wright Mills, Paul Goodman, Lewis Coser, Meyer Shapiro, George Woodcock)[8] during 1946–1948 contributed to his gradual descent "down the slopes of

Dwight Macdonald, the editor of *Politics*, 1940s. Courtesy of Nick Macdonald.

apostasy" (in his words) and thus accelerated his disengagement from Trotskyism.[9] (Howe formally withdrew from the *politics* editorial board in November
1948; the magazine expired a few months later, with both Macdonald's funds and
his fortitude nearly exhausted.)[10]

Nevertheless, though the *politics* and Trotskyist circles moved in overlapping
orbits, Howe still saw himself chiefly as a political man, and his primary reference group was the Shachtmanite sect of Trotskyists. "Half in . . . and half out"
of "our little group" of dissident Trotskyists—WP membership in the mid-1940s
hovered around five hundred, a tiny faction within a faction of the American
Left—Howe's primary reference group in the late 1940s was not the small *politics* circle or the larger *PR* group. Rather, it was Shachtman's Workers Party (renamed the Independent Socialist League in 1949). The Shachtmanite sect had
split with the mainline Trotskyists in 1940 over whether Stalin's betrayal of the
Russian Revolution deprived the Soviet Union of its status as the workers' father-

land. Trotsky said no, blaming Stalin alone for its Stalinism; the Shachtmanites insisted yes, arguing that the real revolution had not yet happened.[11]

It was in the context of these intramural Marxist disputes and practical problems of revolutionary action that Howe responded to Orwell's postwar writings. Presumably Howe took sharp exception to Macdonald's high esteem for Orwell,[12] which was exemplified by Macdonald's commissioning for *politics* an admiring essay-review of Orwell's oeuvre by Orwell's friend, the British anarchist George Woodcock, published in December 1946.[13] Moreover, as Howe started to withdraw further from the Trotskyist movement and also write for *PR* (already by 1948 he had four pieces published there), his ideological animus toward Orwell collided with the high regard for his work shared by almost all of the *PR* writers. Their approval was reflected in the magazine's choice of Orwell to receive the first Partisan Review Award in September 1949, on the American publication of *Nineteen Eighty-Four*, which garnered public accolades from several members of the group (e.g., Lionel and Diana Trilling, Philip Rahv, Alfred Kazin, Daniel Bell, Arthur Schlesinger).[14]

Howe's response to *Nineteen Eighty-Four* at midcentury was much more reserved. Although he had started working part-time as a book reviewer for *Time* and even doing synopses of novels for Paramount Studios, he was still a Marxist in good standing and by conviction.[15] By contrast, although many of the older *Partisan* writers were Trotskyists in the 1930s (and Isaac Rosenfeld was, like Macdonald, a Shachtmanite in the early 1940s), they had already shed their revolutionary socialism and Marxist scholasticism for social democratic politics; Howe was responding to Orwell from a stance that most of the *PR* writers no longer shared.

Howe's essay-review of *Nineteen Eighty-Four*—published in *New International* in November/December 1950—was largely a meditation on whether, deliberately or inadvertently, socialism could be "twisted into something as horrible as '1984,' even by 'we, the good people, the good socialists.'" Howe concluded that Orwell had answered, somberly, in the affirmative. On this point Howe emphatically agreed. *Nineteen Eighty-Four* was a ghastly picture of what socialism could become, "not merely from Stalinism" but even from "genuine socialist efforts." The lesson of *Nineteen Eighty-Four*, said Howe, concerned precisely how to conduct the transition to socialism. Orwell's valuable warning was that democratic practices could not automatically be taken for granted after a revolution. Democracy would more likely be preserved during the transition to socialism if workers shared political and social power with other classes.[16] Still, Howe also noted his "numerous disagreements" with Orwell's democratic socialism and approved Lenin's criticisms of gradualist Eduard Bernstein.[17]

Yet even in 1950 Howe was moving toward his conclusion of a few years later that workers had much more to fear from Leninism than from social democracy. Already he was a wearied veteran of a dozen years of Marxist infighting, feeling a sense of exhaustion and frustration about the political irrelevance and impotence of the Shachtmanites. A socialist at the age of fourteen, an editor at nineteen of *Labor Action*, and one of the original organizers of the Workers Party in 1942, Howe had felt his commitment to revolutionary socialism waning ever since his return to New York after his wartime military stint. Capitalism was not crumbling, he realized, and America was not Nazi Germany.

As his involvement with Trotskyists gradually lessened, Howe concluded that his real calling was that of a writer and literary critic. (The break eventually came when Howe submitted his resignation letter to the Shachtmanites in October 1952.) Already by 1949 he had co-authored (with B. J. Widick) a highly praised pro-labor study on the rise of the industrial unions, *The UAW and Walter Reuther.* It was soon followed by two books of literary-biographical criticism, *Sherwood Anderson* (1951) and *William Faulkner* (1952). And as he began to see himself less as an activist and sectarian journalist-pamphleteer and more as a literary man, Howe began to exchange his old reference groups—first of the Trotskyists and then of the *politics* circle—for the wider, cultivated world of the *Partisan* writers.

During the war years, Orwell had been one of the very few writers whom most of the first-generation members of the *PR* circle—including *Partisan*'s pacifist, revolutionary wing (Macdonald, Clement Greenberg) and more moderate, culturally oriented wing (Rahv, William Phillips, Trilling)—had admired.[18] Their estimations grew enormously after *Animal Farm* (1945), *Dickens, Dali, and Others* (1946), *Nineteen Eighty-Four,* and the posthumous essay collections. Now, with his full entry into the *Partisan* circle and his transition to "writer," Howe's own admiration for Orwell intensified and the range of questions that he brought to his thinking about Orwell broadened and diversified.

III

From the mid-'50s to the early '60s, Howe came increasingly to identify with Orwell, and this second stage of his reception (c. 1955–1963) is marked less by ideological and more by historical, literary, and personal concerns, some of which he shared with other *Partisan* writers. Chief among the former was the nature and development of totalitarianism. *The Origins of Totalitarianism* (1951), that brilliant and controversial masterpiece of Hannah Arendt, an "elder" member of the New York Intellectuals, had an enormous impact on the thinking of the *Partisan* writers and the intellectual world generally. Especially during the period of "de-

Stalinization" in the mid-1950s, when debate raged about the possibility that the Soviet system was altering fundamentally, Arendt's book sparked numerous historical and theoretical discussions as to whether totalitarianism was the form of authoritarian government characteristic of the modern bureaucratic, collectivist age.

Howe's major contribution to Orwell's critical reputation in the 1950s was to help lift *Nineteen Eighty-Four* above mere Cold War polemics and place it within the context of these discussions. Partly as a result of Howe's widely reprinted *American Scholar* essay, "Orwell: History as Nightmare" (1956), *Nineteen Eighty-Four* was soon being treated by journalists and political scientists alike as a work of political theory, an abstract model of the totalitarian state (or, in Howe's phrase, "the post-totalitarian" state).[19] Following Howe's declaration that "no other book has succeeded so completely in rendering the essential quality of totalitarianism" and his detailed examination of Orwell's "view of the dynamics of power in a totalitarian state," critics treated *Nineteen Eighty-Four* as the fictional counterpart to theoretical studies on totalitarianism by Arendt, Richard Lowenthal, Carl Friedrich, and Zbigniew Brzezinski.[20] Indeed, because *Nineteen Eighty-Four* antedated *The Origins of Totalitarianism* and similar political treatises, some critics saw it as inaugurating this emergent tradition and suggested that it had inspired Arendt and later theorists.

Howe contributed to this tendency in his *Nineteen Eighty-Four: Text, Sources, Criticism* (1963). His edition included a supplemental section on "the politics of totalitarianism" that featured extracts from the work of Arendt and Lowenthal designed to present *Nineteen Eighty-Four* as a "typology" of a totalitarian world.[21] By 1983, when Howe edited *1984 Revisited: Totalitarianism in Our Century*, he could fairly write that Orwell's book "occupies a central place" in "the vast literature concerning totalitarianism." It was a place that Howe himself, with his praise of Orwell's "theoretical grasp" of totalitarianism, had done much to establish.[22] "Orwell: History as Nightmare" was published as the closing chapter of Howe's *Politics and the Novel* in 1957, probably Howe's best-known work of literary criticism. Howe placed *Nineteen Eighty-Four* last in a distinguished line of political novels, following works by recognized masters including Stendhal, Dostoyevsky, Conrad, James, Turgenev, Malraux, Silone, and Koestler—and grandly pronounced that *Nineteen Eighty-Four* "brings us to the end of the line. Beyond this—one feels or hopes—it is impossible to go. In Orwell's book the political themes of the novels that we have been discussing in earlier chapters reach their final and terrible flowering."[23]

"Orwell: History As Nightmare" also had an even more direct—though inadvertent—influence on *Nineteen Eighty-Four:* the essay was the germ of the "nightmare" interpretation of *Nineteen Eighty-Four*. Howe argued against critics (e.g., Anthony West) who viewed *Nineteen Eighty-Four* "primarily as a symptom of Orwell's psychological condition." The key word here is *primarily;* Howe was advancing a subtle, syncretistic, psychosocial interpretation of *Nineteen Eighty-Four*. The novel referred not only to Orwell's personal history, insisted Howe, but also to the history of the twentieth century; it was not just a private nightmare but part of "the social reality of our time."[24] Howe was not the first to discuss *Nineteen Eighty-Four* as a "nightmare"; but earlier characterizations were made in passing and were narrowly political.

Howe called *Nineteen Eighty-Four* "the nightmare of the future." Writing amid growing psychobiographical interest in Orwell—three critical/biographical studies and numerous essays on Orwell had already appeared in the six years since his death in January 1950—Howe tried to fuse psychology and politics in discussing Orwell's "nightmare." But the unintended effect of his essay was to give hostile psychological critics of *Nineteen Eighty-Four* another catchword to sling. Following unsympathetic Marxist and psychoanalytic critics, journalists and reviewers began to describe *Nineteen Eighty-Four* as a "nightmarish" projection of a dying prophet's childhood terrors, rather than as a satiric political novel. Likewise, unexpectedly, admirers used Howe's "nightmare" characterization to bolster their psychological argument that Orwell "died" for *Nineteen Eighty-Four,* and that the "nightmare" of tubercular agony he endured to complete his gift to the world testified all the more to his nobility of spirit and love of humanity.[25] Howe closed "Orwell: History as Nightmare" on a benedictory note:

> There are some writers who live most significantly for their own age; they are writers who help redeem their time by forcing it to accept the truth about itself, and therefore saving it, perhaps, from the truth about itself. Such writers, it is possible, will not survive their time, for what makes them so valuable and so endearing to their contemporaries—that mixture of desperate topicality and desperate tenderness—is not likely to be a quality conducive to the greatest art. Perhaps it shouldn't matter to us. We know what they do for us, and we know that no other writers, including the greater ones, can do it.[26]

One notices the adroitly elastic use of first-person pronouns; Howe "knows" what books like *Nineteen Eighty-Four* do for "us," and what should and should not matter to "us." But the concerns here and throughout this essay are Howe's: Orwell and *Nineteen Eighty-Four* are significant and valuable and endearing because they speak to Irving Howe as a writer and radical—and, as we shall see, because they had helped redeem and force him to accept "the truth" about his political self and about the little intellectual groups in New York in whose identities lay part of his own.

For the "we" of this essay's close is Howe's own. By 1954 Howe had "part[ed] company with most of the New York intellectuals I had admired."[27] In January he had founded (with Lewis Coser) the bimonthly *Dissent*. (They tried to raise funds—$6,000 to ensure a year's publication—by using the old *politics* subscriber's list to solicit support.) "The *Dissent* group"—a cluster of unaffiliated radicals dedicated to democratic socialism—was but "a tiny minority within the intellectual world,"[28] Howe admitted, but its members took it upon themselves to keep the idea—and ideal—of socialism alive in midcentury America.

Howe's relationships with several of the early *Dissent* writers (including Meyer Schapiro, Michael Harrington, C. Wright Mills, and Paul Goodman) are profiled in his autobiography, *A Margin of Hope* (1983). The "Dissenters" still considered themselves Socialists (with a capital "s") throughout the '50s.[29] Howe was the intellectual leader of this small yet influential group. And Orwell became his key literary model. For, taking stock of his verbal resources, Howe searched at this early moment of his writing career for suitable literary models—and settled on Orwell. "I decided to work hard to write like Orwell—not, heaven knows, that I succeeded, but it made sense to try, since whatever strength of style I had lay in a certain incisiveness." Orwell and Edmund Wilson became Howe's chief literary benchmarks.[30]

And yet, even before his *Dissent* years, Howe had felt himself growing far apart from the *Partisan* writers on political matters. This became especially evident to him in *Partisan*'s 1952 symposium, "Our Country and Our Culture," in which Howe dissented from the *Partisan* near-consensus that American intellectuals should disavow their "alienation" and become "part of American life." The *Partisan* writers were to Howe "intellectuals in retreat" espousing "a liberalism increasingly conservatized."[31]

All this lay behind Howe's "we"—and behind his insistence on the quality of "desperation" in Orwell's work—at the close of "Orwell: History as Nightmare." The resonances were already clear from Howe's 1955 *Partisan* article on Orwell, "A Moderate Hero." Howe rejected the view of most liberals that Orwell should be seen as a "good" man, a "conscience," or a "saint." Such characterizations, Howe thought, softened or spiritualized Orwell's angry radicalism. Too "cozy" with the conservative spirit of the mid-'50s, liberal critics like Lionel Trilling, V. S. Pritchett, and John Atkins were unnerved by the gritty, irascible, even ill-tempered side of Orwell, claimed Howe. Unable to fathom Orwell's "desperation," they sought to remake him into "a moderate hero," "a down-at-the-heels Boy Scout who voted Labour." Likewise, lacking Orwell's own "fiery" imagination, they were incapable of understanding Orwell's passion for justice and decency, so they recast it in moral terms as a species of "sainthood."[32]

Chafing at what struck him, accurately, as the overcautious neoliberalism of the *Partisan* crowd, and clearly speaking for the embattled radicalism of his new group around *Dissent*, Howe scorned the liberals' "modified" Orwell, averring that Orwell was no moderate and no saint. Trilling had memorialized Orwell as a "virtuous man" in his introduction to the first American edition of *Homage to Catalonia* (1952). But such a figure was too soft for Howe, nothing like his image of a combative Orwell, his refreshingly immoderate hero, his "revolutionary personality." So Trilling's "man of truth" became Howe's "truculent" man, befitting Howe's own more aggressive, less guardedly urbane personality.

> The more one learns about Orwell, the more one begins to doubt that he was unusually virtuous or good. . . . Neither the selflessness nor the patience of the saint, certainly not the indifference to temporal passion that would seem a goal of sainthood, can be found in Orwell. As a "saint" Orwell would not trouble us, for by now we have learned how to put up with saints: we canonize them and thus are rid of them. In fact, one sometimes suspects that, behind the persistent liberal effort to raise Orwell from the mire of polemic to the clear heavens of sainthood, there is an unconscious desire to render him harmless. It is as a man and a writer that Orwell makes his challenge to the writers who follow him. He stirs us by his example, by his all-too-human and truculent example. For he stood in basic opposition to the modes and assumptions that have since come to dominate American and English literary life. He was a writer who rejected the middle-class pattern. . . . He knew how empty, and often how filled with immoderate aggression, the praise of moderation could be. . . . He wasn't a Marxist or a political revolutionary. He was something better and more dangerous: a revolutionary personality.[33]

"One must choose between God and Man," Orwell had maintained in his 1949 essay on Gandhi, "and all 'radicals' and 'progressives' . . . have in effect chosen Man."[34] Orwell had rejected belief in "sainthood" because he had resolutely chosen "Man"; Howe, also an atheist, repudiated literary and spiritual canonization in Orwell's name. One must, Orwell insisted, choose: to wait for Sugarcandy Mountain above or work for a socialist utopia below. Howe drew the necessary conclusion as to the corollary choice: "the clear heavens of sainthood" or "the all-too-human" political "mire."

For Howe, as for Orwell, sanctity meant non-attachment; sainthood and communitarianism were mutually exclusive. Yet Howe's main reservation actually concerned the likely political consequences flowing from use of the term *saint:* moderation, gradualism, quietism. His Orwell, Howe insisted, was no "man of truth"—he was a political figure: an honest radical. Not a "political revolutionary"—but, at this nadir of American socialism, an image of a "revolutionary personality" who could help radicals keep the spirit of revolution alive was "something better." The terms *saint* and *virtuous man,* however, would not do. They evoked in Howe not Atkins's and Trilling's inspiring images of the fully committed, extraordinary ordinary man (Atkins's "social saint"), but rather the figure canonized by British conservative Richard Rees as a "self-mortifying saint." It is the latter image which seemed to Howe almost inhuman and indifferent to temporal passion, which could not serve as the model for those who would launch a political movement, which appeared so far from human capacity that it ceased to "challenge" "us."

Here again we see Howe speaking with plural pronouns. And, once again, it is Irving Howe who was not "stirred" by a "virtuous," "saintly" Orwell—as Trilling, Atkins, Pritchett, and Rees had been. One could well ask Howe, as Richard Rovere, another liberal, soon did in *The Orwell Reader* (1956): "But what is [a 'revolutionary personality'] except another term, one with secular and socialist overtones, for a saint? A 'revolutionary personality' is what the Ethical Culturalist calls Jesus Christ."[35]

But what Howe needed in the mid-1950s was not just a literary model but a model of the radical writer. Orwell's personal importance for Howe was couched in the closing lines of "Orwell: History as Nightmare," in which he seemed inspiring not only to "us" but also to Irving Howe, at a "desperate" moment in American radicalism in the mid-'50s. For Orwell reaffirmed Howe's conviction that "some writers" are indeed "valuable" precisely because they "live for their own age," "help redeem their time," acquiesce to an ephemeral and "desperate topicality," and compel their generation "to accept the truth about itself"—whether or not their work "survives" or is "great art." And Orwell reminded Howe that his own fate and vocation might be to join the ranks of such writers, the ranks of Orwell and Ignazio Silone.[36] Socialism might one day re-emerge as a viable movement in America if dissenting intellectuals preserved a sense of their calling, preserved "a margin of hope."

"I bridled at the notion that the literary life was inherently more noble than the life of politics," Howe recalls. "I bridled because acknowledging this could have been politically disabling at a time when politics remained essential, but also because I knew that it held a portion of obvious truth—otherwise, how explain my inner divisions?" Striving for literary excellence and yet also to keep alive socialism's "animating ethic," Howe found in Orwell the political self which he believed, fairly, Trilling and the *Partisan* ex-radicals had forsaken. Howe wanted "instances of that poise which enables a writer to engage with the passions of the moment yet keep a distancing skepticism." Trilling "spoke for part of what I wanted, yet another, perhaps larger, part of me had to speak against him."[37] Trilling spoke for the skeptical Howe, Orwell for the passionate Howe. "I saw Orwell," Howe recalls, "as a fellow spirit—a radical and engaged writer."[38]

Trilling would not have described Orwell this way. Nor as a "revolutionary" personality. Nor, given his valuation of Orwell's respect for "the familial commonplace" and the "stupidity of things,"[39] as a rebel against middle-class life. But Howe needed a more unbridled, more iconoclastic figure. For Howe, an Orwell hemmed in by the conventional bourgeois pattern was "empty," politically "harmless." "Dangerous" was "better": only a recognizably radical image could truly "challenge" and "trouble us."

IV

In the mid-'60s, partly in strong reaction to the authoritarian radicalism of the New Left, Howe felt impelled "toward a liberalizing of radicalism"—and toward the hesitant renewal of his relationship with Trilling.[40] But Howe's respect and admiration for Orwell remained constant—as did his dissatisfaction with American liberalism, which had merely emerged from "a contagion of repressiveness" in order to enter "a time of structured deceit":[41] the illusion of a Great Society, the tragedy of the war in Vietnam. Looking back in 1969 on Orwell's reception during the Cold War, Howe felt vindicated in his 1955 judgment that the liberals' moderate image of Orwell "tells us a great deal more about the historical moment than about Orwell."[42] The same might be said for Howe's revised image of Orwell in the late '60s.

What changed in this third stage of his reception (c. 1965–1973) was not Howe's esteem but the content and context of his image of Orwell. By this time, after the 1963 publication of *Nineteen Eighty-Four: Text, Sources, Criticism*, Howe was coming to be regarded as Orwell's main American defender and radical champion. Now, however, Howe was defending Orwell not from appropriation by liberals but from denigration by radicals. Fascist, flag-waver, war hawk—the diatribes against Orwell from the American New Left poured forth, variously based on random passages from *Burmese Days*, *The Road to Wigan Pier*, *Animal Farm*, *Nineteen Eighty-Four*, or a *Tribune* column.

In *Mr. Sammler's Planet* (1970), Saul Bellow, a friend of Howe's and a fringe member of the *Partisan* circle, imagined the hostile response to Orwell from some of Mark Rudd's SDS followers at Columbia. Sammler, the Old Left guest lecturer brought in to talk about the 1930s, could well have been Irving Howe.

"Old Man! You quoted Orwell before."
"Yes?"
"You quoted him to say that British radicals were all protected by the British navy . . ."
"Yes, I believe he did say that."
"That's a lot of shit."
Sammler could not speak.
"Orwell was a sick counterrevolutionary. It's good he died when he did."[43]

But Howe could speak, and did. "[S]omething within me—sentimentality, conscience, stubbornness—kept murmuring that I had an obligation to speak."[44] Writing in January 1969, in the wake of the Columbia student uprisings and near the height of the Movement's influence, Howe declared acridly that, when it came to sharing and understanding the experience of workers, the student Left and its older enthusiasts like Murray Kempton had much to learn from Orwell.

He saw them and liked them as they were, not as he or a political party felt they should be. He didn't twist them into Marxist abstractions, nor did he coddle them in the fashion of the New Left populism. He saw the workers neither as potential revolutionaries nor savage innocents nor stupid clods. He saw them as ordinary suffering human beings; quite like you and me, yet because of their circumstances radically different from you and me. When one thinks of so much of the falseness that runs through so much current writing of this kind—consider only the "literary" posturings of Murray Kempton—it becomes clear that Orwell was a master of the art of exposition. . . . Orwell's deepest view of life [was] his faith in the value and strength of common existence: "The fact to which we have got to cling, as to a life-belt, is that it is possible to be a normal decent person and yet to be fully alive." Let that be inscribed on every blackboard in the land![45]

Whereas in the '50s he had felt caught between *Partisan*'s neoliberalism and his own liberal radicalism, Howe now felt boxed in between the New Left's "kamikaze radicalism" and his own Left-liberalism. What the "larger part" of Howe had sought and found in Orwell during the moderate '50s was passion; but the

larger part of him, frustrated and outraged with the excesses of the young radicals, needed Trilling's "distancing skepticism" by the close of the '60s.[46]

This too Howe eventually came to find in Orwell. "I came to appreciate more
deeply the side of Orwell that wanted and needed to get away from politics."[47]
This "outsider" stance was the one that Orwell had arrived at too, and one notices
that in his 1969 essay Howe now spotlights those qualities in his model which he
had previously downplayed. Howe now stresses the nonpolitical dimension—the
moral, literary, and even spiritual aspects—of Orwell, though he rails once more
against those who call Orwell a saint. Howe emphasizes the nonpolitical in Orwell
not by tempering Orwell's radicalism, however, but rather by proclaiming Orwell's rugged virtuousness: "He is the greatest moral force in English letters during the last several decades: craggy, fiercely polemical, sometimes mistaken, but
an utterly free man." Orwell achieved a "state of grace" in his prose by "sloughing
off the usual vanities of composition," which enabled him to speak "as a voice of
moral urgency."[48]

As he had in the '50s, Howe responded to the political climate and his personal situation of 1969, remolding Orwell as he assimilated him, bending him
into the figure he needed, not without a touch of exaggeration and sentimentality. Howe imagined that, as a writer living with workers and speaking to readers, Orwell "solved the problem of narrative distance" involved in sharing and
communicating his experience. In "Hop Picking" and *The Road to Wigan Pier*,
Orwell understood the necessary balance between proximity and distance: he
neither "coddled" the workers nor "twisted" them into "Marxist abstractions."
He was "driven to plunge into every vortex of misery or injustice that he saw,"
but he retained sufficient perspective to "see what looms in front of his nose."[49]
Howe's Orwell of 1969 is the figure Howe wished he might have been in the '60s.
To plunge in without getting sucked into the vortex: this is what both the young
leftists and Howe had not done, why they and he needed a distancing skepticism
to check centripetal passions.

Generational distance prevailed instead. To the New Left, Orwell and Howe belonged to an Old Left "scarred by the past," bearing "marks of corrosion and distrust," "skeptical of Marxism," and "rigidly anticommunist," in Howe's words.[50]
And "middle-aged Socialists" like himself, Howe admitted, though respectful of
the early achievements of the New Left (e.g., the civil rights campaigns, the SDS
community action projects), resented the young for repeating their elders' pro-
communist follies of the 1930s—and for depriving them of "the role of mentor to
the young."[51] Orwell had performed that role for Howe in the early postwar years,
the role Howe himself might have inherited in the 1960s. But in an anguished,
heartfelt tribute, Howe insisted, as if he were Bellow's Sammler giving the student Left a history lesson about a forgotten era, that Orwell was and remained "a

model for every writer of our age."[52] Howe allowed himself, in closing, to imagine that "if he had lived," Orwell would have steered a course similar to his own, lambasting both Establishment politicians and apocalyptic populists:

> For a whole generation—mine—Orwell was an intellectual hero. He stormed against those English writers who were ready to yield to Hitler; he fought almost single-handed against those who blinded themselves to the evils of Stalin. More than any other English intellectual of our age, he embodied the values of personal independence and a fiercely democratic radicalism. Yet, just because for years I have intensely admired him, I hesitated to return to him. One learns to fear the disappointment of fallen heroes and lapsed enthusiasms. I was wrong to hesitate . . .
>
> It is depressing to think that, if he had lived, he would today be no more than sixty-five years old. How much we have missed in those two decades! Imagine Orwell ripping into one of Harold Wilson's mealy speeches, imagine him examining the thought of Spiro Agnew, imagine him dissecting the ideology of Tom Hayden, imagine him casting a frosty eye on the current wave of irrationalism in Western culture!
>
> The loss seems enormous. . . . He was one of the few heroes of our younger years who remains untarnished. Having to live in a rotten time was made just a little more bearable by his presence.[53]

V

By the 1980s, Howe had become publicly identified with his "intellectual hero." In this fourth stage of his reception (1974–1993), Howe came to be admired by many Left-liberals as the American Orwell of his generation. For instance, Sanford Pinsker saw Howe as a "moral conscience," a tribute that echoed V. S. Pritchett's famous declaration that Orwell was "the conscience of his generation":

> The passion of his argument, by turns fiercely moral and scrupulously fair, the clarity of his prose, a voice that speaks with authority and power and the unmistakability of a thumbprint: Howe is a case study in powers that grew more refined, more subtle, even as they retained a kinship with the sheer exuberance of those times, those places. In this regard, Howe retains a position as a moral conscience almost unparalleled in contemporary letters.

Or as Josephine Woll recalled after his death, in a comparison that many of his *Dissent* friends would have endorsed, "For Irving, Orwell was a model of a writer; for me, Irving was."[54]

Indeed, during his last decade, after the deaths of Edmund Wilson (1972) and Lionel Trilling (1975), Howe came to be seen by many observers (except the Right and far Left) as America's leading literary-political intellectual. His achievement was indeed impressive. Not only was he prolific—he wrote eighteen books, edited twenty-five more, penned dozens of articles and reviews, and edited *Dissent* for forty years—but he was proficient and more often brilliant in virtually every literary endeavor of his mature years. While some readers found his work on "politics and the novel" to be most valuable, others prized his contributions to the study of Yiddish literature and Jewish immigrant history.

Even beyond the *Dissent* circle, some admirers began to see Howe as the American Orwell. The "countdown to 1984," which pushed Orwell into the incessant glare of the international media, further solidified the growing perception of Howe as Orwell's American spokesman and successor. Campus speeches on Orwell, conference talks and radio interviews about Orwell, a *New Republic* cover story, a new and expanded edition of *Nineteen Eighty-Four: Text, Sources, Criticism*, the edited volume *1984: Totalitarianism in Our Century:* in 1983–1984 Howe seemed to be the designated American keeper of the Orwell flame. Howe became increasingly identified with Orwell during these years, even as he himself gained a reputation beyond intellectual and academic circles as a result of his widely acclaimed best-seller *World of Our Fathers* (1977).

Moreover, with the neoconservative embrace of Orwell in 1983–1984, Howe assumed, once again, the role of defender of the radical Orwell. "Kidnapping Our Hero": that was how an indignant Irving Howe characterized Norman Podhoretz's claim to Orwell as a forerunner of neoconservatism, insisting that "to the end of his life Orwell remained a writer of the Left."[55] As in the '50s, Howe was guarding Orwell on his right flank, but by the 1980s Howe's own radicalism had attenuated to "radical humanism."[56] Nonetheless, though he now put more emphasis on the "conservatism of feeling" in *Nineteen Eighty-Four*, Howe strongly affirmed Orwell's own socialism, branding Podhoretz's claim to Orwell "vulgar."[57]

Neither Trilling nor I ever said that Orwell "is me" or "is like" me. My construction of Orwell is just that—a construction—and of an admittedly self-serving kind. But it is a clearer and more openly acknowledged image than Trilling's in the '50s, and I make no claims about a "posthumous" Orwell as Podhoretz does.[58]

I would claim that Irving Howe also had his "partisan" Orwell—who was also a highly political and "dissenting" Orwell. But Howe's deepening identification with Orwell after 1950 did not lead him to distort Orwell's politics, but rather to

Irving Howe and his first grandchild, Anastasia Bukowski, in Montreal, 1993. Courtesy of Nicholas Howe.

highlight the elements of Irving Howe in Orwell's work that he discerned. Indeed, we may say that, as much as any Anglo-American intellectual prominently likened to Orwell, Howe was quite indeed "like" him. Even his convictions about prose style, voiced in the preface to the third edition of *Politics and the Novel* — which was reissued just months before his death in 1993 — directly echoed Orwell's famous aspiration to write "prose like a window pane":

Now, especially at a time when critical writing is marked by jargon and obscurantism, my inclination is to care most about lucidity. The writer of

expository prose, I now feel, should strive for that most difficult of styles:
A prose so direct, so clear, so transparent, that the act of reading comes to
seem like looking through a glass.[59]

Orwell is one of "the writers who have meant most to me," one of "the crucial
witnesses," Howe says at the close of his autobiography. "It is with their witness
that, along the margin, I want to identify," a witness to witnesses.[60]

If, in the end, one affirms with Howe that Orwell died a "democratic socialist,"
it is in no small part, I think, also to pay witness—and final respect—to a perception of Orwell's integrity, intelligence, and self-knowledge.

VI

Although the tributes to Howe as "the American Orwell" are exaggerated, it is
indisputable that he and Orwell shared not just similar political convictions but
also significant literary affinities, as Howe himself rightly intuited.[61] Above all,
the two writers had a similar kind of rhetorical and inventive (rather than creative
or purely literary) imagination. Like Orwell, who was the great twentieth-century
master of enduring catchwords and neologisms, Howe carved lapidary formula-
tions in powerfully, and sometimes beautifully, chiseled prose, whereby he too
added phrases to the cultural zeitgeist. (Howe especially admired those passages
in which an author wrote "chiseled" or "clenched" prose—a favorite Howe epi-
thet—and Howe's own best writing possesses a rigorous, taut dynamism.) Indeed,
one could say that the prose gifts of both writers crossed from the rhetorical to the
journalistic. Like Orwell's catchphrases, Howe's coinages were often polemical—
and directed at explicitly political targets: "this age of conformity" (his swipe at
the intelligentsia's conservative turn in the 1950s);[62] "socialism is the name of
our desire" (adapted from Tolstoy's famous assertion about God); "the New York
Intellectuals" (a phrase that he gave wide currency, if he did not invent it, in characterizing his *Partisan Review* circle); "guerrillas with tenure" (perhaps his sharp-
est cut at the New Left's guru scholars); "a world more attractive" (a little-known
phrase of Trotsky's expressing love for art over politics); "confrontation politics"
(what Howe characterized as the New Left's negotiating style); and "craft elitism"
(how arcane literary theory, exemplified by poststructuralism and postmodernism, exploits jargon to exclude the nonspecialist reader), among other phrases.[63]
Orwell did not hesitate to borrow words and phrases for his own purposes and to
reinscribe them—and neither did Howe. This is apparent in the titles of Howe's
books, such as his volume of literary criticism, *A World More Attractive*, whose title
recalls Trotsky's phrase. But it is also evident in his edited volumes, such as *The*

Radical Imagination and *The Radical Papers*, which nod to Trilling's celebrated book *The Liberal Imagination* and to the Pentagon Papers, respectively.

However some of Howe's political adversaries may ridicule comparisons portraying him as "the American Orwell,"[64] this much can be said: Howe chose wisely when he embraced Orwell as his literary and political model, for Orwell helped liberate him from sectarian radicalism. In particular, Orwell's skepticism toward ideology countered the influence of Trotsky's allegiance to Marxist abstraction and the god of System. Moreover, one cannot deny that the ongoing controversy about Howe's heritage does indeed resemble the cultural politics of Orwell's reputation.[65] Indeed, with the exception of Noam Chomsky, probably no American socialist thinker in the post–World War II era has provoked more disagreement within the Left and aroused more vitriol on the Right than Irving Howe.

My own view is that Howe, like Orwell before him, became a conscience of his generation and ultimately even of our nation's liberal-Left intelligentsia. As a result, the stakes involved in disputes about Howe's legacy are high. For to elevate or denigrate Howe—as has long been similarly the case with Orwell in Britain—is to affirm or assault nothing less than the recent history of the American liberal-Left, the status of the radical dissenting tradition, and the relevance of social democracy and democratic socialism to the American polity.

The image of "the conservative mind": Kirk in his fifties.
Courtesy of Annette Kirk.

CHAPTER FOUR

"A Leftist by Accident?"

Orwell and the American Cultural Conservatives

I

Orwell's rising reputation, especially in the United States in the 1950s, coincided with the birth of American cultural conservatism in its contemporary guise. And indeed the enthusiastic reception accorded to him by American conservatives not only contributed strongly to his Cold Warrior status during the decade but also exerted powerful influence upon American conservatism's emerging sensibility and direction.

Chief among Orwell's admirers on the Right was the scholar-intellectual often credited with having inaugurated early postwar American cultural conservatism, Russell Kirk, who discussed Orwell's work frequently and at length. This chapter addresses Kirk's reception of Orwell's oeuvre, especially *Nineteen Eighty-Four*, from the 1950s through the 1980s, drawing not only on his published work but also on interviews that I conducted with him. As we shall see, unlike British conservatives around the Catholic *Tablet*, such as Christopher Hollis, who knew Orwell personally and emphasized their spiritual and political affinities with him—turning him into something close to a "religious fellow-traveler"—Kirk saw Orwell as an atheistic socialist who despaired about socialism yet firmly rejected religious belief and faith in the afterlife.[1]

By the early 1980s, when I began to interview him, Kirk (1918–1993) stood as the nation's most respected student of historical conservatism. To many readers, Kirk seemed the personification of the title of his first and best-known book: *The Conservative Mind*. Since its publication in 1953 and the founding in 1957 of *Modern Age*, which soon became the leading quarterly of the American Right, Kirk had devoted the greater part of his distinguished scholarly and literary career to exploring, chronicling, and explaining conservatism to the American public. That there had occurred a serious revival of intelligent conservatism in America was due, in part, to his work. *The Conservative Mind* identified a line of conservative thought stretching back to eighteenth-century England and established conclusively that there was an intellectual tradition of Anglo-American conservatism.[2] By the time of Kirk's death, *The Conservative Mind* had gone though seven editions. It was—and still is—widely considered the single most influential modern work addressing cultural conservatism.[3]

Kirk spent five years in postwar Britain as a doctoral candidate at St. Andrew's University (1947–1952), where he encountered many British conservatives and socialists.[4] In a series of interviews with me during the mid-1980s, he declared that he credited Orwell with having been a key figure responsible for shifting Anglo-American intellectual opinion rightward, thereby creating a favorable climate for the reception of *The Conservative Mind* on its appearance in April 1953. Kirk placed that contention in the context of his remarks in *Enemies of the Permanent Things* (1969), where he had opened his Orwell chapter with a lavish claim for Orwell's impact less than a decade after his death in January 1950 at the age of forty-six: "No novelist has exerted a stronger influence upon political opinion in Britain and America than Orwell."[5] Or as Kirk wrote in his essay "The Path to Utopia," collected in *Beyond the Dreams of Avarice* (1956): "Orwell has been incalculably influential since his death in turning the minds of Englishmen against collectivistic utopias, more influential by far than he was when he lived."[6] In language that echoed, perhaps ironically, the criticism of some of Orwell's fierce critics within the British New Left (especially E. P. Thompson),[7] Kirk elaborated on that observation in our interview in March 1983:

That influence was, generally, a chastening one. Orwell was, in the midfifties, a dramatic force for turning people away from socialism and progressivism. That was a period of painful reflection for Americans, who no longer believed left-wing ideas about the much-promised benefits of bigger government or the welfare state. Orwell's disillusion with socialism assisted such reflections. He contributed very considerably to the abandonment of the call of progress in the West, whose results are not entirely fortunate.[8]

Or, as Kirk had expressed it in *The Conservative Mind:* "Orwell succeeded in wakening the dread of the British and the American public against the conception of state socialism in *Nineteen Eighty-Four.*"[9]

But Kirk noted in another interview in 1983 that Orwell did not equate his critique of socialism with a new allegiance to conservatism:

In Orwell's case, of course, many conservatives were happy to welcome a convert to the ranks. Orwell was not a conservative, but an anti-collectivist. Not

Russell Kirk in his mid-forties in Scotland, 1961. By this time,
after *The Conservative Mind* (1953) and the founding of his journal *Modern Age* (1957), Kirk had become one of the leading conservative intellectuals in the U.S. Courtesy of Annette Kirk.

all anti-collectivists are conservative. So it was with Orwell. There are, obviously, strongly traditional elements in his personality and his writings. Still,
his general attitude was that of a socialist. Even if he subscribed to nothing
resembling Soviet collectivism, he nevertheless does anticipate rather gloom-
ily a future of equality as uniformity.[10]

Kirk went on to emphasize the postwar context in which both his and Orwell's writings were received. Just a handful of significant contemporary conservative works existed: Friedrich Hayek's *Road to Serfdom* (1942), Richard M. Weaver's *Ideas Have Consequences* (1948), the work of Nazi refugees Eric Voegelin and Leo Strauss, and William F. Buckley's *God and Man at Yale* (1951). It all seemed to bear out Lionel Trilling's statement in *The Liberal Imagination* (1950) that there was virtually no intellectual expression of conservatism "in general circulation" at midcentury.[11] Indeed, to most members of the Anglo-American intelligentsia, the collocation "conservative intellectuals" seemed like a contradiction in terms. Both in Britain and the United States, there seemed to be no conservative movement in the early 1950s.[12]

Acknowledging these historical facts in an interview in 1984, Kirk elaborated on why he believed that Orwell's work exerted such "dramatic force" on intellectual opinion in the mid-fifties. The renaissance of what would be hailed as "the new conservatism" in 1953 coincided with Kirk's book on conservatism that spring and the BBC-TV adaptation of *Nineteen Eighty-Four* in December 1954 (a program that reached millions of Britons and had the largest viewing audience of any BBC production up to that date). As Kirk later recalled:

Orwell's influence is paramount around that time. No doubt his influence accounted in part for the favorable reception of my book. It was a period of sober reflection. The geopolitical picture had been heading in the wrong direction: What came out of World War II was nothing like the Federation of the World. People were foolish to expect that. I argued that we needed to take up conservative views once more and examine their spirit. That was made possible in part by Orwell's general influence. And Orwell's great reputation among neo-liberals, like the *Partisan Review* circle and intellectuals such as Lionel Trilling, also set the climate and contributed favorably to my book's good reception. In fact there were two reviews of mine in *PR*. Neither of them accepted my doctrines, but they were willing to talk about things.[13]

The germ of the substantial essay on Orwell in *Enemies of the Permanent Things* is traceable to an event that occurred almost two decades earlier: the fall 1952 debate on Orwell at Michigan State between Elwood Lawrence and Kirk. Lawrence was a senior professor at Michigan State University and was in charge of the literary competitions there, which Kirk often won when he was an undergraduate. Kirk had been living in Scotland in 1952; Lawrence was on an academic sabbatical in London, and Kirk visited his house in Paddington.[14]

So, both of us having recently been in Britain, my friend Warren Fleischauer at Michigan State conceived a debate between us on Orwell. Lawrence was an American liberal who was enthusiastic about British socialism. That, of course, was a common position in 1950. Lawrence had gotten free health care under Britain's new socialized medicine program, lived for a year in London, and had a great experience abroad. So he didn't see anything really wrong with socialism. He very much resented *Nineteen Eighty-Four* as an attack upon socialism. I said that Orwell was a socialist only nominally. I argued that *Nineteen Eighty-Four* could indeed happen if the socialist mullahs triumphed throughout the world.[15]

The encounter did not have a happy ending for the two men's personal relationship:

Lawrence was angered by the exchange ever after. He had been teaching an edition of John Stuart Mill's *On Liberty* with an introduction by me. And he had the students cut out my introduction! So I never really saw him after that.

Kirk also argued in the debate—as he later did in his 1956 essay—that conservatives in America and Britain were strongly sympathetic to *Nineteen Eighty-Four*.

George Brown, the Liberal M.P. from Belfort, came back around then [1952] from a visit to Poland and said that Poland is "*Nineteen Eighty-Four* realized." In general, that was the attitude of many Britons and most Americans. As a result, there were persons who looked on Orwell as both a fierce anti-socialist and as a thoroughgoing conservative because they were unacquainted with his previous writings and background. I suppose that the average American reader thought: "Now here's someone who speaks up for American principles against communism." It was that kind of naïve attitude. Among persons of some education on the liberal Left, the prevailing view was: "This is the true British socialist." To them Orwell represented the socialist resistance to totalitarianism.[16]

Kirk noted that most Americans casually and erroneously conflated support for British Labour with socialism:

Most Americans failed to distinguish between Labour with a capital L and socialism. The relationship was always sort of tenuous. George Brown was a

Russell Kirk and wife Annette in his ancestral home, known as Piety Hall, in Mecosta, Michigan, in 1968, around the time he was finishing *Enemies of the Permanent Things.* Courtesy of Annette Kirk.

Labour man rather than a socialist per se. Orwell would have liked to have been a wholehearted Labour man, but he couldn't be. He *thought* he was a socialist, but he wasn't. He was always trying to make himself into a member of the working classes and failing to do so.

I think of the episode in one of his essays, in which he is traveling around with the hop pickers. He comes to a hostel to stay the night. There is a former sergeant-major in charge of the hostel for migrant laborers. The sergeant-major says, "You are a gentleman, aren't you, sir?" Orwell says, "Yes, I went to public school." "Oh, what a pity you're in such circumstances, here, let me show you to a better bunk." Orwell is furious at this because he wants to be taken as a man of the people and he can't get away from being taken for a gentleman.[17]

Kirk was aware that British conservatives who had been familiar with Orwell's work didn't conceive him to be a conservative convert or a socialist heading toward conservatism. But American conservatives had generally been unfamiliar with Orwell until the publication of *Animal Farm* (1945): the majority of them thus regarded him as a disillusioned socialist; other American conservatives said that Orwell in *Nineteen Eighty-Four* turned away from socialism completely and was no longer a politically engaged man in any sense. Still others viewed Orwell's emphasis in *Nineteen Eighty-Four* on old books, nursery rhymes, and venerable London churches as an urge to embrace a kind of conservatism, though he didn't formally do it.

All these views differed from what Kirk held, which was that Orwell was indeed a socialist, but that socialism was a faith he could no longer believe in. Orwell was a socialist "only nominally," repeated Kirk. "Really it was a despairing form of socialism that he was finally led to. But most people were not clear on that. . . . The average American reader knew nothing about the man."[18]

Kirk considered *Nineteen Eighty-Four* not so much a warning as a reflection of Orwell's own inner struggles and personal beliefs:

Orwell died, as many people do, of pulmonary diseases and the lack of will to live. The disease gains on those who really have no desire to go on. . . . He would be considered a disillusioned socialist or pessimist if you interpret *Nineteen Eighty-Four* as a direct statement of his belief. He said in a letter that he meant *Nineteen Eighty-Four* clearly as a warning about the dangers to which collectivism was leading . . .

I consider *Nineteen Eighty-Four* a veiled declaration of despair. The power behind INGSOC and the world of *Nineteen Eighty-Four* is thoroughly diabolical. Orwell couldn't admit that to himself because it was in conflict with his freely professed contempt for theology and religion.[19]

Those thoughts elaborated an important contention in *The Conservative Mind:* "When faith in God, duty to family, hope of advancement, and satisfaction with one's task have vanished from the routine of life, Big Brother remains."[20]

Characterizing Orwell as a disillusioned prophet, Kirk elaborated on this theme soon thereafter in his commentary on the 1954 BBC-TV adaptation of *Nineteen Eighty-Four:*

The effect of *Nineteen Eighty Four* upon public opinion goes far to refute the argument that ideas merely reflect the great social and material currents of an age. Orwell's novel reflects his own disillusion. But his prophecies are of the order that create subsequent events. It has been said that Orwell influenced everyone except the people he wanted to move, the intellectuals of the Left, yet they too now are confessing the truth of his indictment. The BBC's presentation of *Nineteen Eighty-Four* was generally commended by socialists. . . . Indeed, the only people who protested against the program were certain persons that felt that such disagreeable possibilities ought not to be discussed in public.[21]

Orwell's example and vision were much on Kirk's mind in the mid-1980s, especially during the ballyhooed "countdown to 1984" in late 1983 and early 1984.[22] Kirk averred that, although he admired Orwell strongly, he accepted that sharp political differences separated them. In an interview in March 1985, Kirk stressed his broad cultural, indeed spiritual, affinities with Orwell. He saw Orwell and himself as allies against "the enemies of the permanent things," in his beloved phrase of T. S. Eliot's. Kirk's identification with Orwell did not lead him to minimize their ideological differences: Kirk regarded Orwell as a socialist who ultimately, in *Animal Farm* and *Nineteen Eighty-Four*, lost hope in a worldly utopia yet harbored a longing for a transcendent order. In *Enemies of the Permanent Things*, Kirk had called Orwell "a Leftist by accident" whose socialism "scarcely can be called a position at all, but only an agonized leap in the dark, away from the pain of consolidated, uniform, industrialized modern existence." Orwell was a "desperado, a man who has despaired of grace," concluded Kirk, "because he could bring himself to believe in no enduring principles of order, or in an Authority transcending private rationality."[23]

In that same 1985 interview, Kirk—who converted in the mid-1960s to Roman Catholicism—developed this argument in a new direction.[24] He argued that Orwell's fiction revealed him to be "a closet believer":

There was an argument that Orwell, in his later work, became a militant atheist. But that really meant that he was a closet believer. In *Nineteen Eighty-Four* he couldn't admit the existence of a diabolical power since he couldn't admit the existence of a beneficent divine power. He had to accept that some terrible force existed beyond man, which is driving people like O'Brien, a force that causes the destruction of the human personality. Orwell was really seeking God. Of course Orwell couldn't profess it.[25]

Kirk concluded:

I took up the other side of the coin, arguing that he accepts the existence of God by accepting the existence of a diabolical power.[26]

Conservatives such as Christopher Hollis, an Old Etonian classmate of Orwell's and later a British M.P. and prominent Catholic convert, focused on Orwell's intimations of divinity and incipient faith, which led them to pronounce Orwell a conservative and would-be believer, rather than a disillusioned socialist.[27] By contrast, Kirk discerned the demonic theme in *Nineteen Eighty-Four* and thus saw Orwell as a self-condemned pagan, a socialist in despair. Kirk agreed with Hollis that Orwell *wanted* to believe, but Kirk held that Orwell's skepticism proved stronger than his faith:

> Orwell's fascination with the demonic is reflected in his attitude toward the supernatural. In one of his letters, he describes drawing a sketch of a ghost in a churchyard. He recalls that he probably had a hallucination. I quote that in my preface to my new volume of ghost stories [*Watchers at the Strait Gate*, 1984]. I believe that it wasn't necessarily a hallucination. But that was the explanation Orwell had to give himself. The only way he could account for that vivid experience was by saying it was a hallucination. That illustrates his yearning for the supernatural and his suppressed faith.[28]

Kirk called this letter to the attention of Robert Aickman, the distinguished British ghost story writer who had harshly reviewed *Animal Farm* in *Horizon*. Kirk recalled:

> Aickman didn't like Orwell at all. Aickman replied to my letter with a tart remark: Well, Orwell is just the kind of person who would see a ghost. Aickman, you see, who wrote all these uncanny stories, professed to be a complete materialist, and also didn't believe in any divine power. His stories are intended to frighten, but also represent a kind of total disorder in which anything may happen. They symbolize the decay of British society.[29]

Kirk said that there was "evasiveness on Orwell's part in coming to terms with religious thought," as if (in Kirk's words) he had secretly lamented, "Oh, how I wish the price were lower so I could subscribe." Kirk also noted that Orwell often expressed "a vicious contempt, even hatred, for Catholics." Kirk attributed that antipathy to the British upper-class tradition in the boarding schools that Orwell attended. "The schools were Anglican, in the sense of being against popery: Resist the wicked papists. Look with contempt upon the sinners, but with fear upon the papists." Unlike Irish Catholic workers, noted Kirk, British Catholic intellectuals tended toward conservatism. "Catholic intellectuals are a far cry from the Irish proletarian Catholics of the cities. That gulf fueled Orwell's contempt for Catholicism."

Orwell was "especially vitriolic toward converts," Kirk noted.

> It was bad enough to be Catholic to begin with, but to convert to Catholicism! I wonder what Orwell would have thought of me! My conversion in 1964 was a long intellectual and emotional process that began in the mid-

1940s. . . . I had written for Catholic magazines for a long time, so it was generally assumed that I was already a Catholic. I really did share their convictions. So I concluded: I might as well declare myself one.[30]

Nonetheless, Kirk also noted that some of the people that were close to Orwell
took rightward turns or even embraced religious faith—such as Arthur Koestler
or Malcolm Muggeridge. Kirk speculated that Orwell might perhaps have changed
in a similar way:

Koestler turned not to orthodox religion but genuine religious mysticism.
His political turn to quietism was connected with that. But I wonder if
Orwell might not have been drawn like Muggeridge to religion. He was one
of Orwell's closest friends and was a socialist of sorts in the late 1930s and
early 1940s. I know him well. He's a gadfly, of course, and feared by some
conservatives because of his unorthodox stands.[31]

Kirk also drew a political comparison between Orwell and George Gissing, the
nineteenth-century British novelist:

One reason I'm so interested in Orwell is that he and I have a Gissing root.
Gissing was a socialist and became politically conservative. Orwell never
went that far, but it's the same trajectory.[32]

Nonetheless, while drawing such comparisons, Kirk also noted the dangers
of anachronistic interpretation. Indeed he remarked on the similarly politicized
receptions of Edmund Burke and Orwell, both of whose work had suffered distortions and willful misinterpretation:

It's an abuse of Burke to claim him for the Left, or certainly the far Left.
And it's an abuse of Orwell to claim him for the Right. But what complicates
the case with Orwell, even more so than Burke, is that these interpretations
are based not only on his straightforward writings, journalism, and essays,
but on an interpretation of his novels. The tricky thing is to decide whether
he himself is speaking directly through his protagonists or if he's even speaking partly through them. That is very different from looking at *Reflections
on the Revolution in France* and asking, "Is Burke sincere?" In Burke's work,
we're not dealing with a fictional creation.
        Let me give you one example. In *Coming Up for Air*, George Bowling
is pretty much a mouthpiece for George Orwell. Critics on the Left insist

that Orwell is mocking Bowling, that the emphasis on Bowling's preoccupation with his childhood points up Bowling's permanent adolescence. In other words, they insist it is a novel and that Orwell is no more George Bowling than Theodore Dreiser is Sister Carrie. But that seems unconvincing to me. Orwell wasn't all that subtle, he was pretty direct in his fictional characterizations.[33]

Kirk noted that there was no significant change in the conservative image of Orwell in the 1960s and '70s—nor in his own response to Orwell—unlike the case on the Left.[34] Conservatives really weren't looking at Orwell in relation to contemporary events as the Left was doing, Kirk noted. But on the Left—after Suez, certainly after Khrushchev's Secret Speech, and even during the Vietnam War—Orwell was thought of as a revolutionary or a reactionary, "depending on which leftist you were talking to."

On the Left, the question that kept coming up again and again in the early 1980s was: "If Orwell were alive today, what would he say?" Not content to speculate in general terms about Orwell's possible political and spiritual trajectory in the decades following his death, Kirk weighed in with his own quite specific prediction during an interview in 1983:

I think he would stand with the present Social Democratic Party—with Shirley Williams and her Liberal colleagues. In 1958, a Liberal Party platform proposed to base some of its policy proposals on Orwell's image of the future.[35]

Kirk considered it misguided, if not absurd, to link a political program to any utopian—let alone anti-utopian—notions about the future. Kirk was no believer in utopias or futuristic blueprints for social betterment. As he wrote in *Beyond the Dreams of Avarice* (1956) about *Nineteen Eighty-Four:*

How much courage does Winston Smith have in *Nineteen Eighty-Four?* The bravest act he performs is to drink to the past. He is living in a realized utopia, which like all realized utopias is hell upon earth. Against such a future as this our chief protection is knowledge of the past.[36]

Russell Kirk sought to safeguard what he called "the permanent things"—the Christian standards of proper conduct derived from revelation, tradition, and reason.[37] And though he and Orwell differed on the means, each of them took up his "sword of imagination," as Kirk proudly termed it. Each of them fought that

common enemy, the nightmare of anti-utopian utopianism, from whatever direction—right or left, past or future—they perceived the threat to come.[38] Kirk believed that he and Orwell were, in that respect—however profound their political
and spiritual differences—comrades-in-arms.[39]

Or, as Kirk expressed it in *Enemies of the Permanent Things:* "In a strange
and desperate way, Orwell was a lover of the permanent things. Orwell's was that
[form of] radicalism which is angry with society because society has failed to provide men with the ancient norms of simple life—family, decency, and continuity. . . . Take him all in all, Orwell was a man, and there is none left in England
like him."[40]

Christopher Hitchens, 2004. Courtesy of Christopher Hitchens.

CHAPTER FIVE

Does Orwell Matter?

Between Fraternity and Fratricide at the *Nation*

I

George Orwell has long been a subject of contention among the writers of the *Nation*. In the 1940s, the *Nation* and the *New Republic* were the only non-communist American magazines to criticize Orwell sharply. In many respects, the reception of Orwell's work in the *Nation* mirrored his treatment by the *New Statesman and Nation* under Kingsley Martin throughout the late 1930s and '40s. Like Martin, several editors of the *Nation* were quite sympathetic to Stalinism, derided Orwell for his vocal anti-communism, and published mixed reviews of *Homage to Catalonia* and *Animal Farm*.

As we shall soon see, *Nation* staff writers and literary contributors have voiced similar reservations about Orwell more than five decades after his death. For instance, whereas Alexander Cockburn (the son of Claud Cockburn, a communist of the 1930s openly hostile toward Orwell) has rebuked Orwell loudly and repeatedly, Christopher Hitchens has expressed lavish admiration for Orwell's achievement. This chapter devotes attention to a few key moments in the *Nation*'s reception history of Orwell as it focuses on Hitchens's response, which spans more than two decades of virtually unqualified homage to Orwell.

II

Because Hitchens's own affiliation (and subsequent break) with the *Nation* figures prominently in his reception of Orwell, it bears noting at the outset that Orwell himself also had a complicated relationship with the *Nation* in the 1940s.[1] Orwell read and valued the *Nation* (and preferred it to the postwar *New Republic* under Henry Wallace);[2] and the *Nation* reviewed the American editions of his major books and evidently respected him and welcomed his reviews.[3] But Orwell was not universally esteemed by *Nation* contributors during his lifetime, let alone thereafter. Orwell's proximity to *PR* and to Macdonald's *politics* doubtless made him suspect in their eyes, even before Orwell's sweeping success with *Animal Farm* in August 1946.

Nation reviewers were ambivalent toward Orwell, prizing his literary prose style and his intellectual acumen, while castigating his outspoken opposition to Soviet totalitarianism and his independent radical stance. In September 1946, Wylie Sypher pronounced *Animal Farm* a "labored satire of Stalinism."[4] Isaac Rosenfeld praised Orwell's style yet found his anti-Stalinist politics shrill and one-sided. Rosenfeld judged *Animal Farm* "a disappointing piece of work," arguing that Orwell should have realized that the fault with the animals' revolution lay with the pigs and their piggishness.[5] (Ironically, this criticism echoed the conservative objection that T. S. Eliot had voiced when he rejected the manuscript for Faber in 1944.)[6]

Rosenfeld's criticism of July 1950 was echoed in Herbert Matthews's three-thousand-word critique of the American edition of *Homage to Catalonia* after Orwell's death. Appearing in July 1952, near the height of the McCarthyite Red scare and the anti-communist witch hunts, Matthews's review merits close attention as the magazine's most substantial treatment of Orwell—and as the *Nation*'s summary verdict on his posthumous reputation.

Matthews's review was (ironically?) titled: "Homage to Orwell."[7] But it was no act of homage. After perfunctorily giving "two cheers" for *Catalonia* and lauding it as "an honest, vivid, personal account," Matthews dismissed it as just "one man's bitter experience" possessing "rewarding literary value" yet no wider validity. If readers approach the book "as history," Matthews argued, "they will be either misled or confused." Matthews continued:

Orwell went to Spain thoroughly ignorant of politics; he came away still ignorant, but with one priceless piece of wisdom—that communism is a counter-revolutionary movement. Spain did not live up to the hopes, the desires, the ideals, the (alas!) illusions that all, Orwell included, harbored.

In order to discredit Orwell more fully, Matthews also took the unusual step of devoting one-third of his review to a letter from Juan Negrin, former prime minister of the Spanish Republic (May 1937–February 1939), which Matthews had solicited in order to gain Negrin's estimate of Orwell. Perhaps unsurprisingly, Negrin's judgment echoed Matthews's own:

After reading his book, I did not change my opinion about Orwell—a decent and righteous gentleman, biased by a too rigid, puritanical frame, gifted with a candor bordering on naïvete, highly critical but blindly credulous, morbidly individualistic (an Englishman!) but submitting lazily and without discernment to the atmosphere of the gregarious community in which he voluntarily and instinctively anchors himself, and so supremely honest and self-denying that he would not hesitate to change his mind once he perceived himself to be wrong . . .

He came to the chaotic front of Aragon under the tutelage of a group *possibly* infiltrated by German agents (reread what he says about Germans moving freely from one side to the other and what the Nazis officially stated after the war about their activities on our side) but *certainly* controlled by elements very allergic not only to Stalinism (this was more often than not a pure pretext) but to anything that meant a united and supreme direction of the struggle under a common discipline.

Putting all this together, one gets more than enough to justify the distorted image in Orwell's mind of the happenings of 1937 in Barcelona.[8]

Orwell did, however, have his admirers at the *Nation*. Diana Trilling, the magazine's regular book reviewer in the 1940s, was—like her husband, Lionel—a staunch supporter of Orwell's and a fellow anti-Stalinist. She too, like Rosenfeld, was a member of the *Partisan Review* circle of New York writers, albeit from an older generation. Writing in August 1949, Diana Trilling wrote a glowing tribute to *Nineteen Eighty-Four* in the *Nation*. Mrs. Trilling called *Nineteen Eighty-Four* "a brilliant and fascinating novel," with Orwell's presentation of Ingsoc "ingenious in the extreme." She then lauded Orwell and *Animal Farm* in terms that even many non-communist leftist supporters no doubt found excessive, especially so because she went on to claim that the fable's explicit targets included Clement Attlee's postwar Labour government, which (implied Mrs. Trilling) might soon be intoning "Beasts of England" at their next Labour Party conference:

Even where, as in his last novel, *Animal Farm*, Mr. Orwell seemed to be concerned only with unmasking the Soviet Union for its dreamy admirers, he was urged on by something larger than sectarianism. . . . In that work, Mr. Orwell fantasized the fate not only of an established dictatorship like that of Russia, but also of Labour England.[9]

Likewise, Irving Howe also praised Orwell highly in the *Nation*'s pages. Reviewing Orwell's last essay collection, *Shooting an Elephant*, published just days before his death, Howe called him "a first-rate journalist" with "a large gift for the observation of significant details."[10] Turning to Orwell's earlier works, Howe pronounced *Down and Out* "superior to anything of its kind written in America,

and [it] should be read by at least those people who think poverty a more significant problem than, say, original sin."[11] Similarly, *Burmese Days* possessed for
Howe "an authenticity and sureness of detail which is possible only to someone
like Orwell, who has seen it from the inside." On the other hand, Howe's lingering Trotskyist sympathies restrained his enthusiasm for Orwell's late work. Echo-
ing Sypher and Rosenfeld, Howe found *Animal Farm* and *Nineteen Eighty-Four*
"static, a mere conjured vision of evil in which no serious attempt is made to seek
out underlying causes."[12] As we saw in Chapter Three, Howe revised his estimate
of Orwell's anti-communist satires in the mid-1950s.

Just as this divergence of opinion among Diana Trilling, Howe, and Rosenfeld
reflected a split view of him that prevailed not only among the New York Intellectuals but also within the early postwar *Nation* itself,[13] so too have the *Nation*'s
editorial staff and contributors exhibited a similar divergence regarding Orwell
in recent years. For example, Alexander Cockburn has condemned Orwell un-
reservedly. "How quickly one learns to loathe the affectations of plain bluntish-
ness," Cockburn bluntly writes in an introduction to Leonard Reed's *Snowball's
Chance*, a fiction rewrite and reply to Orwell's fable. "The man of conscience turns
out to be a whiner, and of course a snitch" (a reference to Orwell's now-infamous
"list" submitted to a British intelligence agent in 1949).[14] Another *Nation* columnist, Katha Pollitt, is likewise no fan of Orwell—nor of Christopher Hitchens.
"Let's say the Communist Party was bad and wrong; why should Orwell help the
repressive powers of the state?" wrote Pollitt. "Let the government do its own
dirty work." Pollitt was also condemning Hitchens's support for Orwell's cooperation with the British intelligence services.[15] Meanwhile Andrew Rubin, an occasional *Nation* contributor, has used another term to repeat, admittedly in more
measured tones, the gist of this polemic. He has contended that Orwell "collabo-
rated" with the British government.[16]

Yet Ian Williams has exalted Orwell as a stellar example of a socialist daring
both to speak out against doublespeak and to think thoughtcrime against the orthodox. Williams has written:

Nothing vindicates Orwell so much as his critics. The intelligence of his
criticism, its effectiveness, is what reduces so many of his attackers to parox-
ysms of adhominemism. In short, Orwell was not a lone voice [against both
fascism and Stalinism], although he was an outstanding voice. He was part of
a large, well-established British tradition that, far from being marginalized
like the Trotskyist sects worldwide or the American Left, became the governing party of one of the world's major nations. It was the clarity and strength
of his voice that set him apart.[17]

In an essay of 2004, Williams adds:

To understand the twentieth century, I regularly reread *Animal Farm, Nineteen Eighty-Four, Alice in Wonderland, Alice Through the Looking Glass,* and *Darkness at Noon.* Orwell's work gives us the intellectual tools to understand what is happening and to combat it—without becoming the unthinking, metaphysically minded enemy that polemics can and do make of people. He offers an outstanding example of a writer and thinker who fights rough and tough, but fairly, for decency.[18]

The *Nation*'s checkered history, especially its sorry record on Stalinism, as well as its continued ambivalence toward Orwell, bears on Hitchens's own identification with Orwell. To understand why Orwell matters so much to Hitchens, we must consider how Hitchens first came to the *Nation* and the role Orwell has played in his intellectual development, which culminated in 2002 with *Why Orwell Matters* (U.K. title: *Orwell's Victory*), a book-length salute to Orwell's achievement as a writer and political thinker.

III

Christopher Hitchens (1949–) is one of our most prominent and controversial public intellectuals. He has criticized Mother Teresa, condemned Henry Kissinger, and nodded to Rilke with his own *Letters to a Young Contrarian* (2001).[19] Along the way, Hitchens has consistently and openly embraced the work and example of George Orwell. No book about Orwell and his intellectual progeny would be complete if it did not examine why Orwell matters to Christopher Hitchens.

Like Orwell before the success of *Animal Farm,* Hitchens was relatively little known outside intellectual circles until the mid-1990s,[20] when he became a much-quoted and frequently interviewed critic of the Clinton administration from the Left, especially during the Monica Lewinsky scandal and the impeachment proceedings against President Clinton.[21] Hitchens reached a still higher level of international visibility in 2001, when he broke with the Left.[22] Just as Orwell became a national figure once he equated Stalinism with rule by pigs in his best-selling fable, so too did Hitchens rise to prominence for his outspoken, rhetorically incisive criticism of the Left following the 9/11 terrorist attacks. Supporting the administration of George W. Bush, Hitchens defended Bush's "war against terrorism" (Hitchens branded the enemy as "Islamofascism") and condemned the Left for its failure to support military intervention to halt terrorists and tyrants such as Osama bin Laden and Saddam Hussein. Hitchens's positions rankled many socialists (Cockburn accused him of becoming "just another conservative porker"), and the ensuing row ultimately led Hitchens to resign his post as a contributing editor and regular columnist with the fortnightly *Nation*. In an article in the *Washington Post* ("So Long, Fellow Travelers"), he came out foursquare against the anti-war Left and in favor of a preemptive strike on Iraq. Hitchens thus gave up his *Nation* column, "Minority Report," quitting the Left's leading journal of opinion in September 2002 (after a twenty-year stint) with the claim that its post-9/11 "paleoliberal" politics marked a sharp sea change. Since he had started writing for it, argued Hitchens, the *Nation* had turned into "the echo chamber of those who truly believe that John Ashcroft is a greater menace than Osama bin Laden."[23]

Of course, Orwell was not alone among radicals in his early condemnation of Soviet communism and his "Left patriot" stance in the 1930s—nor was Hitchens the only leftist to advocate strong military measures against bin Laden's al-Qaeda and Saddam's Iraq. But Hitchens and Orwell expressed themselves unequivocally and in arresting phrases that commanded attention and provoked bitter quarreling. For his part, Hitchens seemed to see his break with the *Nation* in terms comparable to Orwell's estrangement from the *New Statesman and Nation* (after Kingsley Martin rejected Orwell's dispatches from Spain about the machinations of the Stalin-affiliated International Brigades).[24]

Hitchens's goodbye to the *Nation* was not just a personal milestone; it can also be seen as a symbolic event.[25] It signified that he no longer needed the magazine, either as a professional platform or an intellectual community. Outside its orbit, he could affirm (or indulge) his iconoclasm and rebel individualism without restraint, firing salvos at whatever targets and from whatever vantage point he deemed most appropriate.[26]

It was as if he had anticipated this step as ultimately necessary and soon inevitable when he wrote a few months earlier in *Letters to a Young Contrarian:*

Well, no, I don't think that the solidarity of belonging is much of a prize. I appreciate that it can bestow some pride, and that it can lead to mutual aid and even brother- and sisterhood, but it has too many suffocating qualities, and many if not most of the benefits can be acquired in other ways. (105)

While Hitchens's break with the *Nation* triggered a new round of criticism from the Left, liberals and centrists who were reformulating their political stances similarly leapt to Hitchens's defense. Some allies immediately compared Hitchens to Orwell—long before the publication of *Orwell's Victory* in late 2002. For example, former *New Republic* editor Andrew Sullivan made the Orwell connection explicit. Sullivan, a fellow British expatriate residing in the United States with complicated ideological coordinates, wrote for the *Times* of London:

[L]ike Orwell, he quit. Not for the Right, not for social status, not for the 15 minutes of infamy every turncoat gets. He quit for the possibility of think-ing outside any political loyalties at a time when such loyalties are as trivial as they are corrupting. And one day, the Left will come to realise his point.[27]

Going several steps further than Sullivan, Ron Rosenbaum of the *New York Ob-server*, commenting on Hitchens's support for the war in Afghanistan, referred to him as "a George Orwell for our time."[28]

Is he? There are in fact some broad similarities: Both Orwell and Hitchens are public school graduates and brilliant prose stylists. Like Orwell, Hitchens is first a moralist and second a political and cultural critic. For instance, like Or-well, Hitchens—though much less fervently (or publicly)—has reservations about abortion and contraception.[29] Moreover, Orwell was, and remained to his death, a self-avowed man of the Left and anti-Stalinist, as well as an uncompromising atheist,[30] an anti-imperialist, and an anti-Zionist.[31] In each of these respects, Hitchens can be said to resemble Orwell, even though Hitchens has abandoned the self-description "socialist" (though not "leftist"). What remains disputable, however, is whether the ex-Trotskyist Hitchens—who even today harbors not only lingering affection but also guarded admiration for Trotsky (the "Old Man")[32]— has ever been, like Orwell, an anti-communist (as opposed to being merely an anti-Stalinist).[33] Of course, the obvious difference bears noting: unlike Orwell, Hitchens is no novelist or fabulist; he limits himself to journalism, reportage, and the essay. But within those nonfiction limits, his productivity and range of topics easily match, if not exceed, those of Orwell.

Not surprisingly, most of Hitchens's ex-comrades on the Left blanch at the thought of likening him to Orwell. Quite apart from any comparison according to genre or subject matter, they consider Hitchens, at least since September 2001, no "leftist" or radical whatsoever. To them, his recent trajectory represents a rightward lurch far removed from Orwell's "critic within the Left" stance. More-over, they hold that simply in terms of temperament and class attitude, Hitchens lacks Orwell's human warmth and deep feeling for the common man.[34]

So again: Is he an Orwell for our time? The formulation is too simplistic; still, merely to raise the question suggests the scale of Hitchens's significance and achievement. Let us, therefore, move beyond that question and inquire more deeply into the two men's resemblance by examining more closely Hitchens's re-ception history of Orwell.

As we shall see, a look at how Hitchens has identified with Orwell, and how his defense of "why Orwell matters" serves also as a self-defense, not only furnishes insight into the lives and writings of both men. It also has implications for what it means to be a public intellectual today. For it can no longer be done in the manner of Orwell, who largely limited himself to the print media, often indeed the little magazine. To become a prominent intellectual in the postmodern age, one needs to stand within the literary tradition that Orwell represented and yet become an intellectual entrepreneur, adept at using the broadcast media to establish visibility and engage issues with an immediacy and responsiveness that Orwell might not even have understood.

IV

Hitchens grew up in Portsmouth, England, where his father was based as a naval officer. His middle-class parents worked hard to give him the prep school education that helped him gain admission to Balliol College, Oxford.[35] Hitchens has recalled that he was "the first member of my family ever to go to private school or even to university." In 1970, Balliol awarded him a scholarship to study in the United States.[36] Afterward, he returned to Britain and began a string of journalism assignments based in London, writing for the *Times*, the *Daily Express*, and the *New Statesman*. Originally a Trotskyist, indeed a leading activist in the International Socialists (IS) at Oxford,[37] Hitchens moved in the early 1980s toward a radical humanism featuring neutralism on Cold War geopolitics in Europe and sharp overall criticism of Reaganism.[38]

As a young intellectual in the 1970s and early '80s, Hitchens had already adopted Orwell as an intellectual big brother. At the same time, he realized that intellectual life could no longer be pursued the way Orwell had done it.[39] For the older model of an urban intellectual community—whether in London or elsewhere in the British Isles—no longer existed, a victim of the decline of the little magazine, the fracturing of the public sphere, and the flight of intellectuals into universities and academic specialization.

In 1982, Victor Navasky, then-editor of the *Nation*, hired Hitchens as a special correspondent from London. Soon the editor was asking whether Hitchens would move to Washington, D.C.

"You know, the magazine hasn't had a Washington columnist since I. F. Stone," Navasky said to the thirty-three-year-old writer.

"Why the hell not?" came the response.[40]

And so Hitchens did much more than visit the United States. He moved there. In hindsight, the physical relocation suggests the terms in which he might become the Orwell of his generation—i.e., by doing what Orwell failed to do. Moving from Airstrip One to the center of power in Oceania might afford Hitchens the possibility of living the conjunction of political-intellectual life that was still possible in the London of Orwell's day. And so, by emigrating to Washington, D.C., Hitchens soon became a kind of expatriate Orwell, one who has been able to measure the whale from the inside.[41]

Indeed, in *Orwell's Victory*, Hitchens asserts that Orwell was right on the three major issues of the twentieth century—imperialism, fascism, and Stalinism.[42] Orwell's single glaring weakness, Hitchens says, is that he missed America.

It is true that Orwell never visited the United States, despite several invitations to do so when he was London correspondent for the *Partisan Review* (1941–1946), and he paid America little attention, except to condemn its slick magazines and the Hollywood film industry. In *Why Orwell Matters* as well as in his journalism, Hitchens maintains that Orwell can be forgiven for being so Anglocentric. He was a very sick man, bedridden in later years with tuberculosis. Moreover, his entire intellectual network resided in London at a time when Britain still remained a world power, and certainly the leading European power. Indeed, throughout most of Orwell's lifetime, the British Empire's flag still waved on every continent in the world. Although this would change after World War II, coincident with the end of colonialism and a decisive transatlantic shift in the power dynamic from Europe to the United States, the change was, arguably, not yet fully clear even at the time of Orwell's death in January 1950.[43] By contrast, as the Cold War unfolded thereafter, Hitchens realized, in light of the enduring American-Soviet superpower rivalry, that Airstrip One had long become a geopolitical sideshow by the 1980s.

V

Hitchens's public identification with Orwell began long before *Orwell's Victory*.[44] Hitchens often referred to Orwell in his journalism of the 1970s and reviewed Bernard Crick's *George Orwell* admiringly in 1980.[45] In January 1983, shortly after Hitchens settled in Washington, with "Orwellmania" reaching a fever pitch as *Nineteen Eighty-Four* approached its manifest historical destiny,[46] *Harper's* ran a cover story by Norman Podhoretz titled "If Orwell Were Alive Today." Podhoretz argued that Orwell would have stood "with the neoconservatives and against the Left" were he still alive in the title year. Hitchens, in his first lengthy defense of Orwell, countered that Orwell would have remained on the Left, adding that Orwell rejected numerous opportunities to embrace the Right during his own lifetime.

Podhoretz based his argument on selective passages from Orwell's minor journalism. Citing Orwell's opposition to pacifism during World War II, his English
patriotism, his loathing of the Soviet Union, and above all his relentless criticism
of his fellow leftists, Podhoretz claimed that Orwell's overall politics and stands
on specific issues such as the nuclear freeze would have resembled those of neoconservatives such as Podhoretz himself. Orwell surely would have castigated
the "peace" movement as pacifist/neo-isolationist, and he would have stood fast
against détente as an accommodation to "Soviet imperialism." He would probably have also allowed that democratic socialism had failed and should be abandoned, for he might well have accepted, like the neoconservatives, that "the aims
of what *he* meant by socialism [had been] realized to a very great extent under
capitalism, and without either the concentration camps or the economic miseries that have been the invariable companions of socialism in practice." Podhoretz
concluded:

> I find it hard to believe that Orwell would have allowed an orthodoxy to
> blind him [to socialism's failure] more than he allowed any other "smelly
> little orthodoxies" to blind him to the truth about the particular issues
> involved in the struggle between totalitarianism and democracy: Spain,
> World War II, and communism.
>
>   In Orwell's time, it was the left-wing intelligentsia that made it so difficult
> for these truths to prevail. And so it is too with the particular issues gener-
> ated by the struggle between totalitarianism and democracy in our time,
> which is why I am convinced that if Orwell were alive today, he would be
> taking a stand with the neoconservatives and against the Left.[47]

Hitchens was quick to dispute Podhoretz's claims and engaged in a reclamation
process of his own. Selecting different quotations from Orwell's journalism, and
filling in Podhoretz's questionable elisions, Hitchens argued that Orwell, since he
had helped found the anarchist-sponsored Freedom Defence Committee, would
have opposed "the McCarthy persecutions" "unequivocally." And Hitchens disagreed with those, like Mary McCarthy, who supposed that Orwell would have
backed the United States in Vietnam. Orwell "hated colonialism," said Hitchens,
and he "would have seen the essential continuity of American intervention with
the French colonial presence. . . . He would have seen through the obfuscations
(lies, actually) of the Kennedy and Johnson administrations." Hitchens closed:

> I wish Orwell were alive today. The democratic socialist camp needs him
> more than ever. I would also dearly like to have his comments on the sort of
> well-heeled power worshiper who passes for an intellectual these days.[48]

So the pitched battle for Orwell's mantle between socialists and neoconservatives in 1983–1984 turned personal and nasty.[49] It should be noted, by the way, that neither Podhoretz's nor Hitchens's claim to Orwell is without its difficulties. Podhoretz, for example, omits the fact that Orwell, unlike virtually all neoconservatives from the generation of the '30s, was not a former Trotskyist or Stalinist or fellow-traveler disillusioned by "the god that failed." Nor is Orwell's anti-imperialism or his support of the libertarian Freedom Defence Committee any indication as to how he would have acted during the McCarthy or Vietnam eras, as Hitchens supposes.

Hitchens later revisited Podhoretz's argument and his own rebuttal, adding for good measure that Podhoretz's clever use of ellipses resembled that of Orwell's adversary on the Marxist Left, Raymond Williams—and that both men lacked Orwell's literary integrity. Wrote Hitchens:

In 1982 in *Harper's* magazine in New York, the neoconservative critic Norman Podhoretz—perhaps the most unscrupulous man of letters of our time—wrote an essay to prove that Orwell took the American side in the Cold War between the superpowers. He did this by the method of inserting an ellipsis where none belonged, in an extract from Orwell's 1947 *Tribune* essay "In Defence of Comrade Zilliacus." As between Washington and Moscow, Orwell had written:

"If you *had* to choose between Russia and America, which would you choose? It will not do to give the usual quibbling answer, 'I refuse to choose.' In the end, the choice may be forced upon us. We are no longer strong enough to stand alone, and if we fail to bring a West European union into being we shall be obliged, in the long run, to subordinate our policy to that of one Great Power or another."

Hitchens then showed what might be termed the stylistic and hermeneutical affinities between Orwell's chief neocon admirer and his leading Marxist scourge:[50]

Podhoretz employed the simple expedient of leaving out the whole of the third sentence and the whole middle clause of the fourth one. He continued to do this, in reprints of his dull polemic, despite being advised of the fact that he had been rumbled. [*Rumble* is a British slang term, roughly meaning to "see through" or "catch in the act."] Williams, by contrast, chose to omit the second and third sentences. Neither man acknowledged that Orwell drew the conclusion, later in the same year, that the emerging Cold War was a contest between greater and lesser evils, that it did not have to be, and that:

"Therefore a Socialist United States of Europe seems to me the only worthwhile political objective today."

Hitchens concluded by contrasting Orwell's intellectual integrity and honorable
polemical style with "the crudities of Podhoretz and Williams":

> Fighting Stalin and Hitler at the same time was a much harsher business
> than fending off the crudities of Podhoretz and Williams, but it involved
> sticking to the same consistent points—even if they were inconsistently
> expressed—and trusting to the readers to notice who was being honest in
> the long term, or at all. Orwell, incidentally, never paid his foes back in the
> same coin. At the very last stage of the proofs of *Animal Farm*, he altered
> the passage about the blowing up of the animals' hard-built and hard-won
> windmill. It had read: "All the animals including Napoleon flung themselves
> on their faces." Orwell changed this to "All the animals except Napoleon."
> It weighed with him that Stalin had remained in Moscow during the Nazi
> advance on the city. I said earlier that all quotation is necessarily selective
> and out of context. But there is a sort of tradition that, when length or den-
> sity of quotation obliges one to omit a few words, the resulting ". . ." should
> not deprive the reader of anything essential or germane. Podhoretz seems
> to me, by his inept ellipses, to have broken this compact with his readers in
> both letter and spirit.[51]

In this defense of his hero, we see a characteristic way that Hitchens aligns
himself with Orwell: anti-imperialist Orwell needs protecting against false body
snatchers from all directions.

This self-appointed role as Orwell's guardian,[52] based on Hitchens's perception that Orwell often needs to be rescued both from misguided appropriation
and from sugar-coated glorification, is evident throughout Hitchens's Orwell
criticism. For example, writing about Orwell for the *American Enterprise* in mid-
1999, Hitchens first broached his view that Orwell's single glaring weakness was
his inattentiveness to and one-sided dismissal of the United States. "References
to the United States in his journalism are almost always neutral or hostile, and
directed either at the rise of a new imperialism or the spread of a new cultural
vulgarity," he wrote. Orwell had no interest in the half-forgotten British leftist
tradition of considering America the land of revolution instead of Russia. Orwell
was "anti-American" and viewed the United States as "large, friendly, and stupid,
with a mean streak."[53]

Hitchens also argued for the ongoing relevance of the mode of Orwell's writing on the Cold War (a "war" that Orwell condemned as a fraud on the populations of both Russia and the United States, though he reluctantly sided with America). It is the inherent tension and contradiction of Orwell's prose, says Hitchens, that "make his work worth re-reading, precisely because it is so honestly expressed and because he shares his confusions with his readers."

But it is in the conclusion to this short piece that Hitchens is most revealing about his personal stake in Orwell's legacy:

Thus, I believe Orwell's biggest surprise, surveying the 1990s, would be the ambivalent position of the United States, and the amazing conflicts within its state and society. The flatterer of Yeltsin and the liberator of Kosovo . . . the exporter of weapons and the boycotter of sweatshops; the headquarters of human-rights lawyers and the abstainer on the War Crimes Tribunal. . . . An ostentatiously pious society with a firmly non-judgmental public morality. The last, worst hope of mankind. The new-ish world called in to redress the balance of the older. The greatest subject for a journalist or novelist there ever was—and he missed it, and it still took him to its warm old heart and gave his publishers the infinite revenue of which he never saw a penny piece.[54]

This passage, while expressing fondness and admiration for Orwell, also implies an intellectual passing of the torch between the two men. Even though Orwell missed the biggest breaking story of the postwar era—the emergence of the United States as the dominant world power and undisputed leader of the West— Hitchens would not. Hitchens would be there—"on the beat" in Washington, as it were—to project his forerunner's thoughts on contemporary America and to redress any gaps in Orwell's thinking. The summons seems virtually mandated, suggests Hitchens, for Orwell was among the greatest political writers of the twentieth century, and America is today "the greatest subject." Both are thus worthy of Hitchens's full attention and efforts.

In *Letters to a Young Contrarian* (1999), Hitchens openly referred to Orwell as his "hero" and further positioned himself as an antinomian thinker, a rebel, an iconoclast in Orwell's mold. Hitchens exalted Orwell as an exemplary contrarian and a model for aspiring writers because of his mastery of persuasive rhetoric and his penchant for clear, direct prose.[55]

George Orwell said that the prime responsibility lay in being able to tell people what they did not wish to hear. . . . The noble title of "dissident" must be earned rather than claimed; it connotes sacrifice and risk rather than mere disagreement, and it has been consecrated by many exemplary and courageous men and women.[56]

Addressing the civil war that raged in Bosnia during the 1990s, Hitchens also invoked Orwell's example of the clear-sighted, skeptical witness and anti-utopian:

I understood [the need] to beware of overidealising the Bosnians, and to suspect the Utopian tourist in myself and others. The model text here is Orwell's *Homage to Catalonia;* it was surprising, and confirming, to find how often it came up in discussions. Bosnian official propaganda took an internationalist tone; it described Milosevic's army and auxiliary death squads as "Chetniks"—an old antifascist term—rather than as "Serbs."

To train the condemnation upon the Utopians is to miss the historical point (the point made in *Animal Farm,* among other places) that Utopians become tyrants when they start to emulate their former masters.[57]

But it was in his review of Peter Davison's Penguin edition of Orwell's essays and reviews on the Spanish Civil War, *Orwell in Spain* (2001), that Hitchens broached the argument that he would fully develop the following year in *Orwell's Victory*—that Orwell was "the man who confronted three of the great crises of the twentieth century and got all three of them, so to speak, 'right.'" First Orwell was "right" about the menace and legacy of imperialism, and later and more importantly, he was right about the totalitarianisms of the Right and Left, Nazism and Stalinism. Hitchens concluded:

He was right, early and often, about the menace presented by fascism and national socialism not just to the peace of the world but to the very idea of civilization. And he was right about Stalinism, about the great and small temptations that it offered to certain kinds of intellectuals and about the monstrous consequences that would ensue from that nightmarish sleep of reason.[58]

This review offered the first glimpse into the elisions in Hitchens's own portrait of Orwell. For example, while Hitchens's claim that millions know Orwell's name "as a synonym for prescience and integrity" is possible, it is also likely that tens of millions surely know it (in proper adjectival form) as a synonym for terror, tyranny, and totalitarianism. Similarly, his statement that Orwell "died a virtual pauper" is a romantic myth. By the time he died at forty-six, Orwell had become a wealthy man from his last two books. Nonetheless, such exaggerations both disclose the force of Hitchens's impassioned identification with Orwell's personal and literary character and furnish a preview of Hitchens's argument in *Orwell's Victory*.

VI

Orwell's Victory, published in the United Kingdom in November 2002 (coincidentally the same month as his last column for the *Nation*), represents the culmination of Hitchens's thinking on Orwell. Hitchens establishes early on that his study will be less a rationale for Orwell's political prescience than a dressing down of those left-wing critics and right-wing canonizers who have misread or misinterpreted Orwell's work.

"This is not a biography," Hitchens writes, "but I sometimes feel as if George Orwell requires extricating from a pile of saccharine tablets and moist hankies; an object of sickly veneration and sentimental overpraise, employed to stultify schoolchildren with his insufferable rightness and purity."[59]

Thus Hitchens's aim is to rescue an embattled and unfairly exalted "St. George" Orwell and rehumanize him, to bring him back from heavenly plaster sainthood to earth. As for the Right, Hitchens dispatches conservative writers such as Podhoretz, who want to claim Orwell as a political ally for his anticommunist sentiment, in a brief chapter with a terse opening sentence: "George Orwell was conservative about many things, but not about politics."[60] But Hitchens acknowledges that the most powerful assaults on Orwell's reputation have come from the Left. The focus of Hitchens's attention is on Orwell's reception by the Left, and this chapter ("Orwell and the Left") is more than twice as long as any other in the book.

In Hitchens's view, the Marxist Left resents Orwell because he committed the "ultimate sin" of "giving ammunition to the enemy" when he criticized communism in the 1930s and again during the early Cold War era. If leftists today still need proof that Orwell was right about the perils of communism, Hitchens points to the examples of North Korea and Zimbabwe. Many leftists, Hitchens concludes, have been "either too stupid or too compromised" to recognize that Marxism has produced plenty of Kim Il Sungs and Robert Mugabes.[61] Hitchens claims that "the very name of Orwell is enough to evoke a shiver of revulsion among leftists."[62] He goes on to cite E. P. Thompson, Isaac Deutscher, Salman Rushdie, and Raymond Williams, arguing that their criticisms are a representative sample of the "ill will and bad faith and intellectual confusion that appear to ignite spontaneously when Orwell's name is mentioned in some quarters."[63]

Hitchens takes these radical critics of Orwell seriously. But he elides the fact that Orwell has not been a subject of strong contention on either the Left or the Right for two decades. The main writers that Hitchens cites—Edward Said, E. P. Thompson, Raymond Williams—are not only dated voices (their quotes range from 1955 to 1984), but isolated ones.

The truth is that Orwell has been enormously popular across the political spectrum since his death—as Hitchens points out elsewhere—for his willingness to take unpopular stands on important issues.[64] Hitchens quite simply overemphasizes how besieged Orwell is in his "afterlife." By focusing on the responses to Orwell of Williams and Said, Hitchens gives the impression that Orwell has been more unpopular on the Left than he actually has. Williams and Said are unrepresentative. Their castigation of Orwell does reflect his low standing among present-day Marxists. And yet, with the exception of the Marxist or sectarian Left (e.g., Scott Lucas),[65] few radicals have been critical of Orwell in the last two decades—even though Orwell's much-deplored decision to "name names" to the postwar British intelligence service has reinvigorated Left criticism of him.[66] Rather, Orwell has indeed been a catholic "St. George," the patron saint of almost all factions. David Brooks recognized this in his review of *Why Orwell Matters* for the *Weekly Standard:*

[T]o reenter these debates is really to go into an intellectual-history museum. E. P. Thompson may have believed that Orwell was an apologist for quietism. Raymond Williams may have regarded Orwell as hopelessly bourgeois. But aside from a few dozen professors, does anybody really think Orwell still needs defending from these ideological dinosaurs? . . . The Orwell tug of war is over.[67]

Ironically, this development can be seen as the literary-critical dimension of "Orwell's victory." Except on the far Left, Orwell's stature is virtually uncontested today. Hitchens is well aware of this fact when he complains about the proliferation of lavish Orwell admirers. The adversaries form a small minority, and it is far more common to find those who overpraise Orwell. Hitchens himself has been accused of such excesses. Indeed, though Hitchens avoids "sickly" overpraise, he does laud Orwell as "a flinty and solitary loner," "a libertarian before the word gained currency," a man of "sturdy English virtues," and "the outstanding English example of the dissident intellectual who preferred above all other allegiances the loyalty to the truth."[68]

Hitchens does also present a few criticisms of Orwell: Orwell misjudged America; his early novels are mediocre; and he was a man of his time, not above unenlightened remarks about women, gays, and Jews. But Hitchens defends Orwell against these charges immediately: he died before he could travel to America; his early novels constituted salutary "throat clearing" before his two masterpieces of fiction; and his prejudices are forgivable since Orwell's father made him "the victim of a narrow-minded patriarch."[69]

VII

In his 1939 essay on Dickens, Orwell noted that writers "tell you a great deal about [themselves] while talking about someone else."[70] As we have noted in earlier chapters of this study, the same could be said about Hitchens on Orwell. Hitchens defends Orwell partly because Hitchens is writing a veiled self-defense; his Orwell commentary amounts to a self-defense of his ego-ideal of the intellectual whom Hitchens dreams of being—and not merely in the sense of covering a similarly wide range of topics, but rather as a rebel of the Left, as the "conscience" of *his* generation. If Orwell's critics are insignificant, then Orwell does not need defending. By contrast, Hitchens faces significant critics and must constantly defend himself. If he aspires to be the new Orwell, Hitchens can, by becoming Orwell's defender, also defend himself indirectly against his own critics.

I am not alone in discerning the part of George Orwell in Hitchens—and Hitchens's urge to defend that embattled part of himself. Hitchens's identification with Orwell is quite transparent, and it has been noted by observers on the Left as well as the Right. In his scathing attack on Orwell (and Hitchens), *The Betrayal of Dissent: Beyond Orwell, Hitchens, and the New American Century* (Pluto, 2003), Scott Lucas castigates Hitchens repeatedly for embracing Orwell's role as "policeman of the Left" and "the honorable loner," characterizing Hitchens's "strategy" as follows: "Orwell must be exonerated and uplifted for Hitchens to become the beacon for another generation."[71] In his notice of *Orwell's Victory* for the *Village Voice*, the reviewer observes more politely:

> In light of Hitchens' recent departure from the *Nation* after 20 years as the magazine's Washington columnist, the close reader gets the distinct sense that Hitchens is also defending (or, at the very least, explaining) himself and some of the positions and actions he's taken in the last 20 years.[72]

Similarly, Andy Croft noted in the *Guardian:* "Hitchens clearly identifies with his subject, and at times appears to be writing about himself as much as about Orwell."[73] On the Right, Geoffrey Wheatcroft remarked in the *Spectator* that Hitchens's "short Philippic" is "plainly as much about Christopher Hitchens as about George Orwell."[74] Perhaps the conservative *Policy Review* went furthest:

Hitchens has long taken Orwell to be a kind of intellectual father, and so like father, like son. The similarities between the two men are numerous: To name just the most obvious, they are both English liberals with socialist sympathies, who nonetheless depart from liberal orthodoxy on key subjects. But most importantly, both have long wrestled with questions regarding the relationship between politics and language, between the political life and the literary life. In Hitchens' past writings, the figure of Orwell remained in the background of this larger discussion—the source of a quotation or two—but now in his latest offering, *Why Orwell Matters*, Hitchens' mentor has become both the work's subject and its pervading spirit.[75]

VIII

Hitchens's provocative study of Orwell appeared in the United States six months after its U.K. publication under the title *Why Orwell Matters*. The U.K. title, *Orwell's Victory*, however, was more appropriate (even if not Hitchens's first choice).[76] A leitmotif of Hitchens's book is that Orwell "got history right" in terms of the three big questions that arose in twentieth-century Europe, which is a feat with collective autobiographical implications that an educated British audience would inevitably value in a way that American readers do not. During Orwell's lifetime, it was Britain that suffered the Blitz, withstood Hitler's bombs, and never gave rise to a mass communist movement or party, and whose political opinions governed the English-speaking world's stance toward Stalinism; yet whose Left intelligentsia, like others in Europe, also supported Stalin and the Left. And it was also, of course, the British Empire that constituted the world's leading imperialistic force, the group shouldering the white man's burden, the global power on which "the sun never set."

Because it was less likely that a broad American audience would appreciate such matters, let alone the courage and balance of Orwell's early stands on fascism, communism, and imperialism (many Americans do not even know the general history of fascism or communism as a starting point for such a discussion), "Orwell's Victory" would probably have been a title without resonance for most Americans. The title "Why Orwell Matters" carries an implicit question mark, as if to acknowledge the limitations of a less well-informed U.S. readership. Americans, even if they do not know European history, are interested in cultural affairs and in what this important writer has to say to them. The American title reflects Orwell's continued relevance, which is a topic with which U.S. readers can more readily identify.

So then: What answer does Hitchens's American title invite? Why does Orwell matter? In fact, Hitchens never really addresses the question implied in the title

his American publisher foisted on him—why Orwell matters now. As Judith Shulevitz noted in the *New York Times:*

> You can deduce Orwell's relevance from what Hitchens says is important
> about him: his passionate patriotism, his hatred of totalitarianism, his
> skepticism about religion, his independence of mind, his integrity. Hitch-
> ens is too coy, though, to come out and say how Orwell might figure into the
> battle against what Hitchens, elsewhere, has called Islamic fascism. Maybe
> he thinks that stating the matter plainly (which is, after all, how Orwell
> would have stated it) would be crude. It might reveal that Hitchens agrees
> that he's Orwell, or at least that his position after Sept. 11 is the one Orwell
> would have taken.[77]

If the book's title were *Why Orwell Mattered,* Hitchens's emphasis on the past
exclusively would be quite understandable. But the title *Why Orwell Matters*
makes a claim to the present and by implication the future. Unlike so many intellectuals, however, Hitchens largely resisted the "If Orwell Were Alive Today"
reveries.[78] As the Orwell centennial approached in 2003, such speculation would
have been fitting if "Why Orwell Matters *Now*" had been Hitchens's theme.[79] For
example, Hitchens could easily have drawn a detailed analogy that, because Orwell supported Churchill during World War II, he would likely have supported
George W. Bush in waging war after al Qaeda's attack on the World Trade Center.
But Hitchens's book does not make this or any other explicit link between Orwell
and contemporary issues.[80]

Perhaps Hitchens refrained because he recognizes that Orwell matters today
less for political reasons than for moral reasons. And Orwell is, above all, a moralist—or a "metapolitical" writer, in his friend (and literary executor) Richard
Rees's phrase.[81] Indeed, Orwell is frequently regarded as the leading postwar example of how to live the intellectual life, as someone who stood by his convictions
and had the courage to act on them.[82] Of course, in a formal sense, the political
issues on the international scene that most occupied Orwell—such as the conduct
of the Soviet Union and the demise of colonialism as the European colonies established themselves as independent nations—have receded into history. True,
as Hitchens points out, the North Koreas of the world remain a political threat.
But Orwell matters more for the "how" of his example than for the "what" of his
politics. Hitchens acknowledges in his Conclusion that Orwell's "principles" really matter more than his politics.

> [W]hat [Orwell] illustrates, by his commitment to language as the partner
> of truth, is that "views" do not really count; that it matters not what you

think, but *how* you think; and that politics are relatively unimportant, while principles have a way of enduring, as do the few irreducible individuals who maintain allegiance to them.[83]

In emphasizing Orwell's contrarian attitude—exemplified by his extraordinary "power of facing"—and by so strongly identifying with Orwell's principles and principled positions, Hitchens gives voice to the kind of committed intellectual and independent, indeed "antinomian," radical that he himself seeks to be. And yes, Hitchens too possesses a power of facing what can be deemed unpleasant facts—though Hitchens is less truth-seeker and more contrarian, and they're not at all the same thing. It's often too easy to be contrary for the sake of being contrary, as Hitchens himself warns in *Letters to a Young Contrarian* (even though he also concedes that he occasionally succumbs).[84]

IX

Let us ask it again: In the end, *does* Orwell matter? Does he *still* matter to intellectuals in the twenty-first century?

Yes, as the next two chapters of this book will make clear. And yet: Orwell matters less in the way Hitchens argues—indeed rather more in the way that Hitchens himself matters. "Why Orwell Matters" is a question that still has special relevance for those who are pursuing their vocations as writers with political-literary interests, and more specifically as intellectuals.

For Orwell was a writer in the old sense of the man of letters. He never worked in any medium other than print, except during his brief tenure with BBC radio during the war.[85] He wrote in an age when novels and serious intellectual journalism still had great political significance, and when it was possible to reach a "common reader" by writing for middlebrow magazines and intellectual quarterlies.

Today political writing has not only declined in importance; the public that it once addressed is now fragmented beyond recognition. Some of Orwell's journalistic outlets—such as the *New Statesman*, the *New Republic*, and the *Nation*—still exist. But they do not command the kind of attention that they did sixty years ago, when just appearing in them marked a watershed moment for a writer.[86] The postmodern intellectual who writes an essay for a journal of opinion faces the prospect of entering the public arena amid a cacophony of numerous publics and hundreds of media outlets. Whether or not a sufficiently powerful voice might be able to integrate such a plethora of publics, no such voice has emerged since Orwell's death.

What is also clear is that the way Orwell became an intellectual—by affiliating himself with several intellectual circles and maturing his literary voice through and beyond them—is hardly possible today. And since no contemporary journal is closely affiliated with Orwell's example or legacy (unlike, say, the early postwar *Dissent*), it's impossible to identify with Orwell's vision through a literary or political organ. It must be done individually, as Hitchens has done—and as he has continued to do by leaving the *Nation* to align himself more directly with Orwell.

This sea change is significant. It represents not just a different way of relating to Orwell, but a new chapter in intellectual and cultural history. In Hitchens we witness the apotheosis of the intellectual entrepreneur, who is formed by reading and contributing to various periodicals but typically remains on the outside, a freelancer. Hitchens writes for newspapers, highbrow journals, middlebrow magazines, websites, and blogs. He appears regularly as a pundit on radio and TV. He sells what he has in abundant supply—his opinions. And he thereby represents the new breed of serious literary-political intellectual of the twenty-first century.

The post-9/11 Hitchens forgoes limiting allegiances to any one outlet, and he approaches issues ad hoc, without regard to ideology. By implication, though he never stated it explicitly, Hitchens broke ranks with the *Nation* because he would not break faith with his own conception of intellectual integrity, of which Orwell formed a key part. In parting company with the *Nation*, Hitchens sent a clear message about his view of what intellectuals ought to do if they are true intellectuals, that is, if they are intellectuals in the tradition to which Orwell belongs.[87] They must be willing to break with whatever reference group they have been identified with and follow their own consciences—whether they temporarily join sides with the Right or Left or, in Hitchens's case, opt out of both camps and remain intellectual gadflies.

The latter decision was, arguably, even more difficult in Orwell's day. Because ideological categorizing was so rigid and generally followed a schematic Right vs. Left polarity on major political issues, taking a stand on any bellwether controversy almost invariably meant being imputed to hold a series of related, orthodox positions identified with the Right or the Left.

But it is never easy to be a dissenter or contrarian from your own reference group, as Orwell often noted. Orwell was a democratic socialist and called himself "a man of the Left," yet his goal in *Animal Farm* (and later) was to "destroy the myth that Russia is a socialist country"—and many true believers on the Left excommunicated him for his heresy. Hitchens seems to revel more in his contrariness—he is more the intellectual gadfly than the outsider.[88] Hitchens can outrage the Left by skewering Bill Clinton and supporting the war in Iraq,[89] even as he embitters conservatives by condemning Henry Kissinger as a war criminal and Mother Teresa as a hypocritical fraud.

So is Hitchens now a neocon? No, not by a long shot. Has he turned right? Yes, but only slightly. His chief criticism of Clinton is that he *betrayed* liberalism (and seduced the Left); his criticism of Islamofascism is that it's far more unjust and dangerous to international peace than the Bush administration. (Of course, on aesthetic matters, Hitchens has never been a proponent of a radical avant garde, as his allegiance to Orwell, Waugh, and other formal traditionalists makes clear.)

To put it another way, though he no longer refers to himself as a socialist (to the satisfaction of many radicals) and still identifies himself with the Left (to the consternation of many leftists), Hitchens has become less an ideologically motivated than an issue-oriented thinker.[90] He follows his own conscience with no intellectual coterie for support. Such a courageous go-it-alone mission and firm sense of vocational purpose strengthen his self-perception as an individualist and a rebel on the Left.[91] And if all that does not quite make him the "Orwell of his generation,"[92] it does at least suggest how his stance marks a bridge between the eras of the modern and postmodern intellectual.

PART TWO

Orwell's Literary Siblings Today

George Orwell at work in his Islington flat, early spring 1946.

CHAPTER SIX

Iraq, the Internet, and "the Big O" in 2003

A Centennial Report

At the George Orwell Centenary Conference, which was held in May 2003 at Wellesley College, Massachusetts, I had the great pleasure to interview numerous speakers and participants for a documentary film about Orwell's relevance both to their personal lives and to the twenty-first century. My interviewees cooperated fully, despite some awkward moments with our sound equipment and other inconveniences of the filmmaking process. I found it interesting to converse with them about Orwell's legacy. In virtually every case, they credit him with exerting a strong formative influence on their thinking—and even leaving a deep imprint on their intellectual lives. One could say, then, that they too are among Orwell's intellectual progeny.

Since the George Orwell Centenary Conference featured those whom I interviewed and other leading students of Orwell's work, some of whom are prominent intellectual voices in their own right, their responses to Orwell's work today illuminate his current standing among present-day intellectuals.[1] Their views play a crucial role, I believe, in helping Orwell's current readers to understand his ongoing significance in political and cultural affairs. One of the distinctive features of their remarks is that, despite the sea change in world affairs and Anglo-American culture in the last half-century, Orwell continues to be a presence in their lives as well as in political debate. The range of responses also shows that everyone has his or her own Orwell. Still, this diversity notwithstanding, virtually all of the respondents speak of Orwell's skepticism and readiness to go against the prevailing wisdom.

I can credit Orwell himself with furnishing me a good precedent for the interviews in the next two chapters. Orwell's "Interview with Jonathan Swift," which he conducted as a BBC broadcaster in 1942 (and is collected in Davison's Complete Works of George Orwell), was his own attempt to give a dead man a contemporary voice. There he gets Swift to comment on the state of Britain and of world affairs in the 1940s.

The text below is edited from our taped interviews, which I hope will serve as an *oral history of a moment of Orwell's reception among contemporary intellectuals and scholars.[2] A prominent topic was the U.S.-led invasion of Iraq, whose military phase was just concluding at this time.* Much of the dialogue concerned the question of Orwell's possible statements and even positions regarding the Iraq war, as well as speculation about his thinking on a host of subjects and events topical on the occasion of his centennial. *Among the participants were the following:*

- **MARSHALL BERMAN** *is Distinguished Professor at the City University of New York and the author of* Politics of Authenticity *(1971),* All That Is Solid Melts into Air: The Experience of Modernity *(1982),* Adventures in Marxism *(1999), and* One Hundred Years of Spectacle: Metamorphoses of Times Square *(2005). He has served on the editorial board of* Dissent *since 1980.*

- **BERNARD CRICK** *is the author of numerous books, including the classic* In Defense of Politics *(1966) and* George Orwell: A Life *(1980), the first biography of Orwell.*

- **MORRIS DICKSTEIN** *is Distinguished Professor of English at the Graduate Center of the City University of New York. His books include a study of the 1960s,* Garden of Eden *(1977), which was nominated for the National Book Critics Circle Award in criticism,* Double Agent: The Critic and Society *(1992), and* Leopards in the Temple, *a social history of postwar American fiction published in 2002 by Harvard University Press.*

- **TODD GITLIN** *is a professor of journalism and sociology at Columbia University and the author of ten books, most recently* Intellectuals and the Flag *(2006),* Letters to a Young Activist *(2003), and* Media Unlimited: How the Torrent of Image and Sound Overwhelms Our Lives *(2001). His previous books include* The Twilight of Common Dreams: Why America Is Wracked by Culture Wars *(1995),* The Sixties: Years of Hope, Days of Rage *(1987),* Inside Primetime *(1983),* The Whole World Is Watching *(1980), and two novels,* The Murder of Albert Einstein *(1992) and* Sacrifice *(1999).*

- **ERIKA GOTTLIEB** *has taught at McGill and Concordia Universities in Montreal, in the Faculty of English in Budapest's ELTE University, and elsewhere. She is the author of* Dystopian Fiction East and West: Universe of Terror and Trial *(2001) and* The Orwell Conundrum: A Cry of Despair or Faith in the Spirit of Man *(1992), among other works.*

- **CHRISTOPHER HITCHENS** *is a columnist for* Vanity Fair *and* Slate. *He has written books on Mother Teresa, Henry Kissinger, Bill Clinton, and Thomas Jefferson, as well as* Why Orwell Matters *(2002).*

- **RICHARD KOSTELANETZ** *is an avant-garde writer and cultural critic who has been one of the most daring and innovative experimental figures in American literature. Kostelanetz's creative work spans a wide variety of genres, including fiction, verbal and visual poetry, radio scripts, videotapes, holograms, and graphic art. Among his well-known books are* Dictionary of Avant Gardes *(1993) and* Ecce Kosti *(1996).*

- **DAPHNE PATAI** *is Professor of Spanish and Portuguese at the University of Massachusetts at Amherst and the author of* The Orwell Mystique: A Study in Male Ideology *(1984).*

- **RICHARD RORTY** *is Professor of Humanities at Stanford University. He is the author of a number of books including* Philosophy and the Mirror of Nature *(1979),* Consequences of Pragmatism *(1982), and* Objectivity, Relativism and Truth *(1991).*

- **MICHAEL SHELDEN** *is Professor of English at Indiana University at Bloomington and the author of* George Orwell: The Authorized Biography *(1991).*

- **ANTHONY STEWART** *is an Assistant Professor of English Literature at Dalhousie University in Halifax, Nova Scotia, and the author of* Orwell, Doubleness, and the Value of Decency *(2003).*

- **IAN WILLIAMS** *is a journalist and the United Nations correspondent for the* Nation *and the author of* George Bush at the War Front *(2004) and* Rum: A Social and Sociable History of the Real Spirit of 1776 *(2005). In 1987 he was a speech writer for UK Labour Party leader Neil Kinnock during the elections. Since 1989 he has been based in New York City.*

- **DENNIS WRONG** *is Professor Emeritus of Sociology at New York University and the author of many influential books in sociology and political theory, including* Power: Its Forms, Bases and Uses *(1979),* The Problem of Order: What Unites and Divides Society *(1994),* The Modern Condition: Essays at Century's End *(1998),* Persistence of Particular Things *(2004), and* The Persistence of the Particular *(2005).*

MEETING ORWELL

Q: What was your first encounter with George Orwell's work?

Erika Gottlieb: I had the uncanny "privilege" to go through two totalitarian systems when I was a child and a teenager, through the German dictatorship in Hungary and later Stalin's dictatorship in Hungary before I left for Canada. I was in my late teens when I finally read Orwell, who had a marvelous grasp of what it felt like to grow up the way I did. I think anybody who reads Orwell today, even without the personal experience, is hit by the impact of his knowledge. But only those who lived in that society recognize the full insight of a novel written by a man who never had firsthand experience of totalitarianism. Orwell grasped the essence of it so well! It was a miracle.

Todd Gitlin: I read *Homage to Catalonia* when I was in college, probably in 1963. I also read *Wigan Pier* around that time. I read a lot of the essays before I got involved in SDS. I was involved in peace activities as a college student at Harvard. Orwell's big attraction for me began with the publication of the paperback edition of the four volumes of *Collected Essays, Journalism, and Letters,* which I read in 1971. I read them from page one of volume one through to the last page of volume four, at a time when I was trying to rethink my political orientation. I was well aware that the New Left had careened off a cliff. I was virtually obsessed for a couple of years trying to figure out how that had happened, since it had been my life—and it was naturally distressing to see the vehicle flying into an uninhabitable abyss.

So Orwell was extremely important to me at that time for exposing the mental laziness, surrender of intellectual autonomy, and atmosphere of cloying conformity that he anatomized in the late '30s and '40s—we in the New Left had a softer version of it. We had no Communist Party to enforce it, to speak of. Nor was the New Left anything so willfully stupid as the communists were during the period [when] Orwell was writing. But it was close enough to be extremely useful.

One thing I had become extremely critical of was the habit of viewing Third World revolutions as exemplary departures from bourgeois insufferability. The only one of these revolutionary zones that I myself had visited was Cuba, about which I had ambivalent feelings. But it was around this time that some intellectuals in the West began to be aware that the repression of intellectuals in Cuba was intensifying and unconscionable. In particular, there was the case of a Cuban poet Heberto Padilla, who had been jailed for writing insufficiently pro-Castro poems. And so there was a big campaign to defend Padilla. As I observed this going on, I thought, this is the sort of campaign that Orwell would certainly have participated in.

It's a cheap shot, I guess, that Orwell would do "X or Y," but in this one I'm a hundred percent confident. And Orwell reminded me that this sort of fog of totalistic thinking, which Fidel Castro was now edging into, was a grave political crime and needed to be combated. The intellectuals who weren't willing to combat it had made a decision to choose a kind of primitive loyalty over their proper mission as intellectuals.

All this was converging for me. Those four volumes were kind of a touchstone for me at that time.

Dennis Wrong: I remember I was dining with my parents in a very posh restaurant in Paris or Geneva [c. 1937]. I was sort of awed by the decor, plush chairs, gold gilt trimming, and all that. And my father said, "There's a book by an English writer, in which he worked as a waiter in a place like this, and he describes how they stuck their thumbs in the soup and how, if they dropped a steak on the floor, which was full of sawdust and dirty, they picked it up and just lightly brushed it off and went ahead and served it!"

My parents were fans of *Down and Out in Paris and London.* They had the book. I read it then. That was my first real encounter with Orwell.

Back in boarding school in Canada, I encountered him later. I would have been fifteen at boarding school [1938]. When this incident happened with *Down and Out in Paris and London,* I was probably thirteen or fourteen. So that would have been 1937 or '38, just before World War II.

Q: During the 1930s, you felt that Orwell was responding to you as somebody who was trying to make sense of this complex political world that was before you.

Dennis Wrong: Yes. I wanted to be a socialist. I was committed to being a socialist, partly in rebellion against my parents and my prep school, as is often the case. At the same time I could not surrender the view that Hitler was wicked and that the acts of aggression against Czechoslovakia and Poland were evil. That was fundamentally Orwell's recognition when he was a socialist—"My Country Right or Left" was the article that turned me on. He defended what his country had done. He defended its actions. It wasn't just because it was his country that he felt he should support it in the war. And that made an impact on me. Sonia Orwell and Ian Angus took the title of that article for the first of the four volumes of *Collected Essays, Journalism, and Letters.* Volume I is called "My Country Right or Left." It was that more than anything else [that] made me feel sympathetic to him. For me, it was that fact, that he was a socialist, but he was also very much in favor of the Second World War.

I went to a school that had been created for the children of delegates in the League of Nations. My father was a delegate to the League of Nations, which was set up to implement collective security in order to prevent nations from committing military aggression against others. So how could I—as a rebellious adolescent—not support going to war?

Q: You first came to admire Orwell as a socialist patriot during the war, and later as a Cold Warrior. Despite Orwell's shifting positions, your admiration for him endured?

Dennis Wrong: I don't see that there were any shifting positions. He consistently opposed the Soviet Union for imposing its models on Eastern Europe.

"IF ORWELL WERE ALIVE TODAY . . ."

Q: Is there any value in playing the parlor game of "What would Orwell say today?"

Dennis Wrong: It is very difficult to do so, given what a contrarian figure Orwell was. In the most recent case, the war in Iraq, it seems to me that Orwell can be used on all sides of the argument, and so what then does that mean? It can't be taken as self-evident that you have made a good case by citing Orwell in favor of invading or not invading Iraq, since he can easily be used for either side.

Anthony Stewart: If Orwell were alive today, he would have been in agreement with the invasion of Iraq, because he supported Britain entering into the Second World War. If Orwell were alive today, he'd be exactly as he was in his own time. He'd be unpopular with large groups of academics and intellectuals—and he wouldn't care.

Christopher Hitchens: The twenty-first century began, not with a confrontation with the totalitarian principle, but with the recrudescence of an older form of absolutism, namely the theocratic, millennial fanaticism that was met with in Afghanistan and has been able to metastasize itself.

Theocratic absolutism—and millennial religion—metastasized very rapidly, even within the American border, with a secret army.

Orwell teaches us quite a lot about this. The ultimate form, and the most refined form, of tyranny—because it requires us not just to obey, not simply to be a slave but to be a joyful one, to praise our chains, to enjoy our master, to kiss the whip—and it's perhaps therefore the most threatening form—is exemplified by the intellectuals of *Nineteen Eighty-Four* who attempt to change the language and the existence of the secret book. Everything in his writing shows that Orwell prizes liberty and regards the concept of the infallible Vatican as the most menacing tyranny from which you can escape.

Q: Orwell was a committed pacifist in 1938 and 1939, then made a sharp turn toward patriotism. What would he say about the war in Iraq?

Morris Dickstein: I really don't know. I really wouldn't want to say that Orwell would say this or say that fifty years after he died. But on the basis of his attitude toward the Second World War, which really was a dramatic change based on his attitude of just a few years earlier, it seems to me that he would probably have supported a war against Saddam Hussein, but not the cant that went along with it to round up popular support.

There were various red herrings as it turned out. It seems that the claim that Iraq harbored weapons of mass destruction was one of those red herrings. Now I'm not somebody who actually opposed the war, but I suspect Orwell would have identified a lot of the cant that went into the campaign for it, because he detested a lot of the propaganda that went into both sides, though he supported the Allies in World War II.

Q: Do you think Orwell, who was a strong anti-fascist, would respond similarly to so-called Islamic fascism?

Dennis Wrong: I do, yes, think he would have certainly seen a kinship between that and the various anti-democratic nationalist movements based on race or religion. I think he would have condemned those Islamic movements.

Ian Williams: He was strongly against organized religion. He was strongly anti-Catholic—and he would have been strongly anti-Islam, if Islam were the issue. He would be very concerned about the attempt of anybody to force his opinions on other people. And that is the point about Islamofascism.

But it goes both ways. Saddam was basically a secular fascist, but he occasionally invoked Islam. Orwell would not have brooked compromises with Saddam Hussein, but on the other hand, he would have wanted to weigh very carefully the benefits and motives of intervention. I don't think he would have necessarily come out advocating war against Saddam Hussein.

The analogy I came up with was this: remember that Bertrand Russell suggested a preemptive nuclear strike against the Soviets. Orwell never did so. Who hated Stalin and the Soviet Union more than Orwell? But he said: wait, hold on here, think about the consequences. Yes, the USSR is evil, a terrible society. Yes, it's awful, but will nuking them make us any better? Will it create a better world as a result? What is the best way to deal with the USSR? What are the consequences of taking such actions?

Q: Orwell, the anti-imperialist, opposed the British Empire's limitations on the free determination of people. What might he say today, in light of the fact that, in a place like Zimbabwe, the condition of the citizenry seems to be far worse than it was under. the British Empire? You can see a number of other instances across Asia and elsewhere. Was this champion of justice and decency really advocating that kind of changeover and those consequences?

Ian Williams: When he was talking about Burma, about which he felt he was an expert based on his time there, his problems weren't that the Burmese couldn't run their affairs for themselves, it was that the neighbors wouldn't let them. At one point he said that an independent Burma would be dominated immediately, which is what was happening to small and weak countries in Europe at the time.

He was being pragmatic in a global sense there. But he strongly advocated the British pulling out of India. In fact, the British government went further than he had envisaged. He felt they would only be offering some modified form of dominion state when, in fact, they just left governance to the Indians and Pakistanis.

It is interesting that he pretty much excluded Africa from that. Because there weren't enough signs of political development throughout most of Africa. But he did envisage that a united Europe would have to include, with full citizenship rights, North Africa.

Q: Orwell never visited America. Certainly he thought of cultural America as Hollywood films and some of our other exported cultural products. On the other hand, politically, he seemed to see America as the emerging superstate of the century. He hoped for a third way—Europe's way. What do you think Orwell would say about the change from America in the 1940s to America in the twenty-first century?

Ian Williams: Orwell never visited America, but America visited him in a big way. His essays show how much his perceptions were shaped by the arrival of literally millions of American troops in Britain.

He was obviously very interested in American culture, which he did actually think existed. Do you remember what Gandhi said about Western civilization? He thought it would be a good idea! Orwell did actually accept that there was an American culture, which in many ways he appreciated. One of the things he was concerned about was the segregation question with the American troops, which he referred to several times in his essays. The American military police tried to enforce segregation in British bars and dancehalls, because they didn't want blacks and whites mixing. There was a lot of political scandal across the country, even in small towns where this was attempted. It was a major issue because of the suppressed resentment against Americans who were supposedly coming to fight for freedom and were, in effect, imposing something that most British thought inherently unfair. At least in this instance, Orwell's idea about British decency was accurate. The British thought the American Negro troops much more polite than the white troops—"They're coming to defend our country"—and they didn't see why they should be mistreated like that.

Q: What would he have to say about the state of American race relations today?

Ian Williams: I think he would be fairly appalled. He recognized an underclass when he saw them. His trips up to the north of England, his experiences with down-and-outs would sensitize him to notice that most of the American major cities are black, and he would feel there is an institutionalized discrimination here. He wouldn't discuss it in a politically correct way, but he would want pragmatic solutions to it, I suspect.

I think his chief solution would be for more education. I think he would support some sort of affirmative action. But he's very anomalous on these sorts of things. He was talking about putting his son into a public school. (As you know, a public school in Britain is actually a private school.) So basically he was going to buy his son, Richard, a passport to privilege by sending him to a public school rather than giving him to the state education system. So, he was in many respects a person of his times.

Anthony Stewart: I think his work resonates for black people because of his sense of struggle. I think the academic environment, which is still pretty predominated by whites, incorporates a subtle variety of racism that makes up the sense of anxiety that darker skinned people in the academy feel.

One of the things about Orwell's work that is particularly relevant to historically marginalized groups is that Orwell understood us. He writes about his days as a reduced-fees student at his prep school, where he was with a lot of children who were diplomats' kids and professionals' children. And so he spent a lot of time around kids whose parents made an awful lot more money than his parents made. That was a point of real contention—and it allowed him to know what it was like to be ostracized in school. There are, I flippantly say sometimes, two types of literary classes: on days where we read about white people, there are no such things as racial issues—and then on the literary days about black people, it's all race, nothing else.

One of the things that Orwell allows us to do, and one of the things that would make Orwell relevant to black people and others who historically have been excluded from the academy, is to have an excellent model of a white British author who is able to communicate just what it's like on the outside.

Yet one of the great things about Orwell, and one of the great things about his work, is that he never gives up. He doesn't counsel giving up. It's important that we, as members of these historically marginalized groups, recognize that things are still possible. Never give up. That's one of the real lessons of his work.

ORWELL AND THE VICISSITUDES OF THE LEFT

Q: What do you think of the Right's claim that, if Orwell had come to see what welfare capitalism has established—largely what he sought under the name democratic socialism—*he would have strongly endorsed capitalism?*

Dennis Wrong: Well, I think he came close to that position. If you're thinking of socialism as an utterly different, alternative kind of society, he developed as so many socialists did, including myself, in the direction of social democracy. He would have followed the trend that most of the people do who make heroes out of Orwell: he would have remained on the Left, but as a social democrat, a regulated kind of capitalist—a supporter of Tony Blair in Britain and [Gerhard] Schroeder in Germany.

Q: You were involved in radical politics and some of the sectarian issues on the Left during the early Cold War era. Do you think that Orwell would continue to affiliate himself with the Left?

Dennis Wrong: Oh, I think he would have continued to call himself a socialist. To his dying day he did. He was very upset when conservatives in both Britain and the United States enlisted *Nineteen Eighty-Four* in campaigns against the British Labor Party and for Cold War propaganda. I use that term with some misgivings, because I don't think the Cold War was simply a matter of propaganda. I've always been in support of it. In fact, I actually worked for a year for the man who first formulated the American policies in the Cold War, George Kennan. I was his research assistant for a year after he left the State Department, and Dean Acheson was an old friend of my family from Washington days. So one of the reasons I liked Orwell was that he was a socialist and yet he was still strongly anticommunist or anti-Stalinist, supporting foreign policy directed at containment of the Soviet Union.

Q: What would he have to say about American capitalism and the decline or so-called death of socialism?

Ian Williams: I have a slogan: The West is Red. He predicted in 1948 that democratic socialism was possible in Western Europe, and he advocated a united socialist Europe. If you look around the world, the one society that has delivered the most social security, economic security, guarantees of civil liberties, are the social democratic societies of Western Europe—but this is *his* idea of democratic socialism. If we include Canada and possibly Australia, and exclude the United States, we can say: the industrialized societies of Western Europe have really delivered the goods.

I think he would not be talking today about the death of socialism. He'd say, "Look, we *have* socialism. Yes, we can improve it, but it's here."

Q: Many would say that what has been achieved in Western Europe and Canada could never be called democratic socialism, even if it is roughly equivalent to much of what Orwell at the time considered to be a desirable program. Western Europe is welfare capitalism—and so capitalism has shown its resilience. It has brought home the goods. Certainly many neoconservatives have used that kind of argument. Do you think that it is possible to say that capitalism has triumphed, and that, if one traces out Orwell's trajectory, he would have recognized that reality and embraced "capitalism with a human face"?

Ian Williams: The triumph of capitalism is a dubious prospect. You would think from listening to the neocons that there were gulags across Western Europe.

Orwell actually said that his conception of democratic socialism was for the masses to have some form of social security, better health, better housing, and political liberties to express themselves. And none of the communist societies has competed in any way—at least spiritually, democratically—with the Western European countries. And these capitalist societies are where capitalism is mitigated, controlled, regulated.

Michael Shelden: He was such an unorthodox leftist and such an original mind. I think it helped that Orwell was born in India, that his roots began there. . . . He understood what it was to live under British rule, or under imperial rule of any kind, certainly more so than other intellectuals of his time. And if you were British, looking at the map and thinking it very odd that this tiny little island controls so much of the earth's surface that all these tiny little pockets of earth had the British flag flying over them, you couldn't help but see that this was almost inherently unfair. It just didn't make sense . . .

I think Orwell helped to usher in a period of serious doubt about ideology itself, about the assumption that you had to have some lifelong political affiliation to have meaning in your life.

He was always an independent thinker. And the thought that he would align himself with one ideology, one point of view, for a lifetime, I think, was alien to him. Whatever the situation, I think he tried to approach it on his own, thinking independently and making up his own mind about it. In the case of Spain and the Spanish Civil War, he made up his own mind about it. When it looked as though the government might fight its own war in Europe, he had his doubts but ended up supporting it. He just had to make up his own mind, come to his own conclusions. Many people let their conclusions be formed for them. Not Orwell.

Ian Williams: In the category of people who invoke George Orwell as their savior, the neoconservatives claim that he would have been one of them. And I've rebutted this. The necessary stage for them is to go through Trotskyism on their way to the Right—and Orwell was never a Trotskyist.

ORWELL'S POLITICAL RELEVANCE IN THE TWENTY-FIRST CENTURY

Q: Do you believe that Orwell is still politically relevant today?

Ian Williams: I think Orwell is actually more relevant than ever before. He wasn't talking merely about communism. He wasn't talking merely about fascism. He wasn't talking merely about Stalinism. He was talking about totalitarianism and the totalitarian mindset. And I think there's lots of evidence that the totalitarian mindset to varying degrees is still around. Saddam Hussein. North Korea. Even here it's very difficult to read the pronouncements of John Ashcroft and Homeland Security without having twinges of worry about what people would accept here in terms of social control. You see people being locked up. There's something Orwellian, or maybe a cross between Orwell and Kafka, about people being dropped off in places that aren't officially part of the United States because they're officially part of Cuba, not allowed to see lawyers, not knowing what they're charged with, what their status is.

Daphne Patai: I think the question of Orwell's relevance is strictly an empirical one. *Is* he relevant? Yes, because he is constantly cited. . . . There is enormous attention being paid to who he is and what he wrote. So I don't think that's a matter of opinion. He simply *is* relevant. What we *make* of that relevance, how it relates to what he actually wrote, and what it means is a far more complex question.

Q: Some pundits have characterized the twentieth century as "the Orwell century."

Michael Shelden: I think that's pretty grand. But I think that of all the writers in the twentieth century, Orwell has been the greatest. He has a large following among people who are literary, but he also has a following among political types, among those who like science fiction. He has influence over the globe in a way that most British writers don't. He's read in Asia and in Africa and in South America.

Q: So your view would be that his ongoing relevance is disputable in terms of politics because it really was of the age of totalitarianism, and that age is largely past?

Dennis Wrong: Well, I don't see any powerful mass movements around aiming at total transformation of existing societies. That would be the main point. I mean, I suppose communism was the last one with its branches in other countries, as well as the Soviet Union, but I don't think there are any such movements, none that are gathering steam at least. There are tendencies and relics, certainly. There are still people, a few of them, I suppose, who think Stalin was a great leader and even fewer who think Hitler was, but I think on the whole, I don't see any such tendencies.

Pan-Arabism and fundamentalist Islam—those would be the main ones. One could find analogies too often based on the dogmatic assertions of tribal values, but I don't see any such tendencies in the Western world except for very small minorities of political sectarians.

Q: How do you respond to charges that a similar threat indeed is represented by American imperialism?

Dennis Wrong: I think that's all nonsense. That doesn't mean that American foreign policy hasn't made mistakes and bad judgments, often wielding military force where it would have been better not to. But I don't think it represents anything that could properly be called imperialism.

Q: Can't a totalitarianism of medium-size become a Big Brother in the nuclear age?

Dennis Wrong: Saddam is supposed to have been an admirer of Stalin and to have modeled himself a bit on him. I do see a certain similarity between fundamentalist Islamism in the Middle East and the nationalist and the anti-democratic movements of the previous century. But, of course, these are not great powers. There is not a great power there threatening to sweep all before it. The movement is limited to the Islamic world. So I don't think that's quite comparable as a force likely to reshape world history in the way that communism and Nazism might have changed the history of the West.

Q: Moving into the twenty-first century, would you accept that there are still "little totalitarianisms" that may not match Stalinism or Nazism?

Dennis Wrong: Well, he defined totalitarianism as what might be a permanent possibility in urban industrial societies committed to technological progress and mass communication. He certainly saw totalitarianism as a permanent possibility. But possibility is not probability. The collapse of the Soviet Union and of communism pretty well ended the probability of any general trend in that direction.

Of course, there are little things here and there to which his name has been attached as an adjective. For example, photographing people at tollbooths has been called "Orwellian." I believe that's not exactly a misuse of it, but I don't think such practices portend anything like what he was concerned about in the forms of communism and fascism.

Q: Or, as some Bush administration critics claim, is the "war on terrorism" a form of proto-fascism?

Morris Dickstein: It is similar in that we have an American need to define everything in black or white terms, good versus evil. We don't feel our public would be able to deal with more subtle nuances. And therefore you might say that Orwell slogans like "war is peace" and so on are more extreme versions of a tendency to create black-and-white slogans. Orwell saw it as part of a totalitarian system. But it's clearly built into a democratic system where some degree of popular consent is necessary for policy to go forward.

Our political leaders try to gain support not by leveling with the public but by sort of pushing this line. Look at the difference between how George Bush and Tony Blair tried to defend the war, which became especially clear at their joint news conference. We don't have much international support. Blair acknowledged this. . . . Bush on the other hand . . . simply denied that we did not have much international support. He insisted that there are plenty of nations supporting us. This, I think, is also Orwellian. He was not dealing with the issues raised at the time; he was simply sloganeering and pushing the line or the talking points of the day.

Q: What do you think are the key issues to which Orwell's work was relevant in the twentieth century? In what ways may those no longer be pertinent as we move into the twenty-first?

Dennis Wrong: I would say it is mainly Orwell's perception of the totalitarian implications of communism and fascism. He was one of the prime formulators of the concept of totalitarianism as a new kind of tyranny that is very much dependent upon the techniques of surveillance and communication that came into general use only in the twentieth century. That was what was truly distinctive about him—he was the definer and prophet of the age of totalitarianism, in which apocalyptic new societies arose that attracted adherents with the force of traditional religions—*secular religions* was the term that Raymond Aron coined for them.

Orwell grasped that quite early in the game, after his experience in the Spanish Civil War. And to cope with this age of political faiths, he advocated just transformations in the bumbling-along democratic capitalist societies. That's really what Orwell will be remembered for.

I would also put in a strong word for his essays on popular culture. They set a style, a tradition of writing about popular culture, that still exists, for which he is a kind of role model.

NINETEEN-EIGHTY FOUR AFTER 1989

Q: Many pundits were making predictions in 1989 that, with the passing of communism, Orwell's vision in Nineteen Eighty-Four *would cease to have any compelling power and pertinence. Has that been the case?*

Christopher Hitchens: It was a temptation after the great moment of 1989—the implosion and collapse of a one-party state as a theory and practice—to say that the age of totalitarianism was over with the twentieth century.

But probably the most conspicuous feature of contemporary world affairs is the confrontation with aggressive totalitarian leadership. A recent engagement with it—which extended from 1992 to this year—is the case of a twelve-year on-and-off war with Saddam Hussein, a war with global implications. What looks like an inescapable confrontation with Kim Jong Il's North Korea—with the additional terror of nuclear totalitarianism—is now looming. And we are still digging up the graves from the Milosevic era in the Balkans.

So, though I like to avoid clichés as much as the next writer, I know of no writer of any quality who's been able to visit Baghdad or North Korea and avoid the use of the term *Orwellian.* It's simply inescapable. These are places where the citizen is the property of the state, where terror is the theory and practice, where constant aggression and hatred are inculcated and continuous regimentation is employed. It's quite extraordinary to find how one is reaching for the terms that Orwell taught us.

Orwell saw the smallest details of what a dystopian system would be. Not just the hermetic nature of the state, for example, but the rapidly shifting political allegiances that the state demands of people. Yesterday Eurasia was our ally, today we're at war with Eurasia. So we never were allied with Eurasia, after all!

Of course, the American public hasn't been drilled to love Saddam Hussein or even until recently to hate him. But the political Establishment has been able to move with suspicious ease from having Saddam as a patron and a client to declaring him Public Enemy No. 1. I don't know if that quite meets the strong test of making the word *Orwellian* useful in the exact sense—any more than I'm sure that taking extraordinary measures on the home front for national security quite meets the "Big Brother test" either.

I think, however, the word has to be considered, debated, and perhaps discarded. That's an example of its inescapability.

Q: What kinds of criteria might meet the "Big Brother" or "Orwellian" test? What is it that qualifies that adjective to be targeted accurately versus just tossed around for political purposes?

Christopher Hitchens: Those of us who regard ourselves as being in George Orwell's debt are both pleased and displeased when his name comes up. People say that this latest method of surveillance, or this latest campaign against smoking, or anything that requires a government intervention in the life of a citizen, is another step towards the Big Brother State or *Nineteen Eighty-Four.*

Very often at that moment one is compelled to say, "Well, it's good to know that people are aware of the totalitarian temptation and of the tendency of the state, as it were, to take liberties. But it may be ill-advised to use the extreme model of *Nineteen Eighty-Four* or Big Brother." Or if someone says, "Much more of this and we'll be living in Animal Farm." Because there would be something absurd about those comparisons.

So it's a compliment to Orwell in the sense that he continues to live in people's minds, to inhabit people's memories and emotions. But I think he would be very scornful of the employment to which he is put. Just as he was when *Reader's Digest* made use of his books, not just for Cold War anti-communism, but sometimes to campaign against democratic socialism or the New Deal.

In other words, it is probably the vice of dystopian writing that its vividness makes it too easy to use for propaganda. In order to defend Orwell, one must be at odds with the people who use the term *Orwellian.*

Q: So, Orwell matters because—

Christopher Hitchens:—because he saw two secrets. One is that there is a will on the part of many people to dominate, to command, to exact obedience, and to relish the infliction of pain.

But the dirtier of the two secrets is a slavish willingness to be taken care of, to be maltreated. And Orwell knew that this second one is the one we must be on guard against.

Orwell's effort was always to think and to write in a language that was plain, honest, and rich enough to safeguard us against these temptations.

Q: With the passing of 1989, has the relevance of Nineteen Eighty-Four *lessened?*

Todd Gitlin: Nineteen Eighty-Four is primarily a book about Soviet communism. But the enduring value of Orwell's work extends beyond the book and the date. I myself don't feel a great desire to reread *Nineteen Eighty-Four.* I do periodically reread a number of the essays and the journals. There is a great deal there that has value: Orwell as the diagnostician of lazy-mindedness, Orwell as the tough, see-through-it-all anti-propagandist, Orwell as the sometimes-ambivalent celebrant of working-class virtue, Orwell as the dismantler of linguistic obfuscation, Orwell as the debunker of journalistic fatuity, Orwell as the diagnostician of contemporary angst. All of these Orwells are very much to the point today. But I don't think *Nineteen Eighty-Four* is a book about America or a book about the Labour government of Great Britain.

Morris Dickstein: Nineteen Eighty-Four is a novel and not a political prediction. It was an extrapolation of the world around him at a very interesting moment.

That was also the cusp of another important moment, which was the emergence of the Cold War and of two (and soon three) blocs, very much as Orwell described them in *Nineteen Eighty-Four.* Nowadays people feel that that phase of history has passed. People in the United States have written books about the triumph of democratic capitalism. But with that triumph come things that Orwell was really the first to describe. Like advances in electronic technology, advances in methods of mass propaganda, advances in methods of control that came along with not just totalitarian but democratic society. Those things did not end in 1989 or 1991.

If you look at how television was used in the first real televised campaign in 1960 between John F. Kennedy and Richard Nixon and how the use of television persuasion has developed from 1960 to the present, you can see that Orwell was right on the money. He understood that this was a new and evolving form of electronic media. There's a good deal of relevance to that part of Orwell's vision.

Q: Where were Orwell and Nineteen Eighty-Four *wrong?*

Ian Williams: He was wrong about the workers because he was an eccentric English fogy from a particular background. He sympathized with the working class but I don't think he understood them. You almost never see any references to trade unions. . . . His views tended to be a bit romantic. I don't think he ever claimed to be right on all issues. But he was more often right than he was wrong.

Q: With the passing of communism in 1989, in Hungary and elsewhere, does Orwell's Nineteen Eighty-Four *continue to have relevance and compelling power today in the twenty-first century?*

Erika Gottlieb: To get a translation or the original of *Animal Farm* or *Nineteen Eighty-Four* before 1989 could have resulted in imprisonment. All the intellectuals were interested. Since 1989, the interest in Orwell, who is a socialist after all, is diminished. It's an irony. You know, the more something is forbidden, the more interested you become. There is an unfortunate tendency in Eastern Europe to care much less about the history of socialism than we care in the West. People want to forget.

I actually taught in Hungary for one semester in 1992 and visited in 1988 when Orwell was still a marvelous character whom everybody wanted to read. By 1992, there was much less excitement about him. In the West, we are still much more engaged in analyzing his legacy.

Even at this conference, people are very sensitive about their own politics. They ask Orwell, "Wouldn't you accept my politics, please?" And I don't think this is really the issue. What is at stake is Orwell's example of having dared to criticize what most people believed in. And his courage to pursue the truth even if it went against beliefs shared by many of his confrères. This is something we are very much aware of in the West. The concern of readers and admirers of Orwell in the West has to do with a certain way of defending one's stance on the Left or being an intellectual or engaged in politics.

If you go to countries formerly behind the Iron Curtain, the interest in Orwell is quite different. In the East, in countries that experienced dictatorship, it surprises people that Orwell knew how power worked in a totalitarian system. This is what they focus on: how well, psychologically, how accurately he saw the way power works and the way those who don't have power have to behave.

In the West, you have to have a really active imagination to put yourself in the position of Winston Smith. What you are more engaged with is: "What did Orwell want? What did he accomplish?" Sometimes readers in the West are even ashamed of their initially very strong response to the book because they feel Orwell exaggerated. You have Western readers arguing about Orwell's positions, about whether or not Orwell accomplished what he wanted, and so on.

But I think the real question is whether Orwell had the courage to express what he saw that wasn't popular at all. And I think those who admired Orwell in the West probably admired his courage. He had the courage to tell his own friends, his own immediate circle, that it is a myth that Soviet Russia is a socialist country. And I think that's a very important message, even today, even after the fall of Russia. It means Orwell had the courage to talk about the inconvenient aspects of the truth and to face unpopularity among his own friends and people whom he respected. It's not so much that he said, "I *found* the truth; this is what it is." He had the courage to say, "You have to be able to *search* for the truth without being hindered by any kind of censorship, either by the official censor or by your friends and contemporaries." Orwell had this very exceptional courage to *search* for the truth.

ORWELL, PATRIOTISM, PACIFISM, AND NATIONALISM

Q: In 1942, responding to British pacifists, Orwell said, "To oppose British entry into the war is to be objectively pro-fascist." Some Bush administration supporters in effect have said, "To oppose the war on terrorism, the Iraq war, is to be objectively pro-Saddam." Is that a legitimate use of Orwell?

Todd Gitlin: No. This is dishonest propaganda of the worst kind. Look, the Germans had bombarded Britain for how many months? There was a war on. Germany was a superpower in today's terms. It controlled most of Europe. It would have invaded Britain and it came close to doing so. It had killed British soldiers and civilians and it was a threat to civilization. In that setting, Orwell's remarks, although perhaps on the high side of pungency, were defensible.

The current situation is not that at all. Iraq was never a threat to American security. The strongest case for war was the case the administration didn't make, which is: This is a rotten, vile, murderous regime and it doesn't deserve to exist for its own people. That would have been an honest case for war. I think it was actually the prime motive. But to say that the war was necessary because the Baath regime was a threat to American security—or that weapons of mass destruction were present—this is very different from the case that Orwell was making in 1942.

Everybody likes historical parallels, partly because we like to rest on historical predecessors and partly because we are intellectually lazy. This one is especially lazy and dangerous. People fought the Vietnam War on the basis of Munich and the run-up to World War II. By the way, this is also true of anti-war movements. Some people opposed the Iraq war on the expectation that it was going to turn into Vietnam—and that was also a case of historical fancy footwork.

The broadcast media, especially television, have the power to generate a sort of trance, a sort of electronic mob in which people surrender their critical faculties and take a warm bath in reassurance rituals and demonization rituals. American television is convinced that when war begins, or even in the run-up to war, that its mission is to spin a web of emotional engagement. This is something that Orwell, I think, anticipated in the ritualized hate episodes in *Nineteen Eighty-Four.* It's a spirit of doublethink, in which people surrender their independence to the judgment prefabricated for them through the media, the Oceania-has-always-been-at-war-with-Eurasia syndrome.

I still tend to think that of the two great dystopias of midcentury, the one that is actually relevant to our media situation is not *Nineteen Eighty-Four* but *Brave New World,* in which the media are much more a nonstop fun fest whose major consequence is not the propagandistic tilting of people toward a particular political line, but a sort of jamboree of trivial episodes. To put it in the terms of my former NYU colleague, Mark Miller, "Big Brother Is You, Watching." People internalize their own sort of consumer-centered criteria for believing, and then they proceed to feel manipulated by the mass media.

Q: What about events that occurred later in response to 9/11, such as the invasion of Afghanistan, pursuing the Taliban, the "war on terrorism"—was all that also an instance of patriotism? Or did that cross the line into nationalism, in Orwell's terms?

Todd Gitlin: I'm not sure. Orwell is not a systematic political theorist. For me, it was a straightforward case of national self-defense, a case of rights of national sovereignty, which the UN Security Council endorsed. It didn't follow that everything the United States would wish to do in Afghanistan was legitimate, or that the United States was entitled to chase al-Qaeda operatives anywhere it chose forever. In fact, very quickly after September 11, I was also writing in a spirit of warning against the notion of a war on terror which would have no end point. In fact, curiously and perversely, within the first ten days we heard [Secretary of Defense Donald] Rumsfeld, when asked when the war would be over, saying the war would be over "when Americans feel safe."

Well, that is a perverse definition of war. War has an ending, which is the end of hostilities. And if the end of war means anything in the law of nations, it must be because there is a certificate of combat having ceased. Sometimes war ends when there is unconditional surrender. In any case, there is an objective event that must take place to certify that a war is over. In this case, Rumsfeld is defining war as a state of mind, which I find quite Orwellian. "If we feel safe, the war is over. If we feel unsafe, then the war is on."

Orwell takes you to the lip of an important moral distinction, which is also an analytical distinction. But it's not a political program, nor is it a worldview. It is a useful preliminary, but not more than that.

So Orwell matters as someone who has a moral relevance to those issues, not any kind of political program that would still bear relevance today—but rather a sensibility—and a sensibility is very important.

I opposed the war, although I think there are arguments for it. I don't think this one was a no-brainer. There are certainly elements of justification for the war. There is a millenarian streak in the administration's insistence that the war was necessary, which is, in Orwell's terms, nationalist. That is, it affirms that the United States is the proper judge of political systems. There was a great deal of obfuscation and deception in the way this administration readied the country for and approached the war. There was a kind of shell game of arguments—and therefore all the Orwell skepticism about propaganda is very much to the point.

Q: So Orwell is an example of patriotism?

Ian Williams: Yes. Patriotism—and there is a touch of nostalgia and old-fogyness about it. He insisted on being English, which is very interesting—certainly most of the people I know in the north of England feel closer to Scotland. His English patriotism was not jingoism, but a quiet contentment with the conditions of life.

The patriot's real duty is to criticize his or her country when it's wrong, and he certainly wasn't afraid of doing that. There is no element of "my country right or wrong" in his work. And if you can't say "my country right or wrong," then you sure as hell don't say somebody *else's* country right or wrong. You don't have uncritical support for Iraq or Yugoslavia or Stalin or North Korea or anywhere else—or Israel, come to think of it. He held very strongly that you should consider all of the circumstances before giving your support to anything, and you shouldn't come with a preformed loyalty.

Q: You drew attention to Orwell's distinction [in "Notes on Nationalism"] between nationalism and patriotism.

Todd Gitlin: It was a distinction that made sense to me urgently on the day of September 11, when I felt this was a moment to revisit this essay by Orwell. I live a block from what has come to be called Ground Zero.

His fundamental distinction is between patriotism, which is attachment to a way of life, and nationalism, which is fundamentally aggressive. That was the way he couched the distinction, and it was urgent for me at that moment [2001] to find a vocabulary for expressing an attachment to what my neighborhood felt. And to express that attachment without signing over my politics to the political leadership that was likely going to make of the attacks something that I wouldn't want to subscribe to, namely, a nationalist appeal. Certainly, there were other people in evidence who wanted to turn the victimization position into a warrant for unending war.

Orwell was very blunt and matter-of-fact. I remember the distinction from having read the essay in 1971. He affirms that patriotism is attachment to your way of life. Orwell seemed to believe that the English way of life was the best in the world. Now, that's farther than I want to go. I don't feel that way about America or the American way of life, but I do feel there is much that is admirable.

In any case, I feel it is mine. And to have Orwell's essay in my kit bag during those weeks [in 2001] was a little mark of clarity. About ten days after 9/11, I was interviewed by the *New York Times* columnist Clyde Haberman on the subject of people displaying the American flag to symbolize this attachment. Interestingly, Haberman had reread Orwell's essay himself in preparation for his column. Lots of people turned to Orwell, who, after all, was also a citizen of a country under bombardment. They were very much drawn to the iconography of wartime Britain during those weeks.

Q: So flying the flag was an instance of patriotism, not nationalism—according to Orwell's distinction.

Todd Gitlin: Exactly.

ORWELL THE TECHNO-PROPHET?

Q: Has the use of technology become "Orwellian"?

Morris Dickstein: One of the things that's become more Orwellian is subtler, more sophisticated use of language to obfuscate and conceal and even distort the truth. Orwell used extreme and, in the end, not particularly persuasive examples of a society trying to convince its subjects or its slaves that two and two is five.

This is not what's happening today in America. We have political parties that don't necessarily want to show the people at election time what they represent. If I can be partisan, the Republican Party represents the interests of a relatively small part of the public. And every four years it's got to convince a large part of the public to vote against its own interests. And that involves certain Orwellian techniques of persuasion, whereby certain window dressings in the party platform that are superficial or that contradict where the party stands must be inserted and substituted for the actual interests of the people the party tries to defend and sustain. And both parties do this. The Democratic Party tries to convince you it's the party of law and order. The Republican Party tries to convince you it's the party of all the people.

Both of them are lies, and both of them are wheeled out in every election. That's very Orwellian.

Q: Is our historical consciousness waning? In Nineteen Eighty-Four, *Oceania's change of alliance to Eastasia and then Eurasia is similar to the present: the United States supported Iraq in the 1980s, and in 2003 we launched a war against Iraq.*

Ian Williams: Yes. And in *Nineteen Eighty-Four*, Oceania cared enough about history to try and rewrite it. Today we have people who just don't know history.

Q: If you enlarge the memory hole, then you don't have to do the work of rewriting anything—because it just disappears completely.

Ian Williams: Yes. There's nothing there to rewrite. You might remember there is a novel by Robert Harris called *Fatherland*, which is set in a fictional Germany that won the war. I remember Paramount Pictures optioned the book and then dropped the option, because 50 percent of their target audience, when polled, did not know that Germany lost the war! You don't have to rewrite history under these circumstances, because most people have no historical context at all.

Orwell would be horrified about the society that allows this to happen—where memories have disappeared on this scale. I think he'd say, "Britain is bad and it's following in America's footsteps." In Europe, there exists still a sort of collective consciousness of history. But in America, to an incredible extent, people don't know their own history. Recently I was involved in debates about the current Iraq war. People were excoriating the French, who have "always been evil, always been our enemies." France is the enemy this week. Next week it might be Eurasia. People in the United States have no historical memory at all.

Q: What about "consumer" totalitarianism? Does that apply to American advertising, maybe even the Internet?

Dennis Wrong: Adorno would talk that way. It's a metaphorical way of talking. I don't find it terribly plausible. Of course, nobody likes mass advertising, mass culture. It's true that Orwell wrote that those things portend some kind of political oppression or repression. But I don't see that.

Q: What about Orwell's views on advertising?

Ian Williams: In Orwell's critiques, politics and advertising are the same thing. Politicians today *are* sold like snake oil or soap powder. I think he'd be horrified at it.

I think he would have been amused, horrified, and in his own puritanical way, disgusted by your average e-mail inbox, where opportunities to enhance your penis size or your breast size keep flooding in. But people must be trying this stuff! There must be an awful lot of people walking around with some strange organs.

One of the things people forget about *Nineteen Eighty-Four* is that it wasn't about external control necessarily. The key was people wanted to believe these things. People forced themselves to believe it. That's the essence of doublethink, that you convince yourself that this is true.

Michael Shelden: I think our age is an age of slogans. We have words like *sound byte.* And Orwell didn't know about that, but he had a feel for it from working in radio at BBC. And I think that feel gave him the sense that he could come up with slogans of his own that would be far more enduring and just as complex. You could write whole books about Big Brother. He's just one character in *Nineteen Eighty-Four,* but he's such a powerful presence.

Q: What might Orwell have to say about the role of technology in our lives today?

Ian Williams: He'd be awed. *Nineteen Eighty-Four* was science fiction in the 1940s—telescreens were science fiction. That was the one really serious science fiction element of *Nineteen Eighty-Four.* Now we can put tags in clothes that will record every time you enter a store or every time you pass a cash register. We can record every financial transaction. Big Brother today has more means at his disposal than in Orwell's worst nightmares.

Q: What might he have said about the computer?

Dennis Wrong: He would have seen it simply as a possible new instrument for totalitarian rule. He certainly would have seen computer data banks as very useful instruments for any totalitarian ruler. He would say, "Thank God Hitler didn't have data banks and computers," something like that. I don't really object to the term *Orwellian* when applied to these, but it is taking it a little bit out of the historical context in which Orwell wrote.

Q: I'll bet he would have been delighted to have had a computer on Jura when he was faced with revising Nineteen Eighty-Four!

Dennis Wrong: That may well be!

Q: Would Orwell see the computer and the Internet as liberating technologies or in some ways as new forms of enslavement that bear some analogy to what he was warning against?

Michael Shelden: There is the sense that the Internet is a wonderful thing but also a frightening thing. And frightening in the sense that it violates our right to privacy because it keeps such a good record of everything we do—from every keystroke to every website we visit. And I think that the idea of living in a world where all of your footprints are tracked, from physical to electronic, is the kind of world that Orwell understood, saw, perceived long before we came to it.

In many respects Orwell didn't really like machines. He's uncomfortable with complex machines. In *Nineteen Eighty-Four* one of the objects that's so magical is the glass paperweight. Something from the Victorian era, something from a time before the machine age became so dominant. He was comfortable working with his hands. A world in which the machines had become so dominant was a world he found very intimidating.

Morris Dickstein: Many people think of the Internet as a countercultural instrument. Because up to this point it has been quite accessible to everyone, it's not—yet at least—a vehicle of control such as those Orwell described in *Nineteen Eighty-Four,* even though some websites have the clout to get more attention than others.

Orwell would have probably disliked the instantness and pervasiveness of e-mail. Being in many ways a very old-fashioned person, Orwell might have seen that as an invasion of his life. I suspect that he would have been one of those people to continue to type his pieces on a battered typewriter, rather than on a computer. Orwell prided himself on a certain old-fashioned quality. He liked the way things had formerly been done. He was nostalgic for those ways. And I suspect that the further mechanization of the world would have made him even more nostalgic.

Ian Williams: Well, he was a bit of an old fogy. It'd be interesting to see whether he'd graduate to a word processor or cling to a typewriter. He'd have been concerned about the implications of all this technology. He was quite ambivalent about industry and he realized that, for the working class, it was the only way forward, but he didn't like it at the same time.

Take the way technology was used in the Iraq war. We have twenty-four-hour television. We have context-free news: this means that we're sort of a collective memory hole into which everything gets dumped on a daily basis. People are exposed almost all day to one or two simple facts—over and over again—and it's like the passage in *Nineteen Eighty-Four* that announced an increase in the chocolate ration. I got that same feeling when I saw President Bush at the United Nations announce that Iraq was an aggressive force because it attacked Iran and did terrible things to its people. But what about the context here? George, your party and your government supported it when it was doing those things! We're bereft of the context that would allow us to question our leader, because we have this twenty-four-hour stream of infotainment drivel.

Q: Would you say that he would view the changes in privacy, personal freedoms, and so forth as having increased and brought us greater liberty or having represented greater encroachment and more government intrusion in our lives? Are we getting closer or going further away from what he feared about Big Brother?

Dennis Wrong: I think further away—and toward greater freedom. Insofar as the standard of living is certainly much, much higher, you can't find people like the poverty-stricken mining families Orwell wrote about in *The Road to Wigan Pier*, for example, or the down-and-outers in Paris and London. There has been a general rise in the standard of living. One must remember that it was the Depression that seemed to justify everything that Marxists and others had said about the inherent instability and injustice of capitalism.

Q: What do you think he would have to say about popular culture today, especially in America? What might he say about cable television with five hundred channels?

Dennis Wrong: I really don't know what he would say about it, except that he would be quite critical of a lot of it. He would think it trivializes human experiences—what most highbrow intellectuals would feel about it today.

ORWELL'S LITERARY LEGACY

Q: Why were you drawn to him?

Michael Shelden: I was drawn to his essays, not to his stories. The reason I was drawn to his essays first is that I was so struck by hearing someone speak to me plainly, in language that was clearly artistic and yet crafted in plain speech. It was as though you had an uncle whose wisdom you trusted, and yet instead of speaking to you in the plainest prosaic language, he had an eloquence that turned plain speaking into something great. That is something you can listen to all day long. I can pick up Orwell any time any place and immediately be drawn into his work, because his voice is that of a plain-speaking, wise, older character.

Many of the people who knew him told me that they could hear his voice in his writing. And if you know a very distinctive writer and then listen to them speak, you're often struck by how close what they've written is to the way they speak in person.

Todd Gitlin: He's a great essayist. Not long after September 11, I had a conversation with a liberal congressman. I asked him what he was thinking about. He said he'd had a meeting with Donald Rumsfeld. The congressman had given him a copy of "Shooting an Elephant," Orwell's great essay about the colonial mindset. I don't know that Rumsfeld read it. But it was interesting to me that this congressman had turned back to "Shooting an Elephant" at that moment.

Michael Shelden: If you had attacked the Soviet Union in a pamphlet in 1944 or '45, no one would remember your name today. It would be so completely dated. But if you create a fable, a story about pigs on a farm, you create a story that can be appreciated on many levels. You can laugh along with the antics of the pigs and miss the entire political allegory and still have a good time reading it. But if you appreciate its allegory, it becomes a far more meaningful book, and it doesn't even matter that the Soviet system of government has disappeared, because there are a lot of governments around the world that have elements of the Soviet system. There are miniature Stalins across the globe. And the threat of those Stalins is always there. So in many ways *Animal Farm* is an object lesson about tyrants. Whether people are working in some large corporation or in a place where the government is ruled by a tyrant, if they read Orwell's fable, they'll better understand the tools that tyrants employ and be in a position to fight them, whether to undermine them or simply to get the hell out of there.

Q: Do you recall what your response was to Nineteen Eighty-Four *when you first read it?*

Dennis Wrong: Yes. I was impressed. I saw it as a very credible dystopian novel. I recognized the anti-Soviet implication of it. I also connected it very much to a book that enormously influenced me at the time and I still regard as a great book in the philosophy of history—Hannah Arendt's *Origins of Totalitarianism.* I thought of Arendt and Orwell as very much akin in identifying the possibility of all these things in modern industrial society.

I was even a little offended: Arendt was a high-toned German philosopher and didn't give sufficient credit to Orwell. Bernard Crick also says this in his biography of Orwell: Orwell was plain Billy Brown from London Town. He anticipated her. After all, *Nineteen Eighty-Four* came out [two] years before *The Origins of Totalitarianism.*

Q: What was the experience as a teenager under communism in Hungary that you had that so resonated with his vision in Nineteen Eighty-Four?

Erika Gottlieb: The experience of living with fear and the obligation to convert this fear into the love of the dictator. It's a psychological experience that is not easy to explain. Orwell described this conversion beautifully in *Nineteen Eighty-Four,* where out of the tremendous fear and hostility you have to produce love for the dictator in order to stay alive, to justify your actions to yourself. Orwell recognized very well the tremendous role of propaganda. Anybody who lived in a dictatorship would also agree, yes, this is the way propaganda works.

Q: So slogans from Nineteen Eighty-Four *like "War Is Peace, Freedom Is Slavery, Ignorance Is Strength" were viscerally powerful for you.*

Erika Gottlieb: Yes. The personality cult, the worship of the leader. You not only had to imitate, but actually to feel viscerally the slogans that you have to keep repeating, ad infinitum, just the way we listen to a commercial today so many times that it becomes part of our vocabulary. The [communist] slogan became part of our vocabulary.

Q: You first encountered Orwell's work in the 1930s and '40s, as he was still alive. What can a young person today value about Orwell, now that the world has changed so radically?

Dennis Wrong: Well, if you look at the *Collected Essays, Journalism, and Letters,* the pieces on "Boys' Weeklies," on popular songs, on detective stories, "Raffles and Miss Blandish"—all of these still seem to me to have a certain relevance, at least as a model for what can be done today with popular media like detective stories and "Boys' Weeklies." I was actually a subscriber to the *Boy's Own Paper.* Dickens and Kipling are also written about in that volume of essays, and of course it also includes his essay on politics and the English language.

There's something about his writing, especially in the essays, that is immediately and directly appealing. Some of that is a rhetorical effect. He creates an idea of what cant or orthodoxy is at any given moment. And he creates the impression that he is puncturing that cant or orthodoxy, even when he's created it simply for the purpose of the essay. Nevertheless there's something liberating, something appealing about that act of puncturing that cant . . .

It's not so much Orwell as a moralist or decent man that's appealing. It's the directness of his writing. It does seem to have a moral weight and a strong personal signature. Orwell the man seems to be on every page that he's writing. And even when you disagree with him, you're not dealing with someone who has abstracted himself from the issue. That's where Orwell works as a model—where the language, the rhetoric, and the moral position all seem to intersect.

Q: Orwell's crafting of a plain-man persona never seems like a literary performance. It's utterly transparent.

Morris Dickstein: It's the greatest literary performance. Orwell is not Shakespeare. Orwell is not John Milton. Orwell is not in the class with the greatest of all writers.[3] He didn't have a huge imaginative vision. He belongs to a lesser class of writers, who wrote about topical issues, who interacted with many of the awful and wonderful events of their time. Orwell was a model of how to intersect contemporary history without either getting lost in the topical or caught up in your previous positions but simply reacting viscerally.

That immediacy is extremely rare. That directness. The sense of the person responding. Whether he's responding to a totalitarian system as in *Animal Farm* or *Nineteen Eighty-Four,* or whether he's responding to a piece of news that came in from the BBC ten minutes ago, that responsiveness is the core of Orwell's vision. It's the core of his relation to the world, and that's what will remain when the particular issues he talked about have faded from view.

Q: How do you regard The Road to Wigan Pier *and his other reportage?*

Morris Dickstein: Orwell is often praised for his intellectual honesty. But it really is a facet of a larger phenomenon, which is his social curiosity. Orwell had a very matter-of-fact, sort of empirical, commonsensical British sensibility, which was a limitation on his part. He also had an impulse toward downward mobility, to de-class himself and to eliminate some of the vestiges of his middle-class identity.

In the thirties, when a lot of photographers and journalists were also seeking out the milieu of poverty, Orwell went down among the people and tried to show that there were parts of England, the miners in the north, that were essentially invisible to a middle-class audience. Orwell took up that mission of Carlyle in the Victorian period, or of Jack London, and he went on to show how the other half lived. And he wanted to render it not ideologically, that is, from a Marxist perspective, but from an empirical perspective, in order to show people what life was like. That to me is an eternally relevant social project that still moves me deeply.

Q: Can people appreciate Orwell's work without knowing the history behind it?

Michael Shelden: History's only boring when the people writing it forget the word *story*. Orwell understood that in order to make his times memorable and power-ful, in order to make his history enduring, he had to put it in the form of a memo-rable story.

He made himself into a great storyteller. I don't think it came naturally to him. He started as a reporter. That's where his skills began. But he turned him-self into a storyteller with extraordinary success in these two stories—*Animal Farm* and *Nineteen Eighty-Four*—which people can appreciate even though they may not know the history that informs either story. And Orwell understood that to make people appreciate the history of his time, he had to put it in a memorable story and make it timeless.

Q: How relevant is Orwell as a writer as we proceed in the twenty-first century?

Ian Williams: One of the tests of a work of art is whether it survives the context in which it was born. And *Animal Farm* works as a fable and tells its story about the corruption of power, even if you don't have a clue that Napoleon was Stalin and that Snowball was Trotsky. You don't have to know that. The story works in its own right. And that is the perfect allegory because its message about power and corruption is still there. And *Nineteen Eighty-Four* is once again a more chill-ing version of the corruption of power. The fact that it's still being read twenty years after 1984 shows that it wasn't meant to be a prediction of power but a social experiment, a literary experiment. If you accept these premises about social control in a one-party state, this is what life is like. And I think it will stand for a long, long time as a chilling warning that, despite the end of communism, totalitarianism in many forms is around now and will be around, though it might take new forms. But both of those works give us an apparatus to understand what's happening.

When leaders of countries get up and tell obvious falsehoods with a straight face, you can see Big Brother at work. You can see doublethink when you see neologisms coined: "collateral damage," the euphemisms for strikes, "selected take-outs" for assassinations, and so on. Newspeak is a rapidly growing language!

Todd Gitlin: I think the famous plain style is of great value. His mockery of euphemism and intellectual dishonesty via high-flying rhetoric is of enduring value. Since all governments lie, Orwell's critique of deceptive language in "Politics and the English Language" and other essays is a hardy perennial. Its relevance ain't going away.

Orwell as the guy who invites intellectual courage is not such a small thing, who says you don't have to be a herdsman or herd follower to be a writer, that in fact it damages your literary acumen, your powers of observation: all this is exemplary.

In recent years I've several times taught both *The Road to Wigan Pier* and *Homage to Catalonia*. I've taught them as exercises in observation, but also in rhetoric. One thing I love about Orwell—he selectively, but very tellingly, uses the second person as a way of inviting the reader into a sort of complicity with his line of argument. "You must feel this," he says in effect. If it were overdone, it might be Orwellian. He doesn't do that. He's actually quite a master of rhetoric.

I don't think Orwell is the secular saint of politics. But I think he is an indispensable writer. Writers in general are not saintly, but they are certainly deliverers of important news to other writers. I can't imagine anybody who wants to write essays or to think about politics being legitimately spared the discipline of reading and rereading Orwell's essays.

Q: Is it still important to study Orwell for literary—rather than just political or moral—reasons?

Anthony Stewart: Yes. The difference between reading Orwell and reading T. S. Eliot or James Joyce or any of the great writers from the earlier part of the twentieth century is that he wrote books so that people from all classes would read them.

He used the phrase "good bad books." He made a distinction between [highbrow] books that were written to be "important" and books that, while not just written to be serious, were actually still readable years later. One of his examples was *Uncle Tom's Cabin* by Harriet Beecher Stowe. A lot of people have argued that *Nineteen Eighty-Four* is one of those good bad books.[4]

CHAPTER SEVEN

The Man within the Writings

I. "A PRESENCE IN OUR LIVES"

Q: What does Orwell still have to say to intellectuals today?

Richard Kostelanetz: Simply to always see clearly and always tell the truth concisely.

Richard Rorty: He reminds us how easy it is for intellectuals to become, with the best motives in the world, apologists for tyrannies.

Anthony Stewart: We can still learn a lot from Orwell about decency, which is a term that he used a lot. *Decency* has become sort of a cliché. Yet especially in a time where people who look like me, who historically have not had access to positions of power and positions of privilege, now do, there is no better framework for various groups of people to get along than just the simple commitment to treat one another decently.

Bernard Crick: He would say to intellectuals today, use your intelligence to reach ordinary people. Most of his books are demanding, but none of them needs any special vocabulary or special education.

Erika Gottlieb: Orwell's message to intellectuals today is to be found in his definition of the intellectual's duty to face reality, in spite of, or independently of, party affiliations, to recognize that the "smelly little orthodoxies" and the various "isms" are not to define or legitimize any dishonest position abandoning the social function of the intellectual to enlighten public opinion.

Anthony Stewart: Orwell is still an important person to read. Reading Orwell will give you a sense of the twentieth century. His essays give you a very clear sense of how life is a struggle and that—even though it's a struggle—the struggle is not to be feared.

To me, Orwell was unusual in his relationship to the people he was sort of assumed to be peers with, he was never cozy with them and that lack of coziness was a really important part of his identity.

So, to me, he's important because he gives you a clear sense that fitting in and belonging needn't be the most important thing in our lives.

Q: Does Orwell's example of intellectual integrity have something worthwhile to say about the way in which we are conducting our political and intellectual discourse?

Richard Kostelanetz: Yes, certainly, in an age of intellectual/literary opportunism in which too many are guilty of exploiting one or another gravy train.

Bernard Crick: To judge by the number of times he is quoted, sometimes ignorantly, sometimes accurately, he is used as a counter-symbol to a general feeling today of a lack of integrity among political leaders and ingrown, publicly incomprehensible discourse among academic intellectuals.

Richard Rorty: No. We all do our best to avoid what later readers will see as self-deception, and sometimes we succeed. But Orwell's success doesn't give us much help in figuring out how to avoid the temptations to self-deception that permeate the political and intellectual issues of our own day.

Christopher Hitchens: The striking feature of today's political landscape is the way it's often dominated by semi-private languages. The language used by political consultants, political manipulators, and pollsters is the language that isn't expected to be needed by the voters it chooses to influence.

And the language that's used by dictatorships exactly conforms to the sort of thing Orwell warned us against: leaders of the glorious struggle that is to come; the great future that awaits; the hard times that have to be endured meanwhile. And of course, when this [politicized language] supports leader worship or an extreme religion, it becomes a language entirely unto itself. Children are taught not to read or to write, or to consider or to compare, but simply to memorize one sacred language—and the whole text of the Holy Book becomes all they know. It possesses them. They don't possess it. Even the milder type [of propaganda] forms people who surrender their freedom of thought, their independence of mind.

Todd Gitlin: At his best, Orwell is rather unusual for an English writer—he is interested in understanding his own intellectual process. He's not defensive. It's not important for him to establish that he is always right about something. In fact, he changes his mind on various fronts and he's interested in why that might be. He's interested in self-scrutiny. For example, in "Shooting an Elephant," he's interested in the mentality of the colonial, which at that time was himself. There are wonderful passages in *The Road to Wigan Pier* and *Homage to Catalonia*, where he looks at himself not in the kind of obsessive, interminable hyper-psychological fashion that's more congenial to American writers now, but in a more disciplined English fashion. He's interested in what he's feeling at the time, which then becomes useful data.

Related to this, he doesn't take cheap shots. Some of the best stuff in *Homage to Catalonia* are explorations of the mindset and the experience of his enemies. Read him on the fascist soldier, for example. He's very moving. He is not a demonizer. He is interested in why it is that people do things which are immoral. He's curious. And the people on his side are not necessarily exemplars of supreme excellence.

So I think Orwell is a great reminder of how to reflect about one's adversaries. We have an idiotic yes-you-did-no-you-didn't kind of culture. What passes for political debate—perversely influential forms of television, television of crossfire blather which we call debates—I can't imagine that Orwell would show any interest in that sort of childish, schoolyard cheap shot. I think he's an adult about argument and he understands that people are complicated and that intentions are not actions and that actions are not intentions.

The other thing that Orwell might tell us about political discourse is that, in order to be a moral agent, you don't have to and you shouldn't sign up to join a team. Although nobody could have been more anti-communist than George Orwell in 1950, he refused to join the Congress for Cultural Freedom, because they didn't take seriously the problem of colonialism. He didn't think you should blind yourself in one eye because of the urgency of what was going on out of the other eye. All this we would benefit from taking seriously.

Orwell sets an example for us today by his concentrated effort in his own time to diagnose the destructive dynamics in the "realpolitik" of the 1930s and 40s, the perturbing, unprecedented, unpredictable minuet of alliances and betrayals among Nazi Germany, Stalin's Russia, and the Allies. He blames the Right. He also blames the Left. What's more, he has the courage to examine and criticize his own position.

Let us just imagine President Bush and his advisors, for example, reexamining their "analysis of the situation" a couple of years ago and admitting their faults and shortcomings. No doubt, the kind of moral and intellectual integrity demonstrated by Orwell is admirable; however, its efficacy is dubious: Certainly among politicians in power it has not been tried yet.

Michael Shelden: Orwell has become a cultural icon. There are so many people in schools and in private life who read his work that his name has become almost a brand name. It's not enough to simply describe a totalitarian, "Orwellian" universe. There's also the sense that Orwell's name, like Campbell's Soup, is an awfully powerful trademark. And if you want to get your ideas heard, you might package them with the Orwell brand. I think a lot of people like to cover themselves with Orwell's name, ride on his fame. It's a natural instinct.

If you try to align yourself with him, you're in effect saying, "Believe me, because I have the same standards of honesty and integrity that this guy had." That's powerful. Because we're very much tempted these days not to believe anything we're told.

When you pick up something to read, you want to feel that you haven't been cheated. Orwell gives you that sense that you haven't wasted your time but that you've grown a bit, that you've expanded a bit in your own mind as a result of reading him. And that's something that keeps people coming back to him.

Q: Does Orwell matter as an intellectual and even ethical example to you? Do you in any sense agree with Lionel Trilling's perception of him as "a virtuous man"?

Richard Kostelanetz: "Virtuous writer" would be more correct, as recent biographers have uncovered personal failings that cannot be disputed. Need I add that I consider the Trilling encomium a typical example of New York writers making stuff up in lieu of anything resembling verifiable research?

Richard Rorty: I think it would be a mistake to think of him as more virtuous than Shaw, who was tempted by fascism, or than [Eric] Hobsbawm, who is still unable to face up to his role as an apologist for Stalin. Orwell was virtuous, but also lucky. It takes a lot of luck, as well as a lot of virtue, to be viewed by history as always having been on the right side.

Bernard Crick: I find Orwell's honesty and integrity impressive, while remembering that he adopts the persona of the plain, blunt, honest man, which does not always correspond exactly to his personal life. So I find Lionel Trilling's perception of him as "a virtuous man" somewhat misleading. His close friend, Richard Rees, called him "almost saintly," which I think is almost silly. He is not exceptionally virtuous in the moral sense, but he is a writer who espoused, in the old-fashioned sense, republican virtues (as the eighteenth century understood the term) of civic action and personal integrity—much in the manner that Machiavelli used the Roman "virtu," public-spirited skill and courage.

Morris Dickstein: I really see him more as a cantankerous, quite *im*perfect man. I admire Orwell more as a very real, very ordinary, very prejudiced man. . . . For me, among the greatest reasons for his literary relevance are his creative use of the essay and his blurring of the line between fiction, reportage, and creative writing. Many of his essays and book reviews are so meticulously crafted in terms of rhetoric. . . . He really understood that the future of fiction was in an area that was close to documentary.

Michael Shelden: People want heroes. Orwell's as good as anyone. He was a moral exemplar. But people today are very skeptical of that term. They've seen too many heroes cut down to size. And you could find any number of ways to talk about Orwell's flaws. But as a human being, with lots of faults, he still had a side to him that one of his friends called a "crystal spirit." It is a beauty and integrity that has inspired a lot of people. I think many people inspired by Orwell are inspired by his deep sense of integrity.

Erika Gottlieb: Trilling is right in describing Orwell the man as virtuous, although he probably underrates Orwell the writer when praising him for the "virtue of not being a genius." By contrast, Koestler considers Orwell "the only writer of genius among *litterateurs* of social revolt between the two wars" and the "missing link between Kafka and Swift." Maybe one should complete the above definitions of Orwell by looking for a new term, the genius of the moral imagination.

Q: Orwell has sometimes been an object of intellectual hero worship. How do you respond to such treatment of him?

Michael Shelden: There are so many people you might look up to as a hero in your life. But in an ordinary life figures like Orwell come along once in a lifetime or not at all. History offers us these examples of the past and we are profiting from them. . . . You accept something from the past that enriches the present. That's only common sense.

Q: Does it seem to you as if Orwell is overvalued today as an intellectual figure?

Richard Kostelanetz: No, though often misrepresented for one or another vulgar, usually partisan and/or self-aggrandizing purpose.

Richard Rorty: No. He is certainly somebody whom I hope that coming generations will continue to read, and to think about. However, I hope coming generations will continue to read Shaw too—but not because either he or Orwell had
original ideas. They just made certain ideas exceptionally vivid. Like Dickens,
both men were exceptionally useful writers—but *intellectual figure* does not seem
quite the right term.

Bernard Crick: It depends what you mean by "intellectual." He was an intellectual
who tried to reach the common reader—I see the common readers of his day as
those who educated themselves in free public libraries rather than universities.
He understood modernist writers such as Joyce and Henry Miller but deliberately chose not to write in that intellectual way that is only understood by other
intellectuals.

Erika Gottlieb: I'm convinced Orwell is not over-valued; in fact, few people in our
day understand the intellectual complexity and moral courage required to formulate and express his opinions, challenging not only the Right, but even some
widely accepted views of his own friends, of his own side on the Left.

  In fact, he was not the first but definitely the most convincing writer to articulate a comprehensive definition of *any* form of totalitarianism, emphasizing
terror and the lies of propaganda as its most conspicuous features—a definition
encouraging us to fight for democracy by fighting against the forces of the totalitarian mentality—no mean feat for any intellectual.

Morris Dickstein: The prejudices are out there. They are a little bit disconcert-
ing. But the prejudices are the man. And he would often revise his prejudices.
People have written about Orwell's contradictions. But I agree with Christopher
Hitchens that Orwell's contradictions are what make him appealing. . . . There's
something appealing about a writer's ability to change his mind and to be un-
ashamed to do so.

  His penchant for changing his mind was partly a result of the man, partly a result of the times. These were really turbulent times he lived in, the '30s and '40s.
And he responded to really troubled times, and he responded intuitively to those
times. He saw dangers in the formation of totalitarianism, the breakup of totalitarianism, the way democracy was evolving, the way the welfare state was evolving. Orwell's changing views were a response to a changing world. The world has
since become a much more stable place for most people.

Q: Is his literary persona authentic?

Michael Shelden: It's difficult when you're a writer to fake your integrity. And the real issue with Orwell was whether he was ready to practice what he preached. And he proved that to be so in Spain, where he was willing to go out there and fight in the trenches for what he believed and for his pains got a bullet in the throat. He suffered in ways that most writers would prefer not to, simply because he was willing to put his words into action.

You don't lie to yourself and you don't lie to others. That's difficult to do. . . . He was the kind of person who could face facts. He could see something in front of his nose. He was the kind of person who could look something in the eye and not deceive himself or deceive those around him. If the truth happened to be ugly, he was the first to admit it.

Q: Orwell was, above all, a writer, perhaps a great writer. What aspects of his writing have spoken most strongly to you?

Richard Rorty: The same aspects that make Hemingway appealing. He could achieve maximal effects with minimal use of words.

Bernard Crick: There are other ways of writing, but he is a master of the plain style and one of the greatest essayists, both humorous and serious, in the tradition of English writing.

Erika Gottlieb: I don't think we should use the word *perhaps* here, at least not for Orwell's essays and the last two of his novels. That one needs to stand up for one's sense of truth and freedom even when one is a "minority of one," that "truth is not statistical," is probably the most memorable and truly timeless message of Orwell's final satire. Courage to stand up for the uniqueness of the individual, for the liberation of the downtrodden; the nobility of the moral act even when it cannot have immediate, measurable results; to stand up for what is most essential in our human heritage, the uncorrupted consciousness of the word: this is the essence of Orwell's faith in the human spirit. Rooted in his own time, Orwell's satire is a masterpiece of twentieth-century humanism, taking us through tragic irony and militant wit to faith in the "spirit of Man."

Richard Kostelanetz: Need I say more than I've already said, other than that I think he was also an artful fabulist, especially in *Animal Farm*, and a great representational novelist, especially in *Nineteen Eighty-Four*, for portraying the realities of mundane life in totalitarian societies, which oddly he did not know firsthand. I can never forget a young woman in Warsaw in 1982, whom I heard spontaneously testifying that the truest novel about life in Poland at that time was *Nineteen Eighty-Four.*

Marshall Berman: I loved *Animal Farm* (my first Orwell), the *Shooting an Elephant* volume, *Down and Out,* "Politics and the English Language" (which I've taught many times to very different groups in different decades, with uniformly great results), and various other stories and essays. But I couldn't stand the way he was canonized as a Cold War saint.

Q: How damaging are the revisionist claims of Orwell as a snitch (Orwell's infamous "list"), anti-Semite, homophobe, and misogynist? All these claims have been advanced in the last two decades, some of them having received widespread circulation in the mainstream media.

Richard Kostelanetz: This is all *biography* and thus irrelevant to the truth of his writings, which cannot be destroyed, much as those committed to seeing foggily and to writing disingenuously try. Similar attacks were made to undermine the authority of another master aphoristic truth-teller, Oscar Wilde.

Richard Rorty: No more damaging than Eliot's anti-Semitism or Shaw's flirtation with fascism. Nobody's perfect.

Erika Gottlieb: I believe that the four revisionist claims mentioned above are often based on insufficient examination of textual and contextual evidence. Close readers like Hitchens or Rodden, for example, argue convincingly against the accusation that Orwell was a "snitch," aiming to denounce people on his "list" of politically unreliable characters. To acquit him of the accusation of anti-Semitism, readers should take a look at his 1945 "Antisemitism in Britain" and his review of Sartre's *Portrait of the Antisemite.* Even better, they should simply look at the scene in *Nineteen Eighty-Four,* when in the "flicks" Winston is hit by the screen image of a Jewess trying to protect the child in her arms from a bomb—an image that prompts him to start his diary, to embark on a sequence of dreams about his dead mother, and the entire process that leads the emotionally dead member of the Outer Party along the journey of passion and compassion.

As for the accusation that Orwell was a misogynist, the same scene in *Nineteen Eighty-Four* demonstrates that when the adult Winston recognizes the mother's sacrificial, heroic love, this leads to his decision never to betray the love of Julia. When in Room 101 the Party makes him betray this love, he loses the most significant things in being human, his will and his private conscience.

Orwell's tragic humanism speaks against all kinds of oppression. The media often pick up new perspectives on Orwell for their news value, without making the old-fashioned but still useful attempt at finding evidence through closer textual analysis.

Marshall Berman: When the revisionist claims came up a few years ago, I wondered if we'd ever get to the bottom of this guy. It got me interested in Orwell again, because human beings with conflicting feelings are always more interesting and more attractive than plaster saints. Orwell's "plain man" shtick turned me off, though it was interesting as a shtick constructed by an Eton boy. His homophobia depressed me—as if people he called "pansy Left" were wired to misjudge Stalinism because they were gay, as if gay Englishmen were somehow less English than he.

I wondered how many of the people on his Little List were part of his "pansy Left." I was especially fascinated by his remark, "Can't we convict Chaplin of some crime and throw him out of the country?"—Freudianly forgetting that Chaplin was as much a British subject as himself; but also, by the phrase "Can't we convict him . . . ?" which showed a depressing intimacy with the reality of criminal justice behind the scenes. (Gottseidank, the British Home Office were Cold Warriors but not McCarthyites.)

The List episode resonated with other facts of his life, like (1) being a policeman, which was his first job—and he wrote of that job's ambiguities very well; (2) Winston Smith's relationship with police superintendent O'Brien, culminating in "He loved Big Brother," probably the most brilliant line Orwell ever wrote.

Bernard Crick: Orwell was a left-wing socialist who was bitterly anti-communist. This is not understood by many who have accused him of spying on fellow writers, when all he was doing was advising, quite rightly in my opinion, who would not be useful in counter-propaganda at a time when the Communist Party was trying hard, with some limited success, to penetrate British trade unions and even the parliamentary Labour Party. Some deny these things, some forget. The claims of anti-Semitism, homophobia, and misogyny are much exaggerated and usually result from a postmodern failure to appreciate a different context of ideas and beliefs of his time. Some of his best friends were Jews, homosexuals, and women, but he was not a Zionist, a crusader for gay rights, or an advanced feminist. The two latter positions hardly existed in the inter-war period.

Q: What was the personal appeal that Orwell had for you or for your generation, especially with reference to his oft-discussed moral authority?

Richard Kostelanetz: Seeing clearly, epitomized by seeing differently from the herd and yet persuasively, all of which I derived from my first reading of the old Anchor edition of his *Collected Essays* around 1960. And then writing concisely. I can recall a sometime lover, an immigrant about my age from Soviet Russia, educated in the visual arts, who read English with difficulty, telling me around 1990 that Orwell's "Politics and the English Language" was among the most profound essays ever. Nonetheless, I long ago learned not to speak for "my generation."

Unless one sits high in a political/religious hierarchy, isn't moral authority usually gained by going through needlessly difficult professional circumstances in the course of advocating truth against established heresy? To the degree that Orwell was awarded such authority, which he certainly deserved, it came posthumously and therefore was available to be assumed by pretenders whom he, since he was no longer alive, couldn't personally dismiss.

Independent moral authority is an aspiration of mine, sometimes acknowledged by others, thankfully.

Richard Rorty: I am not happy with this term *moral authority.* Like Shaw, Orwell gave us timely warnings. That was his appeal.

Bernard Crick: I saw him as somebody determined to be both a libertarian and an egalitarian. His moral authority comes from treating ordinary people seriously but, unlike modern populists, addressing them seriously and not avoiding difficult issues.

Erika Gottlieb: My generation of people born in East-Central Europe who lived through the totalitarian regimes of Nazism followed by Stalinism has an instinctive admiration for Orwell's probably greatest insight: the opposite of Hitler's Nazism is not Stalinist communism; it is tolerance. (It is worth noting that the two film versions of *Animal Farm* were produced—for better or worse—by two Hungarians, Halas and Halmi.)

Orwell's insight, of course, is borne out by historical events and documents of the last fifty years. Orwell was not the first or the only one pointing out the shocking news that totalitarianism—both on the Right and on the Left—is driven by the government style of terror. He was, however, probably the most convincing writer of fiction who expressed this political truth.

Todd Gitlin: As a young man in the early 1970s, there were only two writers who really mattered to me as moral touchstones. One was Orwell and the other was Camus.

Orwell says that having moral motives as a writer is important. This may seem a small thing. I've often distributed to students Orwell's little essay "Why I Write," in which he says when he hasn't written with a direct political motive, he's written badly. This, of course, is very contrary to the conventional wisdom, which advocates detached writing apart from moral purpose. But I think it's exactly wrong and Orwell is right.

Ian Williams: Well, the terrible thing is, like God, everyone claims him to be on their side. Everyone wants to claim God is on their side and everyone wants to claim Orwell is on their side, and I'm sure he would have been appalled by some of the claims. And I'm sure that God must be a bit upset about this too, when he sees some of the people who claim him!

But Orwell does have a moral authority and that's because what he said proved so triumphantly right. It's interesting that the people who don't really accept his moral authority are those who also don't accept his critique of the Soviet Union. But many who claim him because of his critique of the Soviet Union often tend to miss that he was critical of other totalitarian governments.

He's not "balanced" in the spurious way of giving both sides equal weight, but of looking at both sides and then coming to a conclusion and seeing the good and the bad. And a good example of that is when he actually changed *Animal Farm* because he had been unfair in his depiction of Stalin as Napoleon. Despite his views about Stalin, about the Soviet Union, he had this twinge of conscience that he'd been unfair to Stalin. That's a small but telling example of his intellectual integrity.

Dennis Wrong: It was his style of writing, the directness of it that appealed to me. He said he wanted to write prose that was as clear as a pane of glass. I think to a considerable extent he achieved that. There was just the sense of directness—no adornment, no hype—that turned me on. I read him in books that were not available in the United States at the time, in the Penguin New Writing series edited by John Lehmann.

I think it was the first time I saw a picture of him. I have that picture of him in my bathroom, blown up.

Q: Why does a picture of Orwell hang in your bathroom and what does it make you feel when you look at that picture after sixty years?

Dennis Wrong: I have pictures of many people in my living room—Edmund Wilson, Faulkner, Hemingway. But I only have one in the bathroom, and that is Orwell.

Q: During "sitting meditation" in the bathroom, shall we say, you contemplate Or-
well's political example?!

Dennis Wrong: Well, he was the kind of writer who really told it like it is! (*Laugh-*
ter) And what one wants to do as a writer is to cut through the hype to the truth.
I'm certainly not a postmodernist. I believe in the truth.

Q: And Orwell—the man within the writings—embodies that for you?

Dennis Wrong: Yes. The photo reminds me of his example. In fact, I have another
picture of Orwell in my study, so I have two of Orwell in my house. He's the only
person I have two of. That, I certainly agree, says something. I've felt a deep identification with him. He's been a presence in my life—and indeed, as I talk to the
people at the conference, a presence in all our lives.

II. ORWELL'S MORAL AUTHORITY—OR AUTHORITARIANISM?

The following interview at the George Orwell Centenary Conference warrants special
mention of its immediate context. I was invited to be a guest, along with Daphne Pa-
tai, on the NPR radio program "The Connection," devoted to Orwell's legacy, which
was broadcast in Boston on April 30, 2003. This was the day before the start of the Or-
well Centenary Conference sponsored by Wellesley College. Several callers, along with
Professor Patai, who teaches at the University of Massachusetts at Amherst, raised
questions and advanced allegations about Orwell's "misogyny," so I was not surprised
by the similar turn that our conference discussions took.

Although I viewed the conference, as I explained in my own presentation, as a
"commemoration" rather than a "celebration" of Orwell, it soon became clear that an
international conference devoted to Orwell's legacy would inevitably trigger contro-
versy. The sparring started with a series of frank exchanges on the topic of sexual
politics, which were provoked by some vivid epithets directed at Orwell himself. Dur-
ing her panel session on May 1, Daphne Patai declared Orwell a misogynist, after
which an undergraduate Wellesley student posted a related question on the school's
electronic bulletin board: How, she asked, could a conference "celebrating" the work
of a misogynist take place at her school, a women's college? Indeed, several campus
e-mails condemned the event. Other Wellesley students also deplored the conference,
expanding the indictment into a wholesale dismissal of the entire corpus of "that sex-
ist Orwell."

Yes, it was 2003, and we were approaching the centennial of Orwell's birth on
June 25, and—perhaps inevitably—a new round of deification and deflation had al-
ready commenced.

In an earlier study of Orwell, The Politics of Literary Reputation *(1989), I noted that the most serious challenge to Orwell's stature would come from feminist critics. That remains the case, as the critique by Daphne Patai in this section evinces.*[1] *My exchange with her was lively and indeed sometimes heated, and it strikes me in hindsight that one might regard her vigorous dissent from the acclamations that Orwell typically receives to be morally courageous—even Orwell-like.*[2]

This edited transcript of our interview, which was conducted following her conference talk, forms the entire portion of Chapter Seven, Part II.

Q: My concern here is Orwell's ongoing relevance and appropriate value: what Orwell still has to say and his enormous attraction for others, and what all that says about writers as literary figures today.

A: The question of Orwell's relevance is, first of all, strictly an empirical one. The answer to "Is he relevant?" is certainly, yes, because he is constantly cited. Before I came to this conference I did a Google search with the terms "Orwell and Saddam," and I got 15,000 hits. I also did "Newspeak" and I got 5,500. That tells me there is enormous attention being paid to Orwell and to what he wrote.

So I don't think his relevance is a matter of anybody's opinion. He simply *is* relevant. That is a fact. What we make of that relevance and how it relates to what he actually wrote is a different and far, far more complex question.

Q: What do you make of it?

A: I think the main reason that Orwell is constantly cited is because he has enormous moral authority. People use Orwell for political ends, and the political ends vary because he wrote so much in so many different venues expressing so many opinions. So he can, indeed, be used to support a great many sides in argument, not just one. But I think that the reason that anyone wants to use him at all is because he is seen as a moral exemplar (the "wintry conscience of his generation") and, therefore, whoever uses him to support a particular position seems to feel that that position is strengthened by the invocation of Orwell's name. I have some problems with that.

Q: For instance?

A: Well, first of all, arguments are either valid or invalid in their own right. They have to be articulated, and it's not by appeals to authority that we prove or even strengthen an argument. Orwell may have said "X" and he may have been wrong about "X." Orwell said "such and such" and therefore the assumption "he would support my position or have this position today" does not do anything to validate a particular given position, which has to be defended in its own terms and not simply by reference to preexisting authority. But his stature is such that that's exactly the way he functions as an authority. He has become a symbolic figure. In that sense, it doesn't have a great deal to do with what he wrote in any complete sense, because what he wrote is too complex and too varied.

Q: That's certainly the hard claim: "Look at what Orwell said then and somehow apply it to today."

A: Right.

Q: What about the softer claim which is also quite prevalent, perhaps even much more so: We look to our forebears for guidance, but we need to beware of historical analogies. They are of limited value, but they may also provide insight. If we understand what somebody said and did years ago who stands in a similar yet different position from ours today, that may offer us insight into what we could do and say today.

A: But when the figure is a contrary one like Orwell, it's very hard to support such a position. To take the most recent relevant case—the war in Iraq—it seems clear to me that Orwell can be used on all sides of the argument. That means it can't be taken as self-evident that, once you have sided with Orwell in support of either invading or not invading Iraq, you have made a good case, since he can easily be used for either side.

Q: What about Orwell's coinages? In what way do concepts and phrases such as Newspeak, "Big Brother Is Watching You," doublethink, and so on, have contemporary relevance today? Why do we acknowledge that so-called Bushspeak or the statements from the Iraqi Minister of Information are understood more richly if you give them this Orwellian vocabulary of Nineteen Eighty-Four?

A: It gives the context that the average reader or listener on TV can relate to. Obviously, in this country, people grow up having read Orwell. If he didn't already have the reputation which allows these terms to enter the language, it wouldn't mean anything. Orwell was very, very good with slogans. Those slogans are very useful. So, of course, they're still being used.

That's a slightly different issue than the issue of moral authority for which he is usually invoked. That particular writers are quoted because they had particularly striking phrases seems to me natural and normal. It happens all the time. Look at how many titles of books have been published with brief phrases taken from Shakespeare. But that is a very different thing. Shakespeare doesn't have the moral authority to give us an opinion on the invasion of Iraq. No one would have dreamed of [citing him for] such a thing, but Orwell does get cited about that. So I would distinguish between simply referring to the slogans and the tags that he invented, which are clever and useful, and appealing to him as this moral authority to strengthen one's own position.

Q: Isn't there a legitimate claim for moral authority?

A: There probably is. I just find Orwell a very peculiar one because his authority in some areas is so fully matched by his lack of authority or by even objectionable comments in other areas and sometimes in the same areas. His comments are very often contradictory or self-contradictory. So I'm not at all convinced that Orwell is an appropriate moral authority. I'm very struck by the fact that he can be used by all sides. Nobody used Hitler to make any kind of moral arguments. Orwell is so useful on all sides that he is used on all sides. But doesn't that suggest that that moral authority is in fact a highly, highly ambiguous thing, and that there may not be that much actually solid behind it, because it is so easily appropriated for many, many different uses?

Q: What are the problematic aspects of Orwell's moral authority?

A: I'm not talking about something obscure that may have happened in his personal life. For example, for someone to be considered an example of justice and egalitarianism—when we know the question of gender justice was simply nowhere on his horizon—I don't think that's readily excused by saying that you have to see him in his own time. The '30s and '40s were not a reactionary period in which there were no feminist activities. He was not simply affirming the standard view of his society. Or if he was, people should think, "Is it appropriate to turn him into this moral icon when he has such very, very serious blind spots?"

And the same thing with his anti-Semitism. Of course, it was purely professional. Of course many other British figures had exactly the same views. But they are not held up as moral exemplars.

The many odd, idiosyncratic, phlegmatic, objectionable—however one would want to characterize them—characterizations in his writings are something for us to be concerned about. His own moral authority is actually undermined by what he wrote. What has happened progressively over the years is an increasing separation between his purported moral authority and what the man actually wrote. So he has indeed become an icon.

Q: Is it possible for him to be a man of his time in certain areas and to be far ahead in certain others—and for us to admire those areas in which his critiques are valuable?

A: I think so. I think that is a fair statement to make about most people. I think that, for example, there are many people today who consider themselves to be serious political philosophers and they probably eat meat and they probably do not consider treatment of animals an issue to which they wish to pay attention and we might not want to dismiss all the rest of their work for it. And I don't think I am inviting dismissal of Orwell. What I am doing is saying that I, at least, feel uncomfortable seeing him granted such iconic status when I know, having studied his work very, very carefully, that there are major, major problems with it.

Orwell does not deserve the kind of iconic status that he has enjoyed. If his flaws were generally known and understood, his reputation would probably be modified in some way that is important. I know people like to have role models and icons, but it's very hard not to be critical of an excessive fetishism of a given figure.

Orwell was in many respects a perfectly ordinary human being. He should be studied and appreciated as such and not as someone who at the very mention of his name supposedly brings moral authority to position "A" or "Z." Rather than actually making the arguments that need to be made on their own merits, one appeals to authority. And Orwell, of course, is an ironic person to appeal to as an authority.

Q: Those excesses are indisputably unfortunate. But the question keeps coming back: are these reservations of yours about Orwell himself? Or are they about what has been done to Orwell by inattentive or exploitative readers?

A: That's a very good and interesting way to put it, I think. If that actually is a personal question about my own work, it's extremely pertinent. What energized my work was the sense of Orwell not as a writer, but of him as a moral figure, moral authority, moral exemplar. When I discovered that there were problems with that, that is what energized me to attempt to analyze all of his work, including the reputation he developed, what you call his "afterlife." That's a wonderful word. If I had simply focused on him as a writer of fiction, without taking into consideration the moral claims advanced in his name, I would have written a very different kind of book. The energy behind that book did indeed come from the shock of realizing that someone who is idolized beyond the normal appreciation accorded to a significant writer has great defects.

Q: Let me put it this way: Is your problem primarily with Orwell or with his reception?

A: It's a problem with his work. He lends himself to be used in different directions. He also takes on a persona that invites people to see him as a moral authority. In my analysis, for example, I showed how frequently he writes from what I call the "voice in the wilderness" stance, that he alone is the one who is willing to tell the truth about some difficult subject. Very often, it's not at all the case that he is alone. One of Orwell's peculiarities is that he seemed to think that an issue became important only when *he* began to notice it, so that as late as the summer of 1938, he actually wrote, "Somebody really ought to look seriously into fascism." That's an extraordinary statement for someone to make in 1938. I mean it's extraordinarily late. It would not have been extraordinary for someone to make in 1933.

That shows something about his stance to the world once something came to his attention as a problem. He identified it as a moral issue that he was uniquely able to tackle, and a great many readers believed him. So his reputation—this "afterlife"—is not independent. It includes the excesses of reputation to which I and other people object. The excesses are not independent from what he actually wrote and the way that he presented himself as a public intellectual.

Q: So he's conspired with his kidnappers.

A: In many cases he would not call them "kidnappers." In many cases, he would be perfectly happy to be the authoritative source for a particular point of view. But the fact remains that he can just as easily be used for many other positions— not all positions, obviously, since he had fixed positions about certain things— but many, many of his positions are so contrarian that one can find different versions of the position or a complete turnabout from the position from one work to another. So, indeed, one can understand why it is that people have used him in such a variety of ways. He is a writer eminently able to be used in various ways. I think it relates both to his ambiguous moral authority and to the fact that his moral authority is sometimes hijacked.

Q: Yesterday, on the NPR show, you called Orwell a misogynist. It's a strong word. Could you elaborate on that claim?

A: It is a strong word. Everybody knows he was anti-feminist. There is no controversy about that. But the notion that he was a misogynist certainly does trouble some people. I read all of his published and unpublished work that I could get my hands on and exhaustively analyzed it. The persistent theme of denigrating comments, attitudes, and imagery relating to women is simply much too strong, I think, to contradict. It is not enough to say that he was simply a man of his time. That is simply to excuse him at the same time you are saying, "But in this other respect he was visionary and that is wonderful."

Orwell saw his mission as having to do with social justice. In criticizing Orwell for his misogyny, I advert to his own proclaimed standards, not to the standards of his time or myself, but to the standards that he himself proclaimed. So he had astonishing blind spots for someone making those claims.

Q: What about homophobia?

A: Of course he was homophobic. That has nothing to do with his relations with his homosexual friends. Certainly he had a negative attitude and a certain kind of anxiety, a denigrating attitude toward homosexuality. That is definitely the case. I think his writing reflects that quite fully. Is that unfortunate? That's extremely unfortunate. Is that on a par with being a misogynist? No.

The issue of homosexual identity is a very, very different one from women's rights. Male homosexuals had the vote in England when Orwell was born. Women did not. So women certainly had problems that male homosexuals, if they were of the right level of class and education—as his friends were—did not face. To say that this person, who considers himself to be committed to justice, decency, egalitarianism—terms he himself used—should not have had a blind spot about women, should not have been so ready to ridicule women, so ready to see them as insignificant and to attach all kinds of trivial stereotypes to them in his fiction (not to mention actual comments he made in his nonfiction) is a problem of a different order.

Certainly, Orwell had negative attitudes toward a great many groups. He was a very idiosyncratic and crotchety person. He disliked an awful lot of people and was not at all hesitant to make that clear. On the contrary, I think he prided himself on it, because it fed into his position of being a "voice in the wilderness"—a writer daring to say what other people only dared to think.

Q: Why is it that so few people who knew him very well referred to him in these terms?

A: Well, it depended on the circles in which one traveled. If you look at the literature of the '30s, there certainly were criticisms made of male writers with the attitude that Orwell had. But it was not important to most people. They were looking at a different political scene. They were looking at fascism, at totalitarianism.
Although those isms actually have gender ideologies that are a significant part of
those movements, the kinds of people who were interested in these gender issues
were not the people Orwell was friendly with. We certainly know that he was actively hostile toward feminists.

*Q: Of all the highly informed people that he was in regular touch with about
many issues—and who seemed to have been on the opposite side of many of them—
virtually none of them ever charged him with misogyny, homophobia, even anti-
Semitism. Why?*

A: First of all, the term *misogyny* was not regularly used. Homophobia did exist
as a term and a concept. So partly it's a matter of the rhetoric. He is also a man's
man and a male writer. He's very popular with men. There are not many women
scholars who have written about Orwell.

Many of his supporters had very similar views about women. They also had
other kinds of views that he was happy to disabuse. So I don't think the fact that
those ideas were common in his time excuses someone who sees his role as having been to challenge orthodoxy, to challenge conventional thinking. When such
a figure fails to make those challenges, there is a problem. People need to reconsider who it is they are selecting to be a moral exemplar.

Q: Was he anti-Semitic?

A: I think he was an anti-Semite in a purely conventional sense. Virginia Woolf
was. She made scathing comments about her husband Leonard Woolf's mother,
and about the kind of Jewish stereotype she represented. Orwell made similar
kinds of comments in his writing. I don't think they are terribly serious. Ultimately his being an anti-fascist was more important. His having a political position that is coherent on that issue makes it of less significance than the fact that
he made the typical anti-Semitic remark. That's all very different from his comments on the position of women, given that women had just gotten the vote, and
that the changes in their status were occurring very rapidly, especially when he
was very often in opposition to things like birth control. His odd positions only
make sense if you look at them as in fact being defenses of male authority and

of male superiority over women. I do not think it is excusable for someone like Orwell to hold such positions. For a writer of brilliant fiction who is not a moral figure, it would be fine. I agree with Orwell that it's fine for Ezra Pound to get the Bollinger Poetry Prize, if he is judged on his poetry and not his anti-Semitism; yes, that's fine.

But no one considers Ezra Pound a moral exemplar. So I keep going back to the question of what people make of Orwell because he lent himself to that kind of adulation—as opposed to a much more realistic vision of Orwell, which would cease to make him a touchstone of proper thinking on any side.

Q: Orwell said about anti-Semitism in T. S. Eliot's work: "One has to draw a sharp distinction between what was said before and after 1934." We can quibble about the exact date. But the idea is that there is a historical line, and that, because of changes in cultural consciousness, what gets expressed before and after makes a difference. Is that true and is it a relevant point?

A: I think it's an excuse for Orwell; "1934"—he knows what the date is, where the line is. A lot of people would say Hitler's rise to power in 1933, the book burnings [1933–1934], the Nuremberg laws [1935–1938], all the things that were happening in the beginning of Hitler's reign should have been a warning signal to anyone. For Orwell to say that 1934 is the line doesn't establish that it *is* the line; it only tells us that Orwell found some way to excuse Eliot's statements that no longer were particularly attractive.

I think it's important for people to keep on reading Orwell as well as the many, many other interesting writers of that period in the twentieth century. I don't think it's appropriate for people to go on having a worshipful attitude about Orwell. That attitude in itself makes me uncomfortable.

People need to think for themselves and not use Orwell as such an authority. They need to read Orwell for what he has to contribute, for the tremendous interest of his essays and his novels. They need to understand his historical context, but they should not view him as some saintly figure or heroic icon to whom they can appeal in that way. That strikes me as a substitute for thinking. You substitute somebody else's dicta for your own thoughts.

Q: Can we distinguish between a healthy hero worship and a slavish hero worship? I'd posit that one difference is that healthy hero worship is a form of admiration based in reality. Slavish hero worship, on the other hand, is demeaning, putting oneself at the feet of an icon.

A: I think that *any* kind of hero worship slowly creeps over an acceptable line. It's normal for people to have figures that they admire, but it's also important to be skeptical. It's especially important to be skeptical about our intellectual history. Not only in relation to Orwell but in relation to many other such figures. That doesn't mean you trash them and throw them out. Finding out that Jefferson had slaves does not mean that Jefferson is to be disdained or despised. That is a mistake. To that extent, I agree with you, it's important to be able to hold on to the contributions of a person.

But can we appreciate contributions without somehow rolling over sheer appreciation into a kind of hero worship? That is what worries me. That is what I find inappropriate. It's also not usually based on any sound knowledge of Orwell's work. It's usually based simply on what he's come to symbolize.

He's significant as a writer. His writings should be read. He should not be used as an icon.

Q: Strindberg is a misogynist.

A: Yes.

Q: Norman Mailer is arguably a misogynist.

A: Yes.

Q: If "misogyny" is at the core of someone's work or thinking, then a label like that is accurate. If it's not at the core, it's a smear.

A: My book was an effort to understand his political thinking in terms of his anxiety about manliness and masculinity. I attempted to show how his analysis of totalitarianism missed certain of its features, such as its extremely strong masculinity complex—in Italian and German fascism.

So I attempted to do something that I think is a little more sophisticated than simply saying he had bad characterizations of women. That part is easy to do. The rest is not so easy. But it is important to understand that and not dismiss it.

His admirers are unwilling to accept that his reputation may actually be exaggerated. Because he represents so much to them in some abstract sense, to admit there are very serious problems with Orwell threatens them.

And I don't think the attitude of hero worship is appropriate to him. I think his political thinking is interesting and complicated, but his over-concern with masculinity is also very important.

Q: If a label such as misogyny is hung on an artist, and if it sticks, then it tends to overshadow everything else. It overshadows both the work and the life, so that his or her entire reputation is damaged severely or even destroyed. The difference in Orwell's case is that—at least so far—the label hasn't stuck.

A: And you think that proves that my analysis is wrong. I don't think it proves that. I think it proves that a lot of people are attached to their icons and do not want to reconsider them.

CHAPTER EIGHT

Unlessons from My Intellectual Big Brother

D ear George,
Until you entered my life, I vaguely imagined I would become a professor much like those whom I had admired as an undergraduate and as a graduate student, a specialist in Wordsworth's *Prelude* or a scholar who had mastered the minutiae of literary modernism. Your work and legacy have served as my introduction to intellectual life, indeed my passport to contemporary cultural history.

I am often asked what it was that drew me to you. After all, I've been reading and pondering your work for a long time; indeed, I've written hundreds of pages about your life and work. The answer that I find myself giving is that you inspired me—because you lived what you wrote and you wrote out of the depths of your experience.

As I delved more deeply into your life and work, I also discovered a few surprising personal links between us. In fact, my father worked as a day laborer just two miles away from the Gloucestershire working-class hospital in Scotland in which you convalesced. His peasant father in County Donegal, Ireland, felt sympathy with Irish nationalists (like Sean O'Casey, whom you reviled) and flirted with communism. Certainly you would have castigated my grandfather as a knee-jerk socialist and an Irish revolutionary agitator. (And what about me? Would you, George Orwell, have liked me? I'm a vegetarian, a sandal-wearing religious believer, an Irishman, a Catholic. The odds are against it!)

You also led me to numerous discoveries. Thanks to you, I have met so many interesting people. The portrait that I have painted of you is not altogether flattering, but you wouldn't want that, would you? I do hope that it conveys your courage, your steadfastness, your passion, your faith in a better future, and above all, your intelligence and intellectual integrity. To demonstrate my gratitude, I periodically come to the defense of your reputation.

Now, in this final chapter, let me share directly how you have influenced me. My own case is less important for itself than for what it represents about the changing condition of intellectual life in the half-century since your death.

I

How does one become a writer, or indeed (to use an old-fashioned phrase) a man or woman of letters today? Or, for that matter—to use a newfangled term—a "public intellectual"?

It's not possible in quite the way that it used to be for thinking persons of your generation. The culture of Anglo-American intellectual life has altered permanently and irrevocably from the post–World War II era of your day—the age of the intellectual coteries, little magazines, and highbrow literary quarterlies. Those institutions formed literary journalists, intellectuals, and even men and women of letters like you a half-century ago.

Today they don't. Nor does any other literary institution or group or setting. And nothing since has replaced them—not universities, not think tanks, not Internet chat rooms. No wonder that no intellectual since then has replaced you either.

How does a serious reader with aspirations to contribute to cultural life become an "intellectual" nowadays? *Is* it actually possible, in the age of academe, to become an engaged critic? A political writer? A man or woman of letters? Indeed: an "American Scholar," in the broad, Emersonian sense?

No graduate programs exist to develop such a being; graduate education in the humanities fosters specialists. There were no creative writing programs in your time, and none of today's creative writing workshops cultivates intellectual breadth and daring—in fact, nonfiction is typically excluded altogether from creative writing programs. "Journalism school" is not the place—and certainly not law school. The think tanks are oriented toward policymaking, social science research, or ideological agendas—and are typically unreceptive to younger writers.

Younger people today have been shaped by a system of mass higher education, not the world of books and little magazines. The university has expanded, and corporate journalism has become omnipresent, absorbing all these people who in an earlier age might have aimed a little higher. A number of intellectual magazines still thrive today, in and out of the academy, but none bring together a group in quite the way that *Partisan Review* once did, not *Commentary*, *Dissent*, the *Weekly Standard*, the *New York Review of Books*, or the book review section of the *New Republic*.

So where does one go, now that the little magazines and the New York intellectual scene are dead and gone? That was the dilemma that Russell Jacoby's *Last Intellectuals: American Life in the Age of Academe* meditated on almost two decades ago.[1] Jacoby had no answers then. And, if anything, the institutions and settings that once fostered intellectual life are even fewer and weaker in our own time.[2]

So how is it done today?

I submit that it can still be done the old way: writer to writer. That's chiefly the way you did it, George, and *that* approach can still be taken today. The old way is the self-appointed literary apprenticeship. One looks for a model, one enters the Tradition. It is a tradition of writers and intellectuals who developed public voices. And one listens so keenly and resonates so deeply to the pitch and passion of those compelling voices that one internalizes them. One "ingests" one's literary models. One learns their language—their accent, their rhythms, their intonation. One does all this not in order to slavishly imitate them, but rather to grow in and through them toward one's own unique voice and vision.

To put it slightly differently: to become a public voice today, one must internalize the tradition of "the intellectual" because the intellectual *culture* is now gone. And the only way for most aspiring writers to do this is by seeking out models. I discovered that I had created a culture for myself through the books that I read and the interviews I conducted. Without the immersion in the books, the interviews are meaningless. But without the interviews, the books may not come fully alive.

So I submit that the old way of mentoring is crucial, more indispensable today than ever to the intellectual calling. It is necessary to establish and maintain a connection with the Tradition of thinkers, both dead and alive. For the vocation of a writer is about something more than a career, a profession, or a job. It is indeed a calling—the calling of "the word." Not merely in the sense of becoming a wordsmith but rather an author in the old sense (L. *auctores*, an authority). And all authority comes with corresponding responsibility.

The relationship with one's self-selected literary authorities eventually develops so far that they become even more than one's teachers, more even than one's mentors. One "adopts" them as members of one's intellectual—and even spiritual—family. They become elder brothers and sisters.

Indeed, the directive to learn—and "unlearn"—lessons from an intellectual big brother or sister aims to self-legislate a program for the epidemic of orphaned, would-be intellectuals. Yes, this is actually a big brother and sister program for intellectually hungry boys and girls—precisely because there are no graduate, or journalism, or law schools—or writing programs—that can parent them into sufficient intellectual maturity to become public voices.

II

Of course, as we all know, there are big brothers—and Big Brothers. I realize that the latter, upper-cased phrase immediately evokes images of corrupt tyranny rather than caring tutelage. Fair enough. But there are Bad Big Brothers and benevolent big brothers. It's oppressive when "Big Brother is watching you." But we could also imagine how the final line in *Nineteen Eighty-Four*—if lifted from the novel and let stand alone (and lowercased)—could refer to a benevolent big brother: "He loved big brother." Yes, "loved" because of the gifts given, gifts that many intellectuals, on the Right and Left and Center, have acknowledged receiving from you, George Orwell. And that is why intellectuals across the ideological spectrum have exalted you as their "intellectual hero."

Now I know something about big brothers, because I am the oldest in a family of four boys and have heard a lot about big brothers—both benevolent and not-so-benevolent. Admittedly: a big brother can be a royal pain. (That was never the case in our family, of course.) But one thing that all big brothers, both bad and benevolent, have in common: it seems as if they're always with you. Unlike the father, one doesn't expect they are going to die off in some not-so-distant future. Maybe that's why you, George, chose "Big Brother"—rather than "Big Daddy"—as your image of terror. For all of the Freudian frenzy about the male's hidden urge for patricide, the plain fact is that fear of the father can wane for quite practical reasons—simply because one day you know you'll be stronger than the old man. He'll weaken and die. One day you'll probably even pity him. But that's not the case if the old man is only a year or two older than you. He is *always* going to be there.

Yet a benevolent big brother can also be a great gift. Here too, I speak from experience, because you, George Orwell, have been just that kind of intellectual big brother for me.

I'm not at all sure you would approve me as your "younger brother," let alone be proud about it. But after living in your presence for twenty years and authoring five books about your work and legacy, I've definitely forged a bond with your ghost—you've become a central presence in my intellectual and even personal life. ("So how's life with George?" my friends periodically ask me.)

"George Orwell" has never been a scholarly topic or an academic specialty for me; ever since the day I read *Animal Farm* as a tenth-grader, I've felt a certain kinship with you.[3] It seemed natural to teach university courses such as "The Utopian and Anti-Utopian Imagination" organized around your work, and then to write a dissertation about your legacy. It seemed natural because—as I ultimately came to understand and to accept—I was really engaged in veiled autobiography.

Through my studies of your heritage, I was, in fact, claiming it. And I was also talking about my own imaginative flights and fears. Yes, your legacy was part of my inheritance. (In fact, I've often spoken with such passion about your work in my university course on utopias that, when I mentioned years ago to an undergraduate student of mine that I intended to write an essay with the title "My Life with George Orwell," he asked me: "Was George Orwell really your roommate in college? I heard that he was.")

What did you impart to me? What do you still have to say to young people today, more than a half-century after publication of your last book, *Nineteen-Eighty Four*, and your death?

Repeatedly I've asked that question—I've put it not only to myself and my friends; I've even posed it to your friends and colleagues. In fact, during the 1980s I interviewed several of your old friends for my first book—as well as many intellectuals in the following generation who had been influenced by you—and in turn who influenced me.

I conducted another round of interviews in 2003 on the occasion of the Orwell centennial, with younger intellectuals and scholars who have been strongly influenced by Orwell—a generous selection from which forms the basis of Part Two of the present book, as the previous two chapters made clear.

All that has been part of my intellectual coming-of-age, indeed of an unfolding, half-conscious program to discover my vocation by acquiring a personal visa to the world of my intellectual fathers and mothers.

III

Before going on, I ought to elaborate on the circumstances of my coming-of-age—and where I have arrived, politically and culturally, since gaining intellectual maturity. In *The Politics of Literary Reputation* (1989), I described myself as a "post–Vatican II Catholic liberal." But I doubt a "Catholic liberal" would pass muster with you any more readily than did Graham Greene (your "Catholic fellow-traveler"), let alone Catholic conservatives such as Evelyn Waugh and Christopher Hollis.

Yes, as I surmised earlier, I don't think you, George, however sympathetic you seek to be, would cotton to my Catholic faith, even though I'm an Irish-American cradle Catholic and not one of your hated English converts like those three writers.

Yet, although *liberal* characterizes my politics better than any other term, the "L word" is not a central part of my identity. I believe that, even as one embraces a political tradition, one should acknowledge that conservatism, liberalism, and radicalism overlap in important ways. All three value tradition, liberty, and equality—though they prioritize them differently.

In saying this, I am speaking very personally. Each of the great political traditions attracts and has influenced me precisely because it affirms a fundamental commitment to metaphysical values. I am indebted to them all. So I suggest: Yes, let us honor their profound differences and resist any impulse to collapse them into a hodgepodge. But need we invariably see them as mutually hostile? I think not.

I realize that all this may seem confused or eccentric. But I am not interested in wrangling over the correct terminology for my current political outlook. I do believe a substantial aspect of it is properly termed "nineteenth-century liberalism," but my political outlook also possesses elements of "cultural conservatism" and even "socialism," owing to a strand of populist, rustic, backward-looking English radicalism that you shared with Cobbett, Morris, and other contrarian populists and Tory radicals.

Like theirs, mine is an eclectic radicalism. But the label does not overly concern me. What I do know is that I subscribe to an egalitarian, anti-elitist politics at odds with traditional conservatism—and also to an anti-progressive, tradition-minded politics quite resonant with cultural conservatism. I distrust elites—whether in the form of aristocratic castes or Leninist vanguards. Like both you and Chesterton, both of whose thought also eluded political labels, I share a belief in the emotional sustenance of small property, a distaste for industrialism, an antagonism to monopolistic practices, and a faith in the common sense of common people (like my immigrant, working-class Irish parents).

I have long discerned these features as part of your intellectual physiognomy, too—what Conor Cruise O'Brien once called your "Tory growl." Indeed, both Chesterton and you remind me of a simple truth: Radicalism need not mean progressivism, and a repudiation of Marxism need not imply acceptance of social injustice.

I am also a cultural conservative—as, I think, you were (your love of popular culture, including penny postcards and boys' weekly newspapers, notwithstanding). For me, the value of cultural conservatism is precisely its will to conserve—not just high culture in the narrow sense, but all that sublimely uplifts and nurtures life. It is a practical philosophy that wisely acknowledges human limits. It starts with an acceptance of the conditions of reality—yes, the conditions, but not the outcome. I stress this, because the not-infrequent conservative acquiescence to injustice is unacceptable to me. A "decent" conservatism still battles injustice, but it acknowledges that most human beings need a stable environment and the ownership of property—to know, to see, and to handle something, however small, that is their own. (Neoconservatism, in its championing of progress, business conglomerates, and capitalism, does not prize such values.) Such a conservatism is irreconcilable with a postmodernist weltanschauung because it insists that human beings do need a "ground." And this cultural conservatism parts company with progressivism because it holds that the only secure ground is the unmoved Mover Himself.

I realize that you wouldn't express it this way, George, but I couch my political development in terms of my recent religious development—perhaps much like some of your contemporaries did, especially your Old Etonian friend Christopher Hollis. I realize this isn't the way you would explain your evolution. For you, politics was always paramount. But you took religion seriously, very seriously—"the major problem of our time is the loss of belief in immortality," you once wrote. And later: "When men stop worshipping God, they promptly start worshipping man, with disastrous results." Those are your words.

You were a skeptic and an atheist. Of that there can be no question. But in another sense, you realized that the fundamental problem of our age is spiritual: the problem of the decaying belief in immortality in the modern world. You spoke about the need to restore what you called "the religious attitude." No Marxist would speak that way.

So I know that, despite your hostility toward "Romanism" as the ecclesiastical equivalent of Stalinism, some part of you had respect for a person who values religion and owes much to it. You hated orthodoxy and the violation of intellectual integrity and the betrayal of truth, not Christian truths themselves. You denounced "the stinking RC," yet your real antagonism was toward organized religion because it promoted religious orthodoxy and institutionalized belief. So I know you can respect someone who values "the religious attitude" in religion and owes much to it.

When I say that religion has influenced my political development, I don't mean that in any simplistic sense—as if I've become more conservative (or liberal) *because* I'm Catholic. No, rather, I mean that I tend to ask myself questions from the vantage point of my spiritual and religious values when I consider political issues.

You valued religion seriously even as you opposed some of its unfortunate consequences—just as you did in the case of socialism. In fact, you said in *The Road to Wigan Pier* that "the worst thing about Socialism is Socialists." And you knew full well—though many of your present-day readers doubtless do not—that your line derived from a famous remark by Chesterton: "The worst thing about Christianity is Christians." I agree with both of you. And so I hope you can accept my putting religion before politics, just as you typically did the reverse.

My admiration for you endures. I am still inspired by your moral courage and intellectual integrity. And yet, unlike you, I am not a socialist: I am a social democrat. I am wary of fixing my gaze on dazzling communitarian ideals that are beyond me and my fellow citizens. Better to honor "where people are" in their lives—and to legislate from there—rather than to mesmerize them with a vision that is far beyond their moral reach.[4] Moreover, I disagree with your atheism and anti-Catholicism, though I fully affirm your (largely justified) criticism of the Church's abuses—its support of Franco and Mussolini (and its concordat with Hitler), its too-frequent indifference to and collusion with injustice (even including passivity in the face of the Holocaust), and much more. Indeed, I have no doubt that you would have much to criticize in the contemporary Church as well.

George, I thank you for sensitizing me to these abuses—which, of course, are not limited to the Left! As I'll explain shortly, you've helped me see how important it is to criticize my own side, to hold *my* reference group to a high standard.[5]

Yes, these positions doubtless mark my outlook as eclectic. But I take solace from the fact that both Chesterton and you gloried in an idiosyncratic, Pickwickian politics.

IV

So then: What have you, George Orwell, my intellectual big brother, taught me? What have I learned—or unlearned—from your work and example?

I should stress that a large gap exists between what I've learned and how well I practice it. Your intellectual courage and clarity of mind were extraordinary—not to mention your literary achievement. But you were also blessedly "ordinary," as many of your admirers have marveled—and it's a perception of you as "an extraordinary ordinary man" that gives me the temerity even to proceed to enumerate my debts to you, cognizant that any such list can be misconstrued as an attempt to police your legacy. Or worse: as an act of self-nomination to don your mantle—just the sort of body-snatching and grave-robbing of you I've decried in two full-length studies and also in the chapters of the present book.

So much for my personal disclaimer. Let me frame my answer to my two questions above via your most famous essay. In "Politics and the English Language" (1945), you gave six rules for "good writing" in the sense of prose style.[6] And perhaps we could give six similar rules for "good writing" and "good thinking" in the sense of intellectual integrity, which would represent the very opposite of Oceania *goodthink*. So let me share these six "unlessons" derived from your example, which I might title "Politics and the Literary Intelligentsia."

1) Unlearn Groupthink.

Don't ride along with the intellectual herd. Refuse to accede to coterie politics. Become instead a truly "freelance" writer. Risk becoming the conscience of your reference group, indeed a public conscience. Look to your own failings, your own self-righteous anger and intolerance.

To be an intellectual is to embrace the vocation of a critic. Even American neoconservatives, who are typically uncritical of the major power centers in the culture, are nonetheless critics. They are critics of the intellectual culture, rather than the larger culture. They are critics of their own reference group of intellectuals.

You exemplified a writer independent of all coteries. Such a writer is skeptical of all ideologies and isms. You stayed on speaking terms with many of your ideological enemies, respecting your differences with them and agreeing to disagree.

Unfortunately, this very seldom happens in contemporary intellectual life or even in academe. A dissent is overblown into a betrayal; horrendous disagreement provokes ostracism, even exile. As you once observed, in an inescapably ideological age a dissenter within the ranks seems to get tagged with all the positions of opposition.

2) Unlearn treating the glitterati as more equal than others.

Resist the bewitching attractions of court patronage and courtly politicos. Keep instead a wary distance from power.

You had no truck with ideology and isms. You insisted on seeing what was in front of your nose, and said that the test of intellectual honesty was to speak out against Stalin. (You were rather uninterested in the crimes of Hitler because Hitler was beyond the pale, an obvious fascist on the other side. You were far more concerned with the behavior of Stalin.)

The critical intellectual, ever since the Dreyfus case, keeps a keen eye on all power centers—and especially on his own vulnerabilities to its seductions. Even when the Labour Party achieved victory in 1945, you said that you were a "supporter"—not a member—of the British Labour Party. The critical intellectual cannot be flattered or bought. He or she is a prophet outside the city walls, not a high priest representing the status quo. (You once remarked caustically on those "socialists who are patted on the head by a duke, and are lost to the Labour Party forever after.")

You practiced what you preached about relating at a distance to power, as your bracing criticism of Nye Bevan, even after the Labour Party came to power in 1945, made clear.

3) Unlearn simplistic skepticism.

Renounce the alluring, merely oppositional role of critic and skeptic. Commit also to a constructive vision. Commit wholeheartedly yet not uncritically. Be not just a critic and a conscience. Be both a skeptic and a dreamer, a realist and an idealist. Let us remain responsive to what Gissing referred to as "the intelligence of the heart."

You criticized socialists, not socialism. (As I noted earlier, you once remarked that the worst thing about socialism was socialists.) You believed in socialism. You were not just its loyal critic. You wrote *Animal Farm* in order to create a counter-myth to fight the false myth of Russia as a socialist country. But we must not get lost in our ideals or escape into a dangerous Utopianism or into inhumane abstractions. Yes, we must value principles, but more important is an acceptance of realities: not to get carried away by abstract reason or by ideals, but rather to gain a balanced wisdom, the realism of maturity.

Your positive reception by the neoconservatives is evidence that you ran the risk of being misunderstood and claimed by the opposing side. You may have been an excessively scrupulous conscience, but you flayed the Left in order to strengthen it, not to weaken it or abandon it. Yes, your criticism was directed at socialists, not socialism. You mercilessly assaulted their lies and their orthodoxies. You criticized from within the Left, and that is why you became known as the conscience of the Left.

4) Unlearn politicizing the personal and personalizing the political.

Break the intelligentsia's lazy, knee-jerk habit of lining up people in categories.

Power is not everything. In addition to a politics, there is also an ethics, an esthetics, an erotics of life and literature. Yes, the personal is political—but the personal is also not *just* political. The personal is also ethical, aesthetic, erotic—and so much more. Attend to the level and domain of inquiry at issue, in order to see the extent to which politics is a conditioning or determining factor in any particular case. Here again, dialogue with political adversaries—staying open to rethinking, keeping the conversation alive, respecting differences, and agreeing to disagree—is a mark of the healthy capacity both to honor and to distinguish between the political and the personal.

This unlesson heeds the voice of experience. It acknowledges that intellectual integrity rests on the concrete, the individual, the particular.

5) Unlearn Elitespeak and its Newspeak idioms.

Avoid addressing primarily the cultural elite—and avoid the self-referential allusions and jargon that usually accompany such practices. Address instead the informed layperson, the literate public—not merely the literary intelligentsia.

This unlesson addresses the question of language. Writing to be read by the informed layperson and the literate public, rather than merely for a clique or group of specialists, is a choice. To prize accessible writing is to open oneself to the charge of simplemindedness or "bourgeois liberal empiricism." Accessible writing means avoiding specialized vocabulary and academic jargon. It means writing "prose like a windowpane."

6) Break any of these rules, rather than do something that violates intellectual integrity.

This directly echoes your sixth rule in "Politics and the English Language," whereby you concluded that, however valuable your previous advice, no rules for good writing exist. There are only rules to minimize bad writing. The English language, like all languages—indeed, like the richness and complexity of life—admits of no rule-making. And so, with your example, I too can urge: Treat all of the foregoing unlessons as ad hoc. Treat all of the foregoing "rules" as prisms, not isms.

Let me also summarize now the lessons that I have learned from you, what six "rules" you've taught me—by precept and example. And here let me speak quite personally:

- You tempered my will to systematize and gave me a respect and love for the concrete particular.

- You emboldened me to speak out, to make a commitment, to abide by it.

- Your example fortified me to sustain a process of rigorous self-questioning, to hold my own side to the highest possible standard.

- You showed me how important it is to live what one writes. In practical terms this has meant a concentration on friendship and on lived experience.

• You vouchsafed me a vision of my best self—an image of myself that is truly realistic, not just calculating or pragmatic or willful.

• You taught me to write in an accessible manner and not to embrace elitism or specialness, not to insist on being superior by taking the moral high ground and remaining self-righteous, as if only I myself know "the Right Way."

V

And what did you, George, my intellectual big brother, *not* teach me?

In the end, you did not teach me "the Way" to become an intellectual. You simply modeled *one* way to grow intellectually. For instance, you did see and repeatedly address two of the three political matters that dominate cultural life: race and class. But you did not grapple much with the issue of gender—quite possibly because you did not live beyond midcentury and witness the full development of trends under way in your own day. You did not live to see the rise in the 1960s and '70s of social movements such as women's liberation and feminism, gay liberation, and other forms of gender-based radicalism that have come to dominate academic and intellectual life. As a result, you can—unfairly, I think—seem dated.

In these and other ways, we must acknowledge your considerable limitations and shortcomings. Still, one weakness to which you did not succumb was the lure of System. You, George Orwell, recognized the limitations of logic and method. You had no System or Grand Theory. The passion for a System can slip into dogma. You help inoculate one to resist that.

For all that, I thank you. Admittedly, my emphasis in this chapter has not been on your limitations but rather on your inspirational power. This emphasis is legitimate; it does not entail whitewashing or lionizing you, but acknowledging a debt and a legacy.

You also show us that it is possible to act even when the timing seems premature or our knowledge seems inadequate: "I know enough to act." That's what you did. To know that emboldens one. One can learn by doing—as you did in *Down and Out in Paris and London,* in *The Road to Wigan Pier,* in *Homage to Catalonia.*

And that is something else you have taught me, however poorly I practice it: intellectual courage. You exemplified the willingness to risk going outside one's specialization, to risk failure. Having "failed" so dramatically and completely in prep school—or so you thought—you, Eric Blair, became willing to risk failure for the rest of your life.

VI

So that's my testimonial—or manifesto. I believe that one way to grow intellectually is, as it were, to adopt a big brother or big sister—and thereby enter the intellectual tradition by entering his or her work. To do so self-consciously, by selecting a model of how to do it: that is a slow yet time-tested and proven way.

But it is not a matter of simply entering their writing. One ought to see their
written work in the context of their daily lives and thereby gain an understanding of the larger world of the writer—beyond his or her art—and also the role of
artistic and intellectual activity in that life. All this is pursued not in order to
slavishly imitate that life, but to embrace its strengths and understand its weaknesses—as a way of building one's own strengths and growing beyond one's own
weaknesses.

To adopt an intellectual big brother or big sister means that we, their readers
and would-be heirs, must take the initiative. The potential for an impassioned,
powerful response is always there, because the work is there, and it remains available to us.

On the Ethics of Literary Reputation

I

On reading *Animal Farm*, the poet William Empson, Orwell's wartime colleague at the BBC and the author of *Seven Types of Ambiguity* (1930), wrote him: "You must expect to be 'misunderstood' on a large scale."[1] Yes—and, as the foregoing scenes of "Orwell and the Intellectuals" demonstrate, he often has been. Empson himself reported that his young son, a supporter of the Conservative Party, was "delighted" with *Animal Farm* and considered it "very strong Tory propaganda."[2]

Similar misreadings have occurred with *Nineteen Eighty-Four*—for instance, during the early Cold War era, as I noted in the introduction, the last four digits of the John Birch Society's national number were "1-9-8-4."

Moreover, as happened with both *Animal Farm* and *Nineteen Eighty-Four*, sometimes the author himself inadvertently contributes to such misreadings. "Orwellian" misreadings have occurred partly because readers have identified so strongly with the writer that they have projected their own needs and aspirations on him. Their identifications have been variously induced by Orwell's appeal to readers as a rebel and an intellectual's common man, by the perceived moral heroism of his radical humanism, and by the seeming purity and simplicity of his literary style, among other factors. And then there are also the darker reasons for confusion: because the catchwords of *Nineteen Eighty-Four* could be easily turned back on him, because his aggressive "conscience of the Left" stance could seem like a renegade's anti-socialism, and because politically savvy intellectuals noticed the pilgrim crowds swarming toward his grave—and thus deemed him "well worth stealing."

Should we then partly blame Orwell for cooperating with his kidnappers? Or for a lack of foresight as to the uses and abuses to which his works have been put since his death?

Not at all. Rather, the scrupulous reader's task is to get down to particulars and see how writers sometimes invite or participate in their own appropriation, to see why a writer was so susceptible to such Orwellian "facecrime," as Winston Smith would have (proudly) termed the "Orwellian" distortions.

So all this does not imply that a political writer such as Orwell should somehow become a far-seeing prophet and anticipate both how the course of events may alter and how his work may become liable to abuse beyond the grave, any more than it means that he must tame his style and never exhibit partisanship. Rather, the mantle-snatching of Orwell serves as a warning and a summons to his readers—above all, to the intellectuals who interpret his work and influence the culture's perceptions of it—to approach him and his legacy with particular care. For the politics of reception cannot be divorced from the *ethics* of reception. In fact, we might speak here of an "ethics of admiration" (and even detraction), whose precise formulation and vigilant observance form a special responsibility of intellectuals.

Indeed, perhaps the cultivation of such a moral awareness is not just the responsibility, but rather part of the *vocation* of the historically minded intellectual in the post-ideological age—an era that has witnessed not the "end of ideology," but rather such an all-pervasiveness of ideology that any putatively "objective" claim is deemed intellectually naïve or outrageously polemical.

Such distinctions are important. To observe that all interpretations have degrees of validity, and that "some are more equal than others," is not obtuse or crude. Instead it is merely to insist that differing positions on an issue can be embraced with differing levels of confidence and accuracy, depending on the available evidence and based on whatever criteria such evidence is deemed admissible.

II

If the foregoing reflections sensitize readers to aspire to a more judicial (and judicious) sensibility, and indeed invite intellectuals above all to adopt a heightened moral consciousness toward controversial political figures such as Orwell, two questions arise: What specific concerns should occupy the serious admirer or respectful enemy of an artist's work? And what concrete guidelines should shape his hermeneutic "code of ethics"?

Let the following criteria serve as a prolegomena to an ethics of reception. Among the considerations governing such an ethics—which in Orwell's case might indeed also be termed an ethics of admiration (and detraction)—could be the following four precepts:

First, avoid anachronistic interpretation. Take care to assess the historical context in which the writer has lived. Measure his work against the standards of his own day. Beware the fallacy of presentism.

For instance, by the standards of today, numerous respectable contemporaries of Orwell's—especially conservatives and Catholics, such as G. K. Chesterton, Christopher Dawson, and T. S. Eliot—subscribed to an unconscionable anti-Semitism. All of them have been posthumously castigated for this failing. The failing is real and it is important to cite; but it is equally important to note that we live today by cultural norms very different from those that prevailed in the genteel literary circles of pre-fascist Europe. Similarly, Orwell himself was, at least early in his career, mildly anti-Semitic. And yet, Orwell's own emphasis on the importance of historical context, when he defended Eliot (whom his good friend and *Tribune* colleague T. R. Fyvel had criticized as "anti-Semitic") is worth noting:

One has to draw a distinction between what was said before and what after 1934. Of course all these nationalistic prejudices are ridiculous, but disliking Jews isn't intrinsically worse than disliking Negroes or Americans or any other block of people. In the early twenties, Eliot's anti-Semitic remarks were about on a par with the automatic sneer one casts at Anglo-Indian colonels in boarding houses. On the other hand if they had been written after the persecutions began they would have meant something quite different. . . . Some people go round smelling after anti-Semitism all the time. I have no doubt Fyvel thinks I am anti-Semitic. More rubbish is written about this subject than any other I can think of.[3]

By current standards, Orwell was also both homophobic and anti-feminist. But such a judgment says nothing about his positions in view of his own historical and cultural horizons.[4] Nor does it absolve present-day readers of the obligation to research their claims via painstaking investigation of the life and times of historical and biographical subjects.

Such empirical work reflects a healthy respect for historical and cultural difference—and a recognition of our own limitations (and inevitable presentist bias). For we need to learn better to honor and even to admire that which differs from us, whether the differences owe to an historical gulf or to cultural factors—rather than simply to esteem those ways in which the writer is similar to us or how he anticipated the values and standards of the present.

In other words, as I stressed in my critique of the feminist reception of Orwell in *The Politics of Literary Reputation,* one must understand the figure in relation to his contemporaries. Often this will mean to examine closely the historical context in which his opinions were formed, as well as how events broke in a different direction at the time of his death and subsequently. And that will, in turn, entail a nuanced understanding of both the attitudes that existed in his day and how those evolved and have contributed to a different climate of opinion and values in our own day. For instance, Orwell's attitudes toward gays, women and feminism, and Jews were formed in the 1920s and '30s, both before the current recognition of minority oppression and also before minority rights were widely extended to these groups. Orwell was not ahead of his time in these areas. He was a man of his time on such issues—as well as of his class and gender.

Consider, for instance, gender. Discussing *The Road to Wigan Pier*, the Marxist feminist Beatrix Campbell has explained the near-absence of working-class women as evidence of Orwell's "toxic scorn" toward women, especially female socialists. I devoted a chapter in *The Politics of Literary Reputation* to the historical context in which Orwell was writing, and I concluded there that he was not misogynistic, but rather merely conventional on gender issues for his time and place. So it is heartening to see Peter Davison write: "What must be borne in mind in considering the relative nonappearance of women in *The Road to Wigan Pier* is that this is absolutely typical of such studies, even those by women, in the first 50 years of the twentieth century." Davison cites several works, including Left Book Club publications written by women, all of which devote women miners and wives of miners scant attention—a 1948 book, for example, discusses seventy-five cases of working-class miners; not a single one is a woman. On gender issues, Orwell was unexceptional, a man and a writer of his time.[5]

My larger point is that we need empathy for our predecessors, who, as Milan Kundera observes in *Testaments Betrayed* (1985), always walk "in a fog," by which he means they participate in events whose outcome is obscure. They make decisions, "especially decisions involving large historical events remote from their sphere of control," as one proceeds in a fog. He adds:

> I say fog, not darkness. In the darkness, we see nothing, we are blind, we are defenseless, we are not free. In the fog, we are free, but it is a limited freedom, the circumscribed freedom of a person in a fog: he sees fifty yards ahead of him, he can clearly make out the features of his interlocutor, can take pleasure in the beauty of the trees that line the path, and can even observe what is happening close by and react.

So our predecessors proceeded in a fog. But what about us latter-day critics and historians—as we look back from the present on our forerunners? When we judge people of the past, says Kundera, we usually see no fog on their path. "From our present, which was their faraway future, their path looks perfectly clear to us, good visibility all the way. Looking back, we see the path, we see the people proceeding, we see their mistakes, but not the fog."

And Kundera then pleads: "Yet all of them—Heidegger, Mayakovsky, Louis Aragon, Ezra Pound, Gorky, Gottfried Benn, St.-John Perse—all were walking in fog, and one might wonder: Who is more blind? Mayakovsky, who as he wrote his poem on Lenin did not know where Leninism would lead? Or we, who judge him decades later and do not see the fog that enveloped him?"

Kundera concludes: "Mayakovsky's blindness is part of the eternal human condition. But for us not to see the fog on Mayakovsky's path is to forget what a human being is, forget what we ourselves are."[6]

But *shouldn't*, of course, Mayakovsky have known where Leninism might lead? That is how the prosecutorial critic proceeds further with his leading, indeed rhetorical, question. He awaits our response: "Yes, of course." The conclusion follows, as if in a syllogism. For, without a rich understanding of the historical context—i.e., the fog—the verdict is, invariably: Guilty. (To deplore that knee-jerk conclusion does not indeed mean that, after the careful scrutinizing of the historical context, one condones or approves Mayakovsky's future-blind enthusiasm for Lenin.)

Once again, then, we come full circle: the responsible critic must honor the limits of our foggy human condition.

And what about the prosecution of George Orwell?

I raise the issue of Orwell's testament, here and elsewhere, via Kundera because it reminds us how relatively clear-sighted on the big issues Orwell really was[7]—and yet also that the author of the mildly anti-Semitic *Down and Out in Paris and London* (1933) did not envision the fate of European Jewry in the next dozen years. Nor did the author who enthusiastically cooperated with the British and American intelligence services to translate and distribute *Animal Farm* anticipate that it would soon be denuded of its allegorical correspondences with USSR history and presented instead as a general attack on all forms of socialism. Or that "1984" would become such a Red-Scare symbol that the John Birch Society would soon be using those numerals as the last four digits in its national hotline.

So Orwell's vision was, on some issues, impaired by the fog—but let us see the fog as well as his limitations and errors.

III

My other three corollary precepts flow from the first. A second precept of an ethics of reception involves the acceptance of human imperfection. This means that we acknowledge character blemishes as the inevitable price of heroic achievement. We do not insist—as Kingsley Amis once put it about the need to tolerate Orwell's shortcomings—"on ten out of ten" for our culture heroes and then condemn them for failing to measure up to this inhuman standard.

All this suggests that we must learn not just to look at—but also to *overlook*—some minor flaws in the intellectual and spiritual physiognomy of our literary models. As I have already noted, such a wide-angle view entails no whitewashing of any shortcomings. Instead it mandates both their compassionate recognition and balanced assessment as part of the writer's struggle. In that light, they can then be understood as distinctive features in the context of his life and work, rather than narrowly focused upon and thrust into the sensationalistic glare of the spotlight. Such a "field focus" approach enables us to better see the whole man and not concentrate too much on one part, whether good or bad.

Indeed any ethics of detraction would necessarily mean that the judicially minded critic avoid "*the forgetting of everything not a crime*," as Kundera puts it. He adds that we must not "reduce the writer to a defendant" and the art of biography to "*criminography*" as does Victor Farias (whose *Heidegger and Nazism* is "a classic example" of criminography). According to Kundera, Farias locates the roots of the philosopher's Nazism in his early youth, "without the least concern for locating the roots of his genius"; Kundera adds that, on the Left, to punish someone accused of ideological deviations, "Communist tribunals would put *all* his work on the index (thus, for instance, the ban on Lukács and Sartre in Communist countries covered even their pro-Communist writings)."[8]

So, radical adversaries of Orwell such as Scott Lucas should hesitate to condemn his cooperation with British intelligence services in 1949,[9] even as his admirers need to be careful to avoid reducing him to the plaster "St. George." One needs to remind oneself that he lived in an era at least as complicated as our own; he was no icon but a very human individual—with very human foibles and failings.

A third precept: discriminate the man from the work. Learn to distinguish the writer's personality from his writings and intellectual achievement.

This is an imperative task in the case of a writer such as Orwell, who critics claim "lived what he wrote and wrote what he lived." Such a writer is frequently perceived by his admirers to have so fused his literary work and public personality that the two form a seamless whole. But these perceptions are usually judgments formed at a distance from the life of the writer. The closer the biographical scrutiny, the greater the likelihood that one eventually observes discrepancies, some of them sharp—as has happened with each new biography of Orwell (and has also occurred with the aforementioned examples of Chesterton, Dawson, and Eliot).

Here too, however, this realization need not entail any condemnation of the writer for such inconsistencies. Rather, it invites us to understand the inter-relations between the man and his work in all their complexity—and not to insist on an appealing, simplistic figure. Instead we can distinguish better between self-actualizing and demeaning literary models, between creative and slavish intellectual hero-worship.

None of this means yielding to what Kundera calls "the *biographical furor*," including questions such as: "What was his vice or his weakness?" Such questions lead us to forget the writer's work and instead interrogate his life, following what Kundera calls a "quasi-police method." Kundera cites Proust's condemnation of the critic who, in Kundera's words, "surrounds himself with every possible piece of information about a writer, proceeding to check his letters, to interrogate people who knew him . . ."

Yet, says Kundera, the critic who immerses himself in such a plethora of cir-cumstantial data embraces a positivistic method that usually skews his approach. Readers often find that, by over-focusing on writers' lives, such critics inevitably miss their work. Why? Because "a book is the product of a *self other than* the self we manifest in our habits, in our social life, in our vices"; "the writer's true self is manifested in his books *alone*."

I realize that, in our postmodern and poststructuralist era, such talk of a "true" self seems hopelessly naïve. Even literary artists of the stature of Kundera and Proust have trouble getting away with it. Nonetheless, Kundera and Proust are clear: the biographical method is "blind to the author's *other self*, blind to his aesthetic wishes, to his creative genius, his daimon."[10]

Fourth precept: beware all bounty hunters. Weigh—and discount—the influence of both supporters and skeptics. Judge a political writer not by those who claim or disclaim him for their own side. Adopt instead the motto: "The enemy of my enemy is *not*—on that account alone—my friend."

Orwell attacked Stalinism in *Nineteen Eighty-Four*, and prominent conserva-tives did likewise, but surely that does not mean that Orwell would have sanc-tioned the John Birch Society's use of "1984" in its telephone number—or Nor-man Podhoretz's use of "Orwell Press" in the 1980s as the name for the publishing imprint of the neoconservative Committee for the Free World. Orwell specifically dissociated himself from an anti-communist Conservative group in a 1945 letter to the Duchess of Atholl: "I cannot associate myself with an essentially Conser-vative body that claims to defend democracy in Europe [against Stalinism] but has nothing to say about British imperialism. I belong to the Left and must work inside it, much as I hate Russian totalitarianism."[11] (The John Birch Society was certainly among Orwell's concerns when he noted that INGSOC refers not just to "English socialism" but to "hundred percent Americanism.") And yet, "working within the Left" clearly also had its limits for Orwell—as his attacks on the progressives of his day evince. So the fact that both Orwell (in *The Lion and the Unicorn*) and the Marxist Left—or Maoist Left—denounce corporate capitalism does not mean that Marxists and Maoists are his bedfellows—or that Orwell admirers such as Noam Chomsky are so either.

For in an inescapably ideological age such as our own, any significant figure will inevitably be tagged with positions other than the ones that he formally embraced. Admirers and detractors will smear him with charges and convictions at wide variance from those views he upheld, and even attribute to him beliefs that he could not have fathomed during his lifetime. This is another form of intellectual grave-robbing that has become standard practice with Orwell.[12]

That means that one resists equally the hagiographic urge to canonize Orwell as St. George and the iconoclastic temptation to trash him, which might prove oneself a greater skeptic and rebel than he was, a daring intellectual outsider capable of challenging the historical consensus that Orwell was the "conscience of his generation." Succumbing to that iconoclastic temptation was Louis Menand in a January 2003 feature essay in the *New Yorker*. Titled "Honest, Decent, Wrong: The Invention of George Orwell," Menand's piece denounced the left and right-wing pieties about Orwell, his "army of fans all eager to suggest that a writer who approved of little would have approved of them."[13]

So far, so good: Menand is on the lookout for bounty hunters. But he goes on to commit the historical misjudgment of implying that there was no fog in the 1930s, only clear blue and True North, when he writes that the notion that "Orwell was right" about imperialism, fascism, and Stalinism was nothing exceptional: "Many people were against them in Orwell's time," says Menand. But that is historically misguided—Orwell was one of the few intellectuals in the mid-1930s to stand loudly and firmly against all three.

Meanwhile, an example of hagiography that I consider to be what Orwell would call on the "right side" of hero worship was Leon Wieseltier's column in the *New Republic* (17 February 2003), a reply to Menand. Wieseltier argued that Orwell is worth caring about, is even worth fighting over, because he warned against the possibility that "objective truth is fading out of this world." Wieseltier drew important distinctions that Menand's postmodernist sensibility had effaced, distinctions especially relevant to the emerging historiographical battle about the Iraq war: "not all wars are jihads, indeed there are just wars as well as holy wars; not all moral certainties are terroristic impulses, not all objectivity is proto-fascism."

"Whom to be like?" asks Wieseltier. And he answers, diffidently yet with passion and conviction: "There are many greater mistakes than the aspiration to be like George Orwell. For a long time, admiration of Orwell has been one of the most encouraging features of our political and cultural situation. There are worse masters, much worse." [14]

I agree—Orwell is worth fighting over—which doesn't mean that intellectual war crimes in the "If Orwell Were Alive Today" jousts are tolerable. Hence this proposal for an ethics of admiration and detraction, which might serve as a preliminary set of honorable guidelines for conducting such battles.

IV

So the question remains: Whom to be like? That is the question implied by all critical acts or intellectual judgments that pass via biography toward what Lionel Trilling called "the bloody crossroads where literature and politics meet." [15] Such a question takes Orwell's work, as well as his life and legacy, seriously. It does not assume, let alone assert, that he was a "saint," or a moral exemplar. Whatever our conclusions about Orwell's ethical conduct and intellectual integrity, it is clear today that George Orwell was no "saint." Like all of us, he was a human being with flaws, foibles, and failings—especially in his personal life. He was an unfaithful husband with an ambiguous attitude toward Jews and homosexuals, yet also was a loyal friend, a courageous militiaman, a generous supporter of struggling writers, a master of plain prose, a champion of freedom of speech, and an outspoken scourge of both capitalist profiteers and Stalinist ideologues. A conflicted man, not a plaster saint or pure hero. So let us de-canonize and rehumanize George Orwell. Properly skeptical of the hagiography of Orwell's admirers, we can remain impressed by this noble, insightful, and flawed man; we can appreciate the contradictions between Eric Blair's ambiguous life and George Orwell's radiant reputation. [16]

I believe that, after a careful reading of Orwell's work and of the historical record, his writings hold up in an unusually powerful and compelling way. Whatever the claims and counterclaims about Orwell, he is indeed uniquely attractive as an ideological patron and political mentor. Unlike two other contemporaries, Ignazio Silone and Arthur Koestler, both of whom have been tarred by recent scandals, [17] Orwell's reputation still stands high (despite scattered calls since 1996 to condemn him for cooperating with British intelligence services in the early days of the Cold War). In fact, among contemporary British intellectuals who have been admired and claimed by the Right, Left, and Center, only Isaiah Berlin compares; among postwar American intellectuals, only Lionel Trilling. And both Berlin and Trilling (who coveted Berlin's status) are much narrower figures than Orwell—they are intellectuals rather than men of letters. And they are little known to the wider public or outside their native countries.

Amid all this, Orwell remains standing as an intellectual model, perhaps the leading twentieth-century exemplar of the public intellectual.[18]

V

Whom to be like? I suppose my own intellectual and scholarly pursuits—namely, three books addressing various aspects of Orwell's legacy—serve as an obvious personal answer to that question. Indeed, readers' responses to him are almost invariably personal and even passionate. George Orwell's own directness and buttoned-down commonsense style somehow invite one to speak personally about him. So let me close here with an unguarded, final admission of what I have learned from Orwell—and what I acknowledge gratefully has been his invaluable legacy to me—whereby I am simply honoring the fact of my own intensely personal response to both the man and his work.

In doing so, I am responding, as it were, to the question so often put to me by my family and friends: "So then, what is it like to have lived with George Orwell? After all, hasn't it been more than twenty years?" Those are questions that several other writers—doubtless including his biographers—could perhaps answer even better.

My own response may satisfy no one. It satisfies least of all myself, let alone the Orwell of my imagination. My debt to him is incalculable; it cannot be repaid or discharged, but merely acknowledged. And it is best acknowledged by my own practice of the code of ethics of admiration that I have outlined in this epilogue.

The indebtedness is literary and political—but also existential and even spiritual. It has to do with clear writing and plain speaking, with a comradely insistence on holding one's own side to the highest standards. But more important, it owes to Orwell's repeated emphasis on—and inspiring enactment of—intellectual integrity. And it has also to do with his clear-sighted recognition of its complexity and its difficulty, of the manifold temptations to succumb to *la trahison des clercs.*

How both the writer gave voice and the man gave life to such excruciating intellectual integrity have taught me lessons that can be learned only by living with such a presence as Orwell—lessons about truth-telling, about groupthink, about vocation, and about the life of the mind.

They are lessons that are hard-won and easily forgotten, invaluable lessons that must be repeatedly discovered, honored, and learned anew. Fortunate is the person who learns them by word and deed from an intellectual big brother.

Notes

The final volumes of The Complete Works of George Orwell *appeared in 1997–1998, edited by Peter Davison (London: Secker and Warburg). This collection has superseded the four-volume* Collected Essays, Journalism, and Letters of George Orwell *(London: Secker and Warburg, 1968), edited by Sonia Orwell and Ian Angus. But* The Complete Works *did not appear in paperback until mid-2003 and still is not readily accessible to the non-specialist. For that reason, I have, where possible, cited the 1968 volumes (as* CEJL*) for references that appear in both sources.*

PROLOGUE

1. The conference proceedings have been published as *George Orwell: Into the Twenty-First Century,* ed. Thomas Cushman and John Rodden (Boulder: Paradigm, 2004). Nor were the commemorations of—or controversies about—Orwell limited to the English-speaking world, as I discuss below in note 4.

2. The media glare ranged from the serious to the sophomoric, with the latter increasingly overshadowing the former as the centennial date—June 25—approached. For instance, during "Orwell Week" in San Francisco, the George Orwell Centenary Festival was held at Edinburgh Castle and included readings from Orwell's most important works, film screenings, and "Free Victory Gin." Patrons were told on Orwell's birthday: "Show up tonight and tell them 'cheesebikini is doubleplusgood.' You'll get free admission. . . . And remember: four legs good, two legs bad." Source: http://www .whyteandmackay.co.uk/news.asp?newsid=121.

Not to be outdone by the Yanks, the Isle of Jura distillery developed a special nineteen-year-old single malt whiskey in 2003 in commemoration of the centenary of the birth of its most famous visitor. Its promotional campaign for "Jura 1984" began as follows:

> The remote island setting proved to be the perfect place for both the creation of what was to become his masterpiece, and the limited edition, Jura 1984, a unique and distinctive single malt whiskey. *The creation of Jura 1984 adds another unique and*

original product to our portfolio and is a real first for malt drinkers and Orwell enthusi-asts alike. (Ibid.)

Not surprisingly, the English were more circumspect: the Royal Society of Chemistry in London marked June 25 by publishing the ideal technique for brewing tea, one of Orwell's obsessions and the subject of an essay he wrote in 1946.

But there were also more serious, even ominous concerns raised during the Orwell cen-tennial conference at Wellesley College. Just about everyone discerned an Orwellian note in the name of the Pentagon's recently inaugurated Total Information Awareness (TIA) initiative, a program that was aimed at mining a vast centralized database of personal in-formation for patterns that might reveal terrorist activities. (The name was subsequently changed to the Terrorist Information Awareness program, in an effort to reassure Ameri-cans who have nothing to hide.)

3. As I argue throughout this book, however, Orwell's stature as an intellectual hero and cultural icon also poses grave dangers for the credulous admirer. Not the least of them is the temptation to allow Orwell's vision and choices, quite uncritically, to dictate the admirer's own, which fosters a life quite opposite from Orwell's. It does not lead to a life of radical independence, but rather to a pathetic abdication of personal responsibility. In-variably, that process occurs when someone allows himself to honor others while remain-ing unfamiliar with their lived actions, so that he judges not the reputation by the actions, but the actions by the reputation.

This tendency dominates celebrity culture, whereby the reader (or, more commonly, the viewer) lives life at a remove, partly through the hero or icon. It is as if one believes: "I can't do all the things my hero did, so I'll make him my auxiliary. He'll think and do and write and speak and act for me."

This could be called "virtual living," a process of letting other people lead your life for you, make your decisions for you, and carry your responsibility and even receive the blame whenever things don't work out. It's sometimes not just a relief to do so, but even a rather pleasurable surrender (in a masochistic sense). Fortunately, even Orwell's big-gest admirers have seldom gone this far—unlike, say, the fans of Elvis. Nonetheless, as I showed in my earlier studies of Orwell, the process has gone much, much further in Orwell's case than is usually witnessed among intellectuals. Indeed, because intellectu-als pride themselves on being skeptical and sharp-eyed, they are often outraged if you point out that they have forfeited their lives, or even that they have refused to get a life of their own.

4. As I explained in a previous book, *Scenes from an Afterlife: The Legacy of George Orwell* (ISI Books, 2003), the iconic figure of "Orwell"—the monument rather than the man—ironically came most fully alive for me abroad. Indeed, it was in the course of my travels in the non-English-speaking world (and after 1989—that is, after I had completed my first book on him) that I encountered "Orwell," most unforgettably, in the Newspeak of East German communist society, months before reunification in October 1990. I had written on "Germany's Orwell" in the mid-1980s, but it was not until after the Berlin Wall came down that the East German government permitted me to make a visit.

But an ironic, "Orwellian" dimension to post-reunification Germany is also palpably evident. For instance, at the George Orwell Centennial Conference in Berlin in August 2003, I met a teacher from the George Orwell School in the Berlin district of Lichtenberg. She had told me that the school had adopted its present name in 1995 and that she was still the only faculty member who had read *Nineteen Eighty-Four*, let alone any of Orwell's other works. A new school principal from western Germany had taken over and simply insisted—"in totalitarian fashion," she said—that the school be renamed after Orwell. The school board meeting to make the decision was hilarious, she said. It lasted for hours. Virtually nobody except the principal wanted the change. She explained, "He just wore everybody out, with his insistence on why 'Orwell' should be the name of the school. Ironically, he thought that we English teachers would all be able to teach Orwell, but now he seems to recognize that our student body is just not at the linguistic level where we can do that. We do teach *Animal Farm* in German class in the ninth grade and excerpts from *Nineteen Eighty-Four* in German class in the tenth grade, but the students are just far, far below the level in English where they could read Orwell's books in the original."

For other such examples of Orwell's prominent, if ironic, status in Germany, see my *Scenes from an Afterlife*, Part Two.

5. I have also supplemented these dialogues with subsequent interviews that I conducted in 2004. For readers interested in some samples of German intellectuals' responses to Orwell from the August 2003 centennial conference in Berlin devoted to him, see my *The Walls That Remain: Western and Eastern Germans After Reunification* (forthcoming). See also the conference proceedings from the 2003 Berlin symposium, "Bücher die ins Zuchthaus führten," published under the title *Das Orwell'sche Jahrhundert? Colloquium zum 100. Geburtstag von George Orwell*, ed. Bernd Lippmann and Steffen Leide (Ludwigsfelde: Ludwigsfelder Verlagshaus, 2004).

INTRODUCTION

1. See my *George Orwell: The Politics of Literary Reputation* (New York: Oxford University Press, 1989), reissued by Transaction in 2001, and *Scenes from an Afterlife: The Legacy of George Orwell* (2003).

2. Orwell enjoyed tossing off provocative remarks (e.g., "One has to belong to the intelligentsia to believe things like that: no ordinary man could be such a fool"). Indeed, Orwell was an intellectual notoriously contemptuous of his fellow intellectuals: Chapter One thus also spotlights the irony of showcasing for study an "intellectual who hated intellectuals," in the phrase of William Steinhoff in his *George Orwell and the Origins of 1984* (Ann Arbor: University of Michigan Press, 1975).

Although it may seem paradoxical or even contradictory that succeeding generations of intellectuals have honored Orwell despite his contempt for the breed, the phenomenon is quite common: intellectuals like to fancy themselves as daring iconoclasts even if they are dutiful conformists. Nor is Orwell's contempt for other intellectuals at all unusual. Indeed, the hatred of intellectuals for their peers, or at least for the intelligentsia as a class, is well-known and worthy of further analysis. The present study aspires to contribute, however modestly, to that task by its detailed examination of Orwell's relationship to his intellectual admirers and detractors.

3. Of course, in the 1950s there was also another group in Britain to whom he seems to have appealed—the political generation which became disenchanted with Soviet communism after the invasion of Hungary in 1956 and was associated with what was first called the *Universities and Left Review* and later the *Left Review*. This group included Raymond Williams, E. P. Thompson, Stuart Hall, and Richard Hoggart—although the latter never had anything to do with the Communist Party. (I have also discussed Orwell's relationship with the British New Left in *The Politics of Literary Reputation*.)

4. I capitalize the phrase "New York Intellectuals" to distinguish this circle of writers prominent in the middle decades of the twentieth century (and affiliated with *Partisan Review, politics, Commentary*, and *Dissent*) from other groups of intellectuals and writers active in New York at this time. In his 1968 article in *Commentary*, "The New York Intellectuals," Irving Howe gave the phrase currency (*Commentary*, March 1968, 29–51). See also Carole Kessner, *The "Other" New York Jewish Intellectuals* (New York: New York University Press, 1995).

5. Indeed Hitchens has been especially vilified on the Left—as an ex-leftist, renegade, turncoat, and traitor—since his vocal support for the U.S.-led invasions of Afghanistan and Iraq in 2002–2003. His numerous radical critics view him not as "Orwell's successor" but rather as Paul Johnson's successor. (Johnson is the ex-leftist editor of the *New Statesman* who has turned sharply rightward and become a leading conservative intellectual and Tory pundit.)

As I suggest in Chapter Five, however, within the intellectual coordinates of *Every Intellectual's Big Brother*, a different, arguably more viable, candidate comes to mind. One might argue that Hitchens is less in the line of descent from Orwell than in that of another Orwell admirer, Kingsley Amis. (Hitchens was closely acquainted with Amis, who died in 1996, and he remains a dear friend of Kingsley's son, Martin.)

Such comparisons raise a much larger issue that this book frequently touches on, though it is beyond my scope to treat it systematically or in depth: the fascinating matter of intellectual lineages. In part, virtually all of the intellectuals discussed in this book, whether on the Left or the Right, whether in Britain or the United States, have strongly identified with Orwell's diverse rebel stances, seeing him as a fellow contrarian (Hitchens, Howe), a curmudgeon (Amis, John Wain), gadfly (Dwight Macdonald), outsider (Russell Kirk), and renegade (Norman Podhoretz).

A valuable case study could be written on the complex subject of intellectual genealogies (and indeed pedigrees) in the line of descent from Orwell, a subject that I address at length in *The Politics of Literary Reputation*. For some provocative theoretical observations on the topic, see the work of Thomas Gieryn on reputational "mapping," Randall Collins's general sociology of intellectual linkages and his attention to the "cult of the intellectual hero," and Charles Camic's formulation of reputational claiming (and disclaiming) in terms of "predecessor selection." Thomas S. Gieryn, *Cultural Boundaries of Science: Credibility on the Line* (Chicago: University of Chicago Press, 1999); Randall Collins, *The*

Sociology of Philosophies: A Global Theory of Intellectual Change (Cambridge: Harvard University Press, 1998); Charles Camic, "Reputation and Predecessor Selection: Parsons and the Institutionalists," *American Sociological Review* 57 (August 1992): 421–446.

6. Anticipating a main point in Part Two, Chapter Five suggests that not groups but lone individuals today (such as Christopher Hitchens) are the strongest admirers (or critics) of Orwell. Hitchens was a *Nation* columnist, but his identification with George Orwell contributed to lead him beyond the *Nation*. Hitchens resigned in mid-2002 from the magazine, just as *Why Orwell Matters* appeared in the United States.

7. Most of the interviews took place live and in-person on the occasion of the Orwell Centennial in 2003; a few interviews were subsequently also conducted via correspondence in 2004.

8. In *Public Intellectuals* (2001), Richard Posner exalts Orwell as the model intellectual of the twentieth century and compares contemporary intellectuals (usually unfavorably) to him. Posner calls Orwell "the exemplary figure" for "much of the best public-intellectual work in the past," which "has consisted of seeing through the big new political and economic nostrums." Richard Posner, *Public Intellectuals: A Study of Decline* (Cambridge: Harvard University Press, 2001).

Posner also constructs a list of leading public intellectuals based on citation counts from database searches. Ranked no. 5 by media mentions, Orwell is the highest-ranking deceased intellectual on Posner's media list of the top one hundred public intellectuals and one of only two dead intellectuals (along with George Bernard Shaw at no. 17) who makes the top twenty names. Moreover, the first seven so-called intellectuals on Posner's list, which was compiled in the mid-1990s, are really policy wonks or prominent political figures rather than intellectuals, such as Henry Kissinger, Daniel Patrick Moynihan, George Will, Lawrence Summers, William J. Bennett, Robert Reich, and Sidney Blumenthal. The first bona fide intellectuals on the list are Arthur Miller (at no. 8) and Salman Rushdie (at no. 9). William Safire (at no. 10) is, like George Will and Sidney Blumenthal, in the public eye because his syndicated column is run in hundreds of newspapers and offers him access to the powers-that-be in Washington.

It is an interesting reflection of Orwell's lower status in the academy, which prizes cultural (especially avant-garde) theory, that he does not even rank among Posner's top one hundred public intellectuals by scholarly citations during 1995–2000, a list that is headed by names such as Michel Foucault, Pierre Bourdieu, Jürgen Habermas, and Jacques Derrida. The first American on this list is Noam Chomsky, with Richard Rorty and Edward Said barely making it into the top twenty-five.

9. Of course, one could also address Orwell's relationship with other literary-intellectual circles than the ones I discuss in this book.

For example, during his lifetime, Orwell developed close connections to four groups: the first group consisted of those, like Koestler, Humphrey Slater, Victor Serge, and, earlier, Eugene Adam, who were disenchanted ex-communists. Although they had more significant political differences, a second, more sharply defined group was a circle of London anarchists such as George Woodcock, Alex Comfort, and Vernon Richards, who grew closer to him especially after Orwell's sympathetic portrayal of anarchist Barcelona in *Homage to Catalonia.*

A third group was the circle of conservative London writers that included Hugh Kingsmill, Malcolm Muggeridge, and Anthony Powell. (The latter pair was later also close to Kingsley Amis.) The fourth circle of which Orwell might be considered a member, and exerted something of an influence upon, was the *Tribune* group, which included Aneurin Bevan, Richard Crossman, and Michael Foot, the last two having been part of the Oxford Left before World War II. (I devoted full and separate chapters to Orwell's connections with the London anarchists and with the *Tribune* writers, respectively, in *The Politics of Literary Reputation.*)

10. Certainly other reception histories and other examples of intellectuals who have been deeply influenced by George Orwell could have been selected for study here—for example, the American Richard Rorty, dubbed by Richard Posner as "our Orwell"; or Vaclav Havel, the former president of the Czech Republic, characterized in *The National Interest* as "a latter-day Orwell"; or the political journalist Andrew Sullivan, former editor of the *New Republic* and an iconoclastic individualist in Orwell's mold. Other candidates have also been nominated by various observers: Susan Sontag, Noam Chomsky, Edward Said, and others.

What does this diverse group of intellectuals share in common? Whether academics or freelancers, all of them are politically engaged and are praised by admirers for their independence and outspokenness. In Posner's terms, they are "counterpunchers" who oppose the main currents of the intellectual tides of their time. Posner distinguishes between the "oppositional" intellectual and the dogmatic intellectual. "The oppositional stance is the stance of such public intellectuals as Orwell and Camus, who write from the margins of society and are clearer about what they are against than what they are for. Their negativity and self-conscious marginality distinguish them from such social critics as Sartre, who ground their criticisms in a dogma." Posner, *Public Intellectuals*, 31–32.

In any case, all of these intellectuals, as well as others, have been nominated as "Orwell's successors." For instance, in *Public Intellectuals*, Posner exhorts Orwell as a still-relevant example of the intellectual and compares Richard Rorty to him:

Rorty is our Orwell, in combining an unreflective egalitarianism based on sympathy with human suffering and hostility to fat cats with a strong dislike of the unpatriotic Left, and in expressing his views in beautiful prose, at once limpid and passionate. But apart from having a more limited experience of life than Orwell, who knew poverty and dreadful health and war and communism and colonialism all at first hand, Rorty is an academic and most of his writing deals with philosophical issues and texts that hold little interest for people who are not professional philosophers and no interest for people who are not academics. What is more, the unpatriotic Left that he attacks is not the intellectual manifestation of a totalitarian world power but a comical sliver of university life, the raw material for academic novels and fevered conservative denunciation, while the unreflective leftism that he defends is, given the advance of economic thinking since Orwell's death in 1950, retrograde and nostalgic. Though almost as skillful a writer as Orwell, better educated, longer-lived, and analytically more acute, Rorty simply does not inhabit the historical circumstances that would enable him to have a comparable career as a public intellectual. (Ibid., 342-343.)

11. Cyril Connolly, *The Evening Colonnade* (London: David Bruce and Watson Ltd., 1973), 345.

12. See, for instance, *The Politics of Literary Reputation*, chap. 2.

13. I address the status of the claims to his "moral" legacy because it is as a moralist that Orwell continues to exert his strongest appeal. His influence is less political than moral, for the political world that he wrote about—given the collapse of the Soviet Union and the decline of communism—has passed. Unlike other intellectuals of his generation who were exalted as generational heroes and later discovered to be politically compromised—such as Ignazio Silone, Arthur Koestler, and even Isaiah Berlin—Orwell has had no detractors who have been successful at besmirching his image. Orwell remains today a powerful moral exemplar. It is on moral grounds that one increasingly makes the case for "why Orwell matters"—or indeed why anyone from the past still matters.

CHAPTER ONE

1. See, e.g., Bennett Berger, "Sociology and the Intellectuals: An Analysis of a Stereotype," *Antioch Review* 17 (September 1957): 12-17; Lewis Coser, *Men of Ideas: A Sociologist's View* (New York: Free Press, 1965); A. Gella, ed., "An Introduction to the Sociology of the Intelligentsia," in *The Intelligentsia and the Intellectuals: Theory, Method and Case Study* (Beverly Hills, Calif.: Sage, 1976), 9-34.

2. Charles Kadushin, *The American Intellectual Elite*, quoted in Robert J. Brym, "The Political Sociology of Intellectuals: A Critique and a Proposal," in *Intellectuals in Liberal Democracies: Political Influence and Social Involvement*, ed. Alain G. Gagnon (New York: Praeger, 1987), 208.

3. Brym, "Political Sociology of Intellectuals," 199.

4. Ibid., 206-208. See also Robert J. Brym, *Intellectuals and Politics* (London: George Allen & Unwin, 1980), 70-73.

5. Brym, "Political Sociology of Intellectuals," 208.

6. No attempt is made here to define the term *intellectual* precisely. The word first entered the French lexicon in the 1890s as a description of a group of prominent defenders of Alfred Dreyfus. It should be taken in this essay as a general characterization of those who are producers, rather than merely consumers, of ideas, especially through the medium of writing. On the problem of defining the term *intellectual*, see Alain G. Gagnon, "The Role of Intellectuals in Liberal Democracies," in *Intellectuals in Liberal Democracies: Political Influence and Social Involvement*, ed. Gagnon (New York: Praeger, 1987), 4-6.

7. William Steinhoff, *George Orwell and the Origins of 1984* (Ann Arbor: University of Michigan Press, 1976), 57.

8. Alfred Kazin, "Not One of Us," *New York Review of Books*, 23 January 1984.

9. Stuart Samuels, "English Intellectuals and Politics in the 1930s," in *On Intellectuals*, ed. Philip Rieff (New York: Doubleday, 1969), 247.

10. T. R. Fyvel, *Intellectuals Today* (London: Faber, 1968), 44.

11. D. J. Taylor, "Left, Right, Left, Right," *New Statesman*, 20 May 2002.

12. *New Statesman and Nation* 39 (28 January 1950): 96; and George Woodcock, "Orwell's Conscience," *World Review* 14 (April 1950): 28-33.

13. On this relation, see C. F. Hanson, "Intellect and Power: Some Notes on the Intellectual as a Political Type," *Journal of Politics* 31 (1969): 28-31; and Martin Malia, "The Intellectuals: Adversaries or Clerisy?" in *Intellectuals and Tradition*, ed. S. N. Eisenstadt and S. Graubard (New York: Humanities Press, 1973), 206-216.

14. Robert Ezra Park, *Race and Culture* (Glencoe, Ill.: Free Press, 1950), 373. See also Coser, *Men of Ideas*, 37-82, 171-180.

15. Alan Swingewood, "Intellectuals and the Construction of Consensus in Postwar England," in *Intellectuals in Liberal Democracies: Political Influence and Social Involvement*, ed. Alain C. Gagnon (New York: Praeger, 1987), 87.
Among the other reasons for "British exceptionalism" is the fact that workers have traditionally dominated the British socialist movement, a trend which the CPGB has also reflected since its founding in 1920. Possibly British Protestantism has also played a role. Intellectuals have enjoyed high authority in Catholic France and Italy, where communism has also proven popular, arguably because it has served as a substitute religion.

16. Cf. E. P. Thompson, "The Peculiarities of the English," *Socialist Register* 2 (1965), reprinted in his book *The Poverty of Theory and Other Essays* (London: Secker and Warburg, 1978), 35-91. Thompson was replying to Perry Anderson's critical history of the English intelligentsia, "Origins of the Present Crisis," *New Left Review* 23 (1964): 26-53.

17. Coser, *Men of Ideas*, 11-26. On the differences between the French and British intelligentsias, see Keith A. Reader, "The Intellectuals: Notes toward a Comparative Study of Their Position in the Social Formations of France and Britain," *Media, Culture and Society* 4 (1982): 263-273.

18. Noel Annan, "The Intellectual Aristocracy," in *Studies in Social History*, ed. J. H. Plumb (London: Longmans, Green, 1955), 241-287.

19. See Brym's chapter, "Radicals and Moderates," in his *Intellectuals and Politics*, 14-34.

20. Ibid., 25.

21. Fyvel, *Intellectuals Today*, 39.

22. Cf. Paul Hollander, *Political Pilgrims: Travels of Western Intellectuals to the Soviet Union, China and Cuba* (New York: Oxford University Press, 1981), especially chaps. 3 and 4.

23. Samuels, "English Intellectuals," 196.

24. See ibid., 198-211. As Spender put it decades later, "[A]t Oxford it was possible to forget human injustices or at least to think that they were not the business of 'the poet.'" See his contribution to *The God That Failed*, ed. Richard Crossman (New York: Bantam [1950] 1965), 211.

25. Stephen Spender, "Oxford to Communism," *New Verse* 26-27 (November 1937): 10. Quoted in Samuels, "English Intellectuals," 202. See also Spender, *The Destructive Element* (London: Faber and Faber, 1935).

26. See Samuels, "English Intellectuals," 201-204. Also Humphrey Carpenter, *W. H. Auden: A Biography* (Boston: Houghton Mifflin, 1981), 96-110.

27. Spender, *The God That Failed*, 212.

28. Samuels, "English Intellectuals," 206.

29. Michael Roberts, ed., *New Country* (London: Hogarth Press, 1933), 12. See also Samuel Hynes, *The Auden Generation: Literature and Politics in England in the 1930s* (London: Bodley Head, 1976), especially chap. 3, "1933"; and Edward Mendelson, *Early Auden* (New York: Viking, 1981), 137-151. See also Michael O'Neill and Gareth Reeves, *Auden, MacNiece, Spender: The Thirties Poetry* (Basingstoke, Hampshire: Macmillan, 1992).

30. Samuels, "English Intellectuals," 238. On CPGB membership figures, see Neal Wood, *Communism and British Intellectuals* (New York: Columbia, 1959), 23-24.

31. Hynes, *The Auden Generation*, 125-293; Wood, *Communism and British Intellectuals*, 60-63; Stuart Samuels, "The Left Book Club," *Journal of Contemporary History* 1 (1966): 65-86.

32. Wood, *Communism and British Intellectuals*, 69.

33. Fyvel, *Intellectuals Today*, 46.

34. Samuels, "English Intellectuals," 228. Orwell considered the attitude, "We're all socialists nowadays," hypocritical and dangerous to the socialist movement. In *Keep the Aspidistra Flying* (1936), the beau monde girlfriend of wealthy Ravelston remarks that she finds workers "absolutely disgusting," and then says to him a moment later:

> Of course I know you're a Socialist. So am I. I mean we're all Socialists nowadays. But I don't see why you have to give all your money away and make friends with the lower classes. You can be a Socialist *and* have a good time, that's what I say. (George Orwell, *Keep the Aspidistra Flying* [London: Gollancz, 1936], 98.)

35. See *The Collected Essays, Journalism, and Letters of George Orwell*, ed. Sonia Orwell and Ian Angus (New York: Harcourt, Brace and World, 1968), vol. 1, p. 4. All further references are to this edition and will be cited as *CEJL*.

36. On Orwell's life during this period, see Bernard Crick, *George Orwell* (Boston: Little, Brown, 1980), 104–180. Subsequent references to Crick's biography are to this edition and are cited as *GO*.

37. Cf. "Such, Such Were the Joys," *CEJL*, 4:330–369. On Orwell's compulsion to place himself, with anatomical precision, in the "lower-upper-middle class," see *RWP*, 121–153. One old colleague of Orwell's at the BBC, Henry Swanzy, has also recalled a conversation around 1942 with Orwell about being "the poorest boy in the school" at Eton (Crick, *GO*, 281).

38. Cyril Connolly, *Enemies of Promise* (New York: Macmillan, 1948), 164.

39. Richard Rees, *George Orwell: Fugitive from the Camp of Victory* (Carbondale: Southern Illinois University Press, 1961), 123–124. See also George Orwell, *The Road to Wigan Pier* (London: Gollancz, 1937), 138.

40. Writing just four years after Orwell's death, Angus Wilson expressed the opinion, still widespread at that time, that Orwell lost far more than he gained by his lack of an Oxford education. Wilson sees Orwell in terms similar to those expressed by Orwell's Oxbridge coevals and pays Orwell the backhanded compliment that, despite this huge gap in his education, he achieved much as a writer:

> The truth is that by leaving Eton not for Oxford or Cambridge, but for 'experience of the world,' he lost more than he gained. He lost touch with those in all classes whose lives were in fixed patterns, the *rangés* [orthodox, traditionalists] of the world. . . . The essay 'Looking Back on the Spanish War' wonderfully illustrates his deep understanding of the lost, the wandering, and the submerged, but there is hardly a single well-observed 'conventional' character in all his work. To see Orwell's contribution to English letters in the shadow of theses defects is surely only to appreciate more fully the peculiar intensity of his vision and [the] extraordinary brilliance of the craft with which he expressed it.

Angus Wilson, "Orwell and the Intellectuals," *TLS*, 24 January 1954, 8.

41. John Wain, "Here Lies Lower Binfield," *Encounter* 17 (October 1961): 75.

42. On the influence of Eliot and Joyce on Auden and his circle, see Hynes, *The Auden Generation*, 27–37. See also *The Thirties Poets: The Auden Group*, ed. Ronald Carter (London: Macmillan, 1984).

43. This "outsider" stance of a man who had once been "inside" was first identified by Q. D Leavis in her influential *Scrutiny* essay-review on Orwell in September 1940. She noted that Orwell belonged, "by birth and education," to "the right Left people," a leftist "nucleus of the literary world who Christian-name each other and are honour-bound

to advance each other's literary career." But she noted that Orwell was "in" yet not "of" his generation: "He differs from them in having grown up. He sees them accordingly from outside, having emancipated himself, at any rate in part, by the force of a remarkable character." Quoted in Jeffrey Meyers, ed., *George Orwell: The Critical Heritage* (London: Routledge & Kegan Paul, 1975), 187.

Note also John Wain's shrewd observation that Orwell was "able to observe the intelligentsia both from the inside and the outside," because he was an intellectual yet with much of the commonsense temper of a non-intellectual. Wain, "Orwell and the Intelligentsia," *Encounter* 21 (December 1968): 75.

44. Francis Hope's analysis of Orwell's reputation as a "witness" is acute:

He always overgeneralized from his own experience: just because he went to Lancashire or to Catatonia, exposed himself to something he did not enjoy, and then wrote it up very well, he was taken as The Authority on a much wider problem—the communists and the Spanish Civil War as a whole, or British working class life in general. But at least he went there, and if his first-hand reports were then made to bear more general application than they should have, it is largely because so few other reporters put themselves forward. . . . It is remarkable how few people go even as far as Orwell did. ("My Country Right or Left," *New Statesman* 78 [19 December 1969]: 893)

45. Samuels, "English Intellectuals," 247.

46. Rayner Heppenstall, *Four Absentees* (London: Barrie and Rockliff, 1960), 59. Heppenstall adds that, at thirty-two, Orwell seemed to him and Sayers "a great age," and they thought it "a little odd in itself that he should have wanted to share premises with us rather than with men more precisely of his own generation."

47. On Orwell's "outsider" stance toward all political groups, see my essay "The Separate Worlds of George Orwell," *Four Quarters*, Summer 1988.

48. On the generational consciousness of "the Auden generation," see Hynes, *The Auden Generation*, 17–37. Hynes does note that other 1930s writers possessed Orwell's guilt for having been too young and having missed World War I. The key generational break between them, as we have seen, was Orwell's five years in Burma.

49. Cf. S. N. Eisenstadt, "Generational Conflict and Intellectual Antinomianism," *Annals of the American Academy*, 68–79. Indeed, perhaps Orwell's six-year age difference with Spender was also a factor accounting for why Orwell and he ultimately became friends. While it is true that Orwell kept his distance from the rather cliquish Oxbridge-educated Left intelligentsia of the 1930s, he did make an exception of Spender.

Spender was virtually the lone exception. He admired Orwell's work and befriended Orwell in 1937 while he was recuperating from TB in a sanatorium near London. (Curiously enough, when Orwell was interviewed for his job at the BBC in 1941, his interviewer reported him as belonging to the same leftist intellectual group as Spender—probably out of ignorance.) During the war Orwell was invited to speak to an Oxford student club—the

English Society—so by that time, at least, his reputation among budding intellectuals must have been on the rise. (Inez Holden makes the point in her wartime diary that his name was by then widely recognized in London.)

50. Crick, *GO*, xx. As we have seen, Angus Wilson is among those who argues that Orwell, "by leaving Eton not for Oxford or Cambridge, but for 'experience of the world,' . . . lost more than he gained." As a result, says Wilson, Orwell looked down on education and never understood well the English middle class and professional tradition. Wilson, "Orwell and the Intellectuals," 8.

51. Or as Angus Wilson wrote in 1954:

The circumstances of his life had made him a *deraciné* English intellectual, at once familiar with the inner sanctum of the intelligentsia and yet not quite on the respectable visiting list; his temperament made him prefer to cock a snook through the window at the mandarins inside, even after they were prepared to give him the place of honour at dinner. From this vantage point, he saw more clearly and earlier what was happening to the English intellectual world than the most sensitive member of the cosy little family group inside. He saw them threatening Hitler and refusing the arms to make their threats real; he saw them swooning over Spanish heroism and ignoring the terrible reality; he saw them flirting coyly with Stalin and frowning when Siberia was mentioned.

Ibid., 8.

52. "Comment," *Horizon* 1 (1940): 5; Cyril Connolly, *The Unquiet Grave* (London: Gollancz, 1942), 1.

53. Already by 1937–1938, however, as "Macspaunday" became disillusioned with communism, they were "reintegrating" themselves within British society, partly for careerist reasons. By 1938 Auden had accepted the King's Gold Medal for poetry, Day-Lewis had joined the Book Society selection committee, and Spender had begun writing for Geoffrey Grigson's highbrow *New Verse*. On the tensions within the Auden group over these decisions, see C. Day-Lewis, *An English Literary Life* (London: Weidenfeld & Nicolson, 1980), 115–117.

54. Fyvel, *Intellectuals Today*, 49. Fyvel also quotes a BBC acquaintance of Orwell's, Lawrence Gilliam, head of the BBC Home Service during the war, on the socially integrative effect of the intellectuals' war contributions as *intellectuals:*

. . . above all I remember no separation between people. What was happening here was a closing of the gap between intellectual and community. The intellectual found himself not out on a limb, not on a small magazine, writing his poems or articles or critical essays for a tiny audience, but temporarily reunited with the community as a whole and able to service it with his special talents, without losing his poetic identity or his independence.

55. Swingewood, "Consensus in Postwar England," 94.

56. Indeed, as late as April 1955, Edward Shils could ask in his report on the British intelligentsia: "Who criticizes Britain now in any fundamental sense, except for a few Communists and a few Bevanite irreconcilables?" Shils went on:

[I]n the main . . . scarcely anyone in Great Britain seems any longer to feel that there
is anything fundamentally wrong. . . . To the British intellectual of the mid-1950s
[Britain is] fundamentally all right and even much more than that. . . . Never has an
intellectual class found its society and its culture so much to its satisfaction. ("The
Intellectuals in Great Britain," *Encounter* [April 1955]: 8)

57. On the optimistic "revolutionary socialism" briefly espoused by Orwell, Fyvel,
Fred Warburg, and a few others associated with the Searchlight Books group, see Fyvel,
George Orwell: A Personal Memoir (London: Macmillan, 1982), 125–135.

58. For an overview of these positions, see Gagnon, *Intellectuals in Liberal Democracies*,
6–10.

59. Karl Mannheim, *Ideology and Utopia* (New York: Harcourt Brace, 1936), 137–138.
For this summary I have relied chiefly on Gagnon's overview and Brym's analysis in *Intellectuals and Politics* and "The Political Sociology of Intellectuals." Malia is quoted in the
latter (200).

60. Brym, *Intellectuals and Politics*, 13.

61. Brym, "The Political Sociology of Intellectuals," 206, 208.

62. Neglecting the historical dimension of political sociology not only blurs the process whereby radical movements form and fragment. It can also impose a false set of po-
larized categories on the past, which, if they persist, skew analyses of subsequent political configurations. And, as George Watson argues, the dissident politics of the 1930s has
bred precisely such distortions. That single, aberrant decade of British radicalism has
drawn a false line of demarcation between supporters of the "Left" and "Right" which
stretches to the present. The very language of "spectrum" politics, imported from the continental (especially French) tradition of ideological politics, is historically inappropriate
to the liberal British political heritage. Indeed, the entry of the terminology of "Left" and
"Right" into the English political lexicon around 1930 invited the "reclassification" of figures from the Victorian age—who had not thought in terms of the sharply dichotomous,
near-monolithic, party-line ideological taxonomies of Left and Right. Thus Dickens, Cobbett, and others soon became "writer[s] well worth stealing" by Marxists and Tories alike.
The irony is that Orwell's reputation, subject to repeated grave-robbing by intellectuals of
all political stripes, has fallen victim since his death in 1950 to the very same oversimpli-
fications from the 1930s which he so clearly saw through. See George Watson, *Politics and
Literature in Modern Britain* (Totowa, N.J.: Rowman and Littlefield, 1977), 85–97.

63. Indeed, as Richard Posner reminds us, Orwell intended O'Brien in *Nineteen Eighty-
Four* to be a model of the intellectual enthralled by totalitarian ideology: "O'Brien, the
Orwellian Grand Inquisitor, is an intellectual of the most sinister kind: the ideologist of a

totalitarian regime. He is a parody of the English communist intellectuals who so infuriated Orwell." Posner, *Public Intellectuals*, 73.

64. For an overview of these two traditions and their exponents, see G. de Huszar, ed., *The Intellectuals: A Controversial Portrait* (Glencoe, Ill.: Free Press, 1960).

65. Julien Benda, *La trahison des clercs* (Paris: B. Grasset, 1927), translated as *The Betrayal of the Intellectuals* (Boston: Beacon Press, 1955), 32.

66. *CEJL*, 4:410–411, 407–408. I have inverted the order of the last quotation.

67. Ibid., 413–414. One is struck by the similarity of Camus's formulation of the problem in his interviews of the 1950s (e.g., "The Artist and His Time [1953]," in *The Myth of Sisyphus and Other Essays* [New York: Vintage, 1982], 147, 149–150):

> Artists of the past could at least keep silent in the face of tyranny. The tyrannies of today are improved; they no longer admit of silence or neutrality. One has to take a stand, be either for or against . . .
> Considered as artists, we perhaps have no need to interfere in the affairs of the world. But considered as men, yes . . .

Camus admired Orwell's work, which may have influenced Camus's thinking on the artist's responsibilities. Cf. Herbert Lottman, *Albert Camus* (Garden City: Doubleday, 1979), 413.

68. George Orwell, "Annotations to Swingler's 'The Right to Free Expression,'" *Polemic* 5 (1946): 53.

69. Noam Chomsky, *American Power and the New Mandarins* (New York: Pantheon, 1967), 95–102, 144–148. The second quotation is from Chomsky's interview on Melvyn Bragg's BBC-TV program on Orwell, "The Road to the Left," broadcast 10 March 1971. See also Chomsky's distinction between "responsible" and "combative" intellectuals in *Intellectuals and the State* (Amsterdam: Het Wereldvenster Baarn, 1978), 12–13.

70. Wain, "Orwell and the Intelligentsia," 76–77.

71. On Orwell's excruciating integrity, see Arthur Koestler, "A Rebel's Progress to George Orwell's Death," in *The Trail of the Dinosaur* (New York: Harcourt Brace, 1955), 102–105.

72. Watson, *Politics and Literature*, 45.

73. *CEJL*, 2:229.

74. *GO*, 237; Pritchett, "George Orwell," in Meyers, *Critical Heritage*, 96.

CHAPTER TWO

1. On Orwell's reception by some of these groups, see my "Ideology, Revisionism and the British Left: Orwell's Marx and the Marxists' Orwell," *Papers in Comparative Studies*

5 (1984): 45-60, and "Orwell on Religion: The Catholic and Jewish Questions," *College Literature* 11 (1984): 44-58.

2. Blake Morrison has discussed Orwell's influence on Larkin in *The Movement* (Oxford: Oxford University Press, 1980), 178, 234.

3. John Wain, *A House for the Truth* (London: Macmillan, 1972), 1.

4. John Wain, "Dear George Orwell: A Personal Letter," *American Scholar* (February 1983): 22.

5. See Amis, "Why Lucky Jim Turned Right," in Kingsley Amis, *What Became of Jane Austen and Other Questions* (New York: Harcourt Brace Jovanovich, 1971), 202.

6. Wain, "Dear George Orwell," 31-32.

7. See Morrison, *The Movement*, 10-54. Wain and Amis also reviewed regularly for the *Spectator* during the key years of the emergence of the Movement, 1954-1955.

8. Quoted in ibid., 89.

9. Indeed, the Movement's character owes something to the rise of logical positivism and the postwar vogue in the British academy for the ordinary language philosophy of the later Wittgenstein and Gilbert Ryle. To some degree, the Movement writers received this influence through Orwell; Hartley calls the author of "Politics and the English Language" and "Notes on Nationalism" the "great popularizer of logical positivism" in the 1950s. See Anthony Hartley, *A State of England* (London: Hutchinson, 1963), 50.

10. On the role which "consolidation" played as a key concept in the *Movement*'s vocabulary, see Morrison, *The Movement*, 89-91.

11. Wain, "English Poetry: The Immediate Situation," *Sewanee Review* 65 (1957): 359.

12. Morrison, *The Movement*, 73.

13. Wain, "The Last of George Orwell," *Twentieth Century* (January 1954), 71.

14. Ibid.

15. Wain, "Orwell," Spectator, 19 November 1954, 632.

16. On the "Orwell-derived manner" of much Movement prose, see John Lucas, "Aspidistra Flyers," *New Statesman* 99 (23 May 1980): 286-287.

17. J. D. Scott, "In the Movement," *Spectator*, October 1954. This article was anonymous. Scott discusses it and its role in the publicity campaign launched by the *Spectator* to promote the Movement in "A Chip of Literary History," *Spectator*, 16 April 1977.

18. Robert Conquest, "George Orwell," in *George Orwell: Selected Writings*, ed. George Bolt (London: Heinemann Educational Books, 1958), 1.

19. Conquest, Introduction to *New Lines* (London: Macmillan, 1956), 4.

20. Wain, "Dear George Orwell," 22.

21. John Wain, interview with the author, 14 March 1985.

22. Morrison, *The Movement*, 92.

23. Kingsley Amis, "The Road to Airstrip One," *Spectator*, 31 August 1956, 292.

24. John Wain, "The Last of George Orwell," *Twentieth Century* (January 1954), 78.

25. "Inside the Whale" is printed in *The Collected Essays, Journalism, and Letters of George Orwell*, ed. Sonia Orwell and Ian Angus, 4 vols. (New York: Harcourt Brace and World, 1968), 1:493-526. On Miller's view of Orwell as a foolish idealist for going to fight Spanish fascism, see "The Art of Fiction," *Paris Review* 7 (1962): 146-147.

26. Amis, *Socialism and the Intellectuals* (London: Fabian Society, 1957), 8.

27. On Williams's similar volte-face between 1955 and 1956, see his essay-review "George Orwell," in *Essays in Criticism* 5 (1955): 44-52, and his chapter on Orwell in *Culture and Society* (London: Chatto and Windus, 1958), which was written during 1956.

28. On the relation between the Movement and the Angry Young Men phenomenon, see Morrison, *The Movement*, 246-248.

29. Wain, "English Poetry: The Immediate Situation," 359.

30. Cf. Morrison's discussion of the impact of the events of 1956 on some of the Movement writers in *The Movement*, 249-251.

31. Thompson's influential, hostile essay on Orwell of that title is in his *Out of Apathy* (London, 1960), 158-165, 171-173.

32. Williams, *George Orwell* (New York: Viking, 1971), 96.

33. Hartley, *A State of England*, 53-55.

34. Cf. Daniel Rogers, "Look Back in Anger—to George Orwell," *Notes and Queries* (August 1962): 310-311, and Geoffrey Camall, "Saints and Human Beings: Orwell, Osborne and Gandhi," in *Essays Presented to Amy G. Stock*, ed. R. K. Raul (Jaipur: Rajasthan University Press, 1965), 168-177.

35. John Wain, interview with the author, 14 March 1985.

36. Anthony West, "Hidden Wounds," *New Yorker*, 28 January 1956, 71-79.

37. Wain, "Orwell in Perspective," *New World Writing*; reprinted in *George Orwell: A Collection of Critical Essays*, ed. Raymond Williams (Englewood Cliffs, N.J.: Prentice-Hall, 1974), 89.

38. Ibid., 90.

39. Some of Wain's other poetry and fiction of the period also bore the marks of his Soviet experience. *Wildtrack* (1965) included several couplets titled "Attitude of Humanity

toward the Irreducible I." His novel *A Winter in the Hills* (1970) told the story of individualistic Welsh nationalists resisting creeping totalitarianism.

40. Wain, *Sprightly Running: Part of an Autobiography* (London: St. Martin's Press, 1962), 233-234. "John Wain," interview in *The Writer's Place*, ed. Peter Firchow (Minneapolis: University of Minnesota Press, 1974), 327.

41. Conor Cruise O'Brien, "Orwell Looks at the World," in *George Orwell: A Collection of Critical Essays*, ed. Raymond Williams, 158.

42. Wain, "Here Lies Lower Binfield," *Encounter* 17 (October 1961): 71.

43. Ibid., 74, 79.

44. Ibid., 76.

45. Amis, "The Road to Airstrip One," 292.

46. "Kingsley Amis," interview by Clive James, *New Review* 1 (July 1974): 24.

47. For "callow Marxist," see Amis, *Socialism and the Intellectuals*, 5; "name-calling and walking-out stage" is quoted in Morrison, *The Movement*, 252.

48. Amis, interview with the author, 12 March 1985.

49. I discuss the duality of Orwell's appeal in *The Politics of Literary Reputation: The Making and Claiming of "St. George" Orwell* (New York: Oxford University Press, 1989).

50. Martin Green, interview with the author. Green, a longtime English expatriate, first became friendly with Amis when they were colleagues at Cambridge University in 1961-1962. For Green's views of Orwell's influence on Amis, see *A Mirror for Anglo-Saxons* (New York: Harper, 1961), and *Children of the Sun: A Narrative of Decadence in England after 1918* (New York: Basic Books, 1972).

51. Amis, "Why Lucky Jim Turned Right," 202.

52. Amis, "Lone Voices," in *What Became of Jane Austen and Other Essays*, 161.

53. For a discussion of Amis's outspoken cultural conservatism, see Morrison, *The Movement*, 252-255. See also Philip Gardner, *Kingsley Amis* (Boston: Twayne, 1981), 13-22, 144-152.

54. Amis, *Daily Express*, 19 March 1969.

55. Cf. *Authors Take Sides on Vietnam*, ed. Cecil Woolf and John Bagguley (London: Peter Owen, 1967), 48-49.

56. Mary McCarthy, "The Writing on the Wall," *New York Review of Books* (6 January 1969), 3-6.

57. See Amis in *Authors Take Sides on Vietnam*, 48.

58. Wain, "Our Situation," *Encounter* (May 1963), 8.

59. Wain, "In The Thirties," in *The World of George Orwell*, ed. Miriam Gross (London: Weidenfeld and Nicolson, 1971), 79. Interestingly, whereas New Left radicals sympathetic to Orwell seized on his revolutionary zeal in *Homage to Catalonia* comparing American imperialism to Spanish fascism and seeing Orwell as an erstwhile Ché Guevara, Wain and anti-radical critics emphasized the anti-Communism in *Catalonia*. One comparison of Orwell and Guevara is in a letter to the *New Statesman*, 13 December 1968. See also Noam Chomsky, *American Politics and the New Mandarins* (New York: Pantheon, 1969), 95-102, 144-148.

60. Wain, "In the Thirties," in Gross, ed., *The World of George Orwell*, 90.

61. Wain, "Orwell and the Intelligentsia," *Encounter* 21 (December 1968): 74.

62. Ibid., 80.

63. See, for example, Norman Podhoretz, "If Orwell Were Alive Today," *Harper's*, January 1983, 30-37.

64. Amis, interview with the author, 12 March 1985.

65. Ibid. Amis's politics were strongly influenced by the anti-Communism of Conquest, a layman Soviet scholar of Stalinist Russia. Amis's view of the inherent bad faith of radicals is represented by what he sardonically referred to in the interview as "Conquest's Law." This "law" holds that one's radicalism extends only to those issues irrelevant to one's interests or sphere of competence; one is invariably "conservative" about issues one has a stake in or is knowledgeable about. Transforming various institutions (family, education, law, etc.) sounds appealing to a radical outside those institutions, Amis says, but he or she tends to emphasize the need to "understand" the "difficulty" and "complexity" of such schemes when radical proposals involve overturning arrangements benefiting him or her.

66. Wain's proprietary attitude toward Orwell was nothing new for him. See his heated exchange with Tom Hopkinson, author of the first book on Orwell (*George Orwell* [1953]) in the *Twentieth Century*, March 1954, 235-236. Also see Wain's accusations that George Woodcock, one of Orwell's anarchist friends, was "out to steal [Orwell], to kidnap him and keep him in the 'anarchist and libertarian' menagerie" ("On George Orwell," *Commentary* [June 1969]: 28-29). Wain also castigated Williams's "Left Establishment" view of Orwell in his review of Williams's *George Orwell* in the *Observer*, 10 January 1971. By the late 1960s, Wain was among the most prominent of the so-called "Encounter Orwellians" who themselves have been accused by the Left (e.g., Conor Cruise O'Brien and Bernard Crick) of "stealing" Orwell.

67. Wain, "Dear George Orwell," 26-27.

68. Podhoretz, "If Orwell Were Alive Today."

69. Wain, "Dear George Orwell," 26.

70. Ibid., 30-31.

71. Ibid., 22.

72. Wain, interview with the author, 14 March 1985.

73. One easily overlooked source of Wain's impassioned identification with Orwell is surely the striking resemblances of their schooldays and adolescence. In his *Sprightly Running*, Wain recalled in language that echoes Orwell's "Such, Such Were the Joys" his miserable schooldays and how they shaped his outlook. Even the characters and themes of some of Wain's novels, not to mention his prose style, bore a direct relation to Orwell's work. For example, one cannot help but wonder whether Wain's already discussed psychological reading of *Coming Up for Air* reflected his own struggles with his novel *The Contenders*, written near the same time (1958) as his critical essay, and also about a fat man (Joe Shaw) who is really a thin man ("Clarence") inside.

74. Ernest Becker, *The Denial of Death* (New York: Free Press, 1973), 127–158.

75. Cf. Wain, "Orwell and the Intelligentsia," 76–77; and Wain's award-winning biography, *Samuel Johnson* (London: Macmillan, 1975), passim.

CHAPTER THREE

1. The sectarian political battles of the 1940s within the Trotskyist movement were complex. A faction led by Max Shachtman split off from the Socialist Workers Party (SWP) in 1940 to create the Workers Party (WP). They were the minority and claimed they were expelled; the majority, led by James Cannon, claimed that Shachtman had split.

2. "Pro-imperialist": Irving Howe, "The Dilemma of *Partisan Review*," *New International*, February 1942, 24. See also Howe, "How *Partisan Review* Goes to War," *New International*, April 1942. "Half in": Howe, *A Margin of Hope* (New York: Harcourt, 1983), 114.

3. Quoted in Gerald Sorin, *Irving Howe: A Life of Passionate Dissent* (New York: New York University Press, 2002), 51.

4. Macdonald joined the Socialist Workers Party in the fall of 1939, after the Nazi-Soviet Pact was signed that August. Ever whimsical, he adopted the party name "James Joyce." He then followed the disgruntled minority faction out of the SWP, joined them in forming the WP in April 1940, and resigned from the WP in spring 1941.

Macdonald was a valued Trotskyist polemicist during his party career. For instance, he provided editorial assistance to *Labor Action* in the spring of 1940 and wrote a monthly column and numerous pieces for *New International* during 1938–1941 (just as Irving Howe began contributing regularly to the journal), a couple of which were collected in his volume of early political journalism, *Memoirs of a Revolutionist: Essays in Political Criticism* (Cleveland: Meridian, 1957).

On Macdonald's Trotskyism, see Stephen J. Whitfield, *A Critical American: The Politics of Dwight Macdonald* (Hamden, Conn.: Archon Books, 1984), chap. 3, and Michael Wreszin, *A Rebel in Defense of Tradition: The Life and Politics of Dwight Macdonald* (New

York: Basic Books, 1994). See also Macdonald, *Memoirs of a Revolutionist*, and *Interviews with Dwight Macdonald*, ed. Michael Wreszin (Jackson, Miss.: University of Mississippi Press, 2003), 104–105, 133.

5. To his credit, Macdonald tolerated public slights from his young assistant, such as Howe's mocking characterization in *New International* (October 1947) that Macdonald's rejection of Trotskyism for pacifist anarchism made him "the man who went from Karl Marx to Paul Bunyan." Quoted in Edward Alexander, *Irving Howe: Socialist, Critic, Jew* (Bloomington: Indiana University Press, 1998), 29.

6. Moreover, Howe was soon at odds with the WP because of its failure to support the Marshall Plan and to align itself with the democratic West against Stalinism. Those political differences came on top of his literary disagreements with WP and other Trotskyists over the high value that he placed on numerous modernist writers.

7. Howe recalled in *A Margin of Hope:* "Sharp and amusing, feckless and irritating, *politics* for most of its short life was the liveliest magazine the American Left has seen for decades. That I was now working for *politics* made some friends in the movement uneasy, as hard-shell Baptists must feel when a congregant succumbs to soft-shells. It was solemnly agreed—such are the distinctions spun in sects!—that I could work for *politics* as a technical aide but not an editorial collaborator." *A Margin of Hope*, 115–116.

8. Coser, of course, became one of Howe's closest friends, a colleague at Brandeis University, and co-founder of *Dissent*. All these other *politics* contributors joined *Dissent's* editorial board and wrote for the magazine, a fact that both reflects the important continuities between the two magazines and suggests their significant contribution to defining the emergent Cold War in the early postwar era.

Howe also became acquainted at *politics* with the work of the magazine's most important European contributors (Albert Camus, Nicola Chiaromonte, Victor Serge, Nicola Tucci), whose libertarian anti-communist (not merely anti-Stalinist) politics resembled Orwell's own convictions. This immersion in intelligent anti-communist writings of leading European authors surely further eroded Howe's weakening allegiance to the WP and Trotskyism. On the *politics* community, see Gregory D. Sumner, *Dwight Macdonald and the POLITICS Circle: The Challenge of Cosmopolitan Democracy* (Ithaca: Cornell University Press, 1990).

9. Howe, *A Margin of Hope*, 116. Nevertheless, Howe still adhered to the Trotskyist line, writing to Macdonald about one of his *politics* submissions: "[O]ur political lines have diverged so widely that all we can really do is note the differences and let it go at that. I should of course be pleased if you'd print [my response], because it is the only contribution sent you by a practicing Marxist; that is, one who functions in a group." Quoted in Sorin, *Irving Howe*, 53.

10. In 1951 Howe and Plastrik tried to persuade the ISL, which sponsored *Labor Action*, to also sponsor a quarterly journal that would be similar in style and substance to the defunct *politics*. The ISL refused.

11. All this occurred in the wake of the Hitler-Stalin Pact of 1939, which caused a crisis in the SWP when the Soviet Union attacked Poland and the Baltic States. The result was a situation common to the sectarian Left generally and Trotskyist politics in particular: more factional infighting and more split allegiances. Some intellectuals associated with Shachtman, such as James Burnham, announced that the U.S.S.R. was a new form of class society, but Shachtman's view of "the Russian Question" was still in formation. The rupture came to a head in April 1940 over organizational issues, and in subsequent months (after the split) Shachtman's new views of the U.S.S.R. evolved: at first the U.S.S.R. was superior to the Western imperialist countries, then both were equally bad, and finally Shachtman advocated critical support for the West. The name switch from WP to ISL in 1949 mainly came from the WP's recognition that it couldn't regard itself any longer as a party when it was basically a political agitprop group. (Those SWP members who followed Shachtman out of the SWP in April 1940 joined the WP and became known as the Shachtmanites.)

12. Indeed, Macdonald was the only member of the New York Intellectuals closely acquainted with Orwell. The two even carried on an extensive correspondence during 1942–1949, much of which appears in *The Complete Works of George Orwell*, edited by Peter Davison (London: Secker and Warburg, 1986–97). Macdonald and Orwell were contrarians, though Orwell was a more serious-minded writer and more of a political pragmatist than the gadfly Macdonald. Nonetheless, their similarities led the American historian John Lukacs, a friend of Macdonald's, to call him "the American Orwell" for his spirit of independence and defiant outspokenness, his capacity to go "against the American grain," in the phrase of Macdonald's 1962 essay collection of that title. See Michael Wreszin, ed., *Interviews with Dwight Macdonald*, xix.

13. Titled "George Orwell, Nineteenth Century Liberal," Woodcock's essay ended by quoting Orwell's now-famous closing lines in "Charles Dickens": "It is the face of a man who is always fighting against something, but who fights in the open and is not frightened, the face of a man who is generously angry—in other words, of a nineteenth-century liberal, a free intelligence—a type hated with equal hatred by all the smelly little orthodoxies which are now contending for our souls" (Meyers, *Critical Heritage*, 246). Woodcock's laudatory essay was, however, not uncritical. From an anarchist-pacifist standpoint Woodcock deplored Orwell's shallow understanding of social evils, his vague conception of the socialist state, and his misplaced belief in the value of patriotism. Finally, however, Woodcock could "readily forgive [Orwell's] inconsistencies and [the] occasional injustices that accompany them" (ibid., 245). Both Orwell's liberalism and his anarchism shared, Woodcock noted, in opposition to state socialism, a respect for the freedom and dignity of the individual.

Woodcock, a good friend of Orwell's in London anarchist circles throughout the 1940s, later joined the *Dissent* editorial board. This is a clear example of how the "Orwell connection" was passed on from *politics* in the 1940s to *Dissent* in the 1950s—and indeed from the London anarchists to the *politics* circle before that. Woodcock was an important presence in the 1940s at Freedom Press, a London-based group of anarchists

(Vernon Richards, Marie Louise Berneri, Herbert Read) who befriended Orwell and esteemed him highly. Woodcock edited the anarchist papers *War Commentary, Freedom,* and *Now* (to which Orwell contributed his famous essay "How the Poor Die"). These publications thus formed the hub of still another circle of writers that valued Orwell and promoted his work and postwar reputation. As Woodcock told Macdonald's *politics* readers in 1946: "Ask any circle of anarchists or independent socialists who regard opposition to totalitarian communism as an important task, and you will find Orwell's name respected."

For my treatment of Orwell's influence on and reception by the Freedom Press group of anarchists, see *The Politics of Literary Reputation,* chap. 3.

14. See the reviews of Orwell's work by Diana Trilling, Rahv, and Daniel Bell in Meyers, *George Orwell: The Critical Heritage.* Kazin boosted *Nineteen Eighty-Four* in the July 1949 *Book-of-the-Month Club News,* and Schlesinger reviewed *Animal Farm* enthusiastically on page one of the *New York Times Book Review* in August 1946.

15. Alexander, *Irving Howe,* 19. As late as 1949, as Alexander notes, Howe was still writing under the name R. Fahan in *Labor Action.* For instance, in one article titled "Washington Case Raises Civil Liberties Issue: Should Stalinists Be Permitted to Teach?" (ibid., 42–43), he opposed all measures that would prevent Stalinists from teaching, disagreeing with Sidney Hook. (While Hook opposed legislation that barred communists from the classroom, he advocated that universities take action, arguing that communists had to accept party discipline and were therefore not free minds.) Howe wrote a similar piece under his own name, published as "Intellectual Freedom and Stalinists" in *New International* (December 1949).

16. Howe, "1984—Utopia Reversed," *New International,* November/December 1950, 366–368.

17. Ibid., 366.

18. On the wartime rifts among the *Partisan* editors, see S. A. Longstaff, "*Partisan Review* and the Second World War," *Salmagundi,* Winter 1979, 108–129.

19. Howe, "Orwell: History as Nightmare," *American Scholar,* Spring 1956, 193–207. In addition to its appearance in *Politics and the Novel,* the essay was reprinted under the title "*1984:* History as Nightmare," in *1984: Text, Sources, Criticism,* ed. Irving Howe (New York: Harcourt, 1963), 188–196.

20. Ibid., 190, 194.

21. Ibid., 249.

22. Howe, Preface to *1984 Revisited: Totalitarianism in Our Century* (New York: Harper and Row, 1983).

23. Howe, "1984: History as Nightmare," 196.

24. Ibid., 190.

25. For an example of the latter, see George Steiner, "True to Life," *New Yorker*, 29 March 1969. Reprinted in Meyers, *George Orwell: The Critical Heritage*, 363–373.

26. Howe, "1984: History as Nightmare," 196.

27. Howe, *A Margin of Hope*, 211, 213–214, 229.

28. Ibid., 242, 217–218, 238.

29. Ibid., 293.

30. Ibid., 146. In *Decline of the New*, Howe says that his culture heroes include Silone, Orwell, Sholom Aleichem, and Edmund Wilson.

31. Howe, *A Margin of Hope*, 237, 227–228.

32. Howe, "Orwell as a Moderate Hero," *Partisan Review*, Winter 1954–1955, 105–106.

33. Ibid., 106–107.

34. *The Collected Essays, Journalism and Letters of George Orwell*, ed. Sonia Orwell and Ian Angus (London: Secker and Warburg, 1968), hereafter *CEJL*, vol. 4, 449.

35. Richard Rovere, Introduction to *The Orwell Reader* (New York, 1956), xx.

36. Howe mentioned throughout his lifetime his high estimate of Silone as another of his intellectual heroes. What then might Howe have had to say concerning recent revelations about Silone's preference for means over ends and his choice of expediency over morality as an Italian socialist? Silone's radical credentials and noble image have been soiled by evidence discovered in the 1990s, in the files of the Italian Fascist secret police, that he was an informant for the Fascists in the 1930s. Other documents establish that Silone was knowledgeable about CIA funding of the Congress for Cultural Freedom and other anti-Soviet cultural activities of the Western intelligence services in the "cultural cold war"—activities that Howe castigated in "This Age of Conformity" and in *Dissent*'s pages throughout the 1950s and '60s. In light of these findings, Howe's praise of Silone sometimes rings most ironic: "The memory of [Silone's] refusal to accommodate himself to the fascist regime stirred feelings of bad conscience among literary men who had managed to become more flexible. Alas, men of exemplary stature are often hard to accept. They must seem a silent rebuke to those who had been less heroic or more cautious" (*Decline of the New*, 288).

37. Ibid., 232, 321–322.

38. Howe, interview, 8 October 1983.

39. Trilling, Introduction to *Homage to Catalonia*, xvi, xviii.

40. Howe, *A Margin of Hope*, 324.

41. Ibid., 295.

42. Howe, "As the Bones Know" (1969), reprinted in Meyers, *George Orwell: The Critical Heritage*.

43. Saul Bellow, *Mr. Sammler's Planet* (New York: Viking Press, 1970), 35.

44. Howe, *A Margin of Hope*, 314.

45. Howe, "As the Bones Know," 102.

46. Howe, *A Margin of Hope*, 324.

47. Howe, interview, 8 October 1983.

48. Howe, "As the Bones Know," 103.

49. Ibid., 98–99.

50. Howe, *A Margin of Hope*, 291–292.

51. Ibid., 315.

52. Howe, "As the Bones Know," 97.

53. Ibid., 97, 103.

54. Howe's close friend and *Dissent* co-founder Lewis Coser, who was to outlive him by a decade and reach the ripe old age of ninety, phrased a similar thought more expansively:

> Lionel Trilling once told me how he had been looking for an appropriate word to characterize George Orwell, whom he wished to eulogize. It finally seemed to him that a very old-fashioned word was most appropriate, the word virtue. This word seems to me also most appropriate to characterize Irving Howe. He was a virtuous man, one who tried to live up to the self-imposed moral standards and moral duties.

See Lewis Coser's tribute to Howe in John Rodden, ed., *The Worlds of Irving Howe* (Boulder, Colo.: Paradigm, 2005), 323. Coser's reflections first appeared in *Dissent*'s Fall 1993 memorial issue devoted to Howe.

55. "Kidnapping Our Hero": Subtitle of address delivered by Howe at West Chester University, 8 October 1983.

56. Howe, *A Margin of Hope*, 345. Or as he wrote in the preface to the 1992 edition of *Politics and the Novel:*

> This work [of 1957] bears distinct signs of a Marxist outlook. [Today] I still hold firmly to the socialist ethos which partly inspired this book. But the ideology to which these essays occasionally return no longer has for me the power it once had. . . . A pedantic title for this book might have been *Revolutionary Politics and the Modern Novel*. For it pays little attention to the kind of novel written by George Eliot, George Meredith, and Trollope.

57. Howe, interview, 8 October 1983.

58. Ibid.; Howe, *A Margin of Hope*, 350.

59. Howe, *Politics and the Novel* (1992), xi. Howe had already expressed similar sentiments more than a decade earlier when he spoke of his commitment to the "discipline of

the plain style." In a November 1982 letter to his friend Bernard Avishai, he confided: "Writing is a life-long struggle, if you take it seriously; and if you stop doing so, you can slip right back into the worst habits. . . . Achieve clarity and the rest may follow—may. But at least you'll have clarity." Quoted in Gerald Sorin, *Irving Howe*, 361.

60. Howe, *A Margin of Hope*, 350.

61. By contrast, Macdonald shared more Orwell's occasionally quixotic, antinomian streak and his strongly libertarian outlook, and his aversion to mass culture—rather than Orwell's democratic socialist politics. In my view, however, the characterizations of Macdonald as "the American Orwell" are even more inflated than such tributes to Howe (or, for that matter, Christopher Hitchens). See, for instance, the following articles co-authored by John Rodden and John Rossi: "Macdonald: Dwight or Left," *American Prospect* (20 March 2006); "Dethroning the Lords of Kitsch: Dwight Macdonald, the Unmaking of a Journalist," *Common Review* (Winter 2006); and "Rebel with a Cause: Dwight Macdonald Remembered," *Commonweal*, 22 February 2006.

62. Howe also used the phrase in the 1980s and '90s to characterize radical professors who favored multiculturalism and postmodernism over the classical literary canon and the traditional liberal arts curriculum.

63. One measure of the immediate influence of Howe's January 1954 essay of this title in *PR* is that a book by Alan Valentine appeared later that year under the title *The Age of Conformity* (Chicago: Regnery Press, 1954). An essay also appeared in the *American Scholar* in 1956: "American Literature in an Age of Conformity," by John W. Aldridge.

64. Joseph Epstein mocked such tributes in a 1998 *Commentary* essay, collected in John Rodden, *Irving Howe and the Critics: Celebrations and Attacks* (Lincoln: University of Nebraska Press, 2005), 71–80. As we have seen, however, Howe's friends and junior colleagues certainly embrace the comparison of Howe with Orwell.

65. See my *George Orwell: The Politics of Literary Reputation* (1989; repr., New Brunswick: Transaction Publishers, 2002).

CHAPTER FOUR

1. I discuss the reception of Orwell's work by British conservatives and Catholics in *The Politics of Literary Reputation*, chapter 6.

2. Kirk's influence on the direction of conservatism was felt throughout the early postwar era, with the publication of several more books on similar themes: *A Program for Conservatives* (1954), *The Intelligent Woman's Guide to Conservatism* (1957), *Edmund Burke: A Genius Reconsidered* (1967), *Eliot and His Age* (1971), and many others. Before Kirk, conservatism and extremism were one and the same to most liberal intellectuals. *The Conservative Mind* made conservatism intellectually respectable.

3. Kirk was also a prolific publicist and journalist for conservatism. In addition to launching *Modern Age*, he was the founding editor of the *University Bookman*, an educational quarterly. For a quarter-century he wrote a column on education called "From the

Academy" for the *National Review*, and for thirteen years he wrote a newspaper column distributed by the *Los Angeles Times* syndicate. Speaking at a testimonial dinner in Kirk's honor in Washington in 1981, Ronald Reagan, then newly elected, said: "Dr. Kirk helped renew a generation's interest and knowledge of 'permanent things,' which are the underpinnings and the intellectual infrastructure of the conservative revival of our nation."

But not everyone on the Right applauded Kirk—not even in the 1950s and '60s, before the rise of neoconservatism, when his reputation among conservatives was at its height. For instance, Frank Meyer's attack on the "New Conservatism," as he called Kirk's views, appeared in the July 1955 issue of the *Freeman* under the title "Collectivism Rebaptized." Meyer, a libertarian conservative, took exception to Kirk's rejection of individualism and argued that Kirk's position was rhetorical and without substance. Because Kirk "presents himself and his beliefs always rhetorically, never on a reasoned basis, he can succeed in establishing the impression that he has a strong and coherent outlook without ever taking a systematic and consistent position." In *In Defense of Freedom: A Conservative Credo* (1962), Meyer further elaborated his criticism of what he called "the New Conservatism." He felt that Kirk and those of similar views, with their emphasis on order and tradition, were inclined to subordinate the individual to society. For him the primary end of society is to vindicate the freedom of the person, and the proper end of the individual is to use his freedom for the attainment of virtue. His book presented the extreme libertarian position of conservatism. In a reply headlined "An Ideologue of Liberty" in the *Sewanee Review*, Kirk counterattacked: "Disdainful of duty and 'the contract of eternal society,' Mr. Meyer . . . can appeal to little but the arrogant ego." See Russell Kirk, "An Ideologue of Liberty," *Sewanee Review* 72, no. 2 (Spring 1964): 350. Meyers's criticism of Kirk is quoted in Henry Regnery, *Memoirs of a Dissident Publisher* (New York: Harcourt Brace Jovanovich, 1979), 158–159, 189–190.

4. Kirk wrote in his autobiography, *The Sword of Imagination* (1993), "The oldest university in northern Britain, St. Andrews conferred upon Kirk its highest arts degree—which was then held by only one other living scholar." And later: "When Kirk returned to the United States in August 1952, it was clear that the American electorate was turning conservative—even if most people entertained only a vague notion of what the word 'conservative' meant" (*The Sword of Imagination: Memoirs of a Half-Century of Literary Conflict* [Grand Rapids, Mich.: William B. Eerdmans, 1995], 134, 139). (The entire work is written in the third person.)

5. Russell Kirk, *Enemies of the Permanent Things* (New Rochelle, N.Y.: Arlington House, 1969), 133.

6. Russell Kirk, *Beyond the Dreams of Avarice* (Chicago: Regnery, 1956), 191.

7. See E. P. Thompson, "Outside the Whale," in *Out of Apathy* (London: New Left Books, 1960).

8. Kirk, interview, 16 March 1983.

9. Kirk, *The Conservative Mind*, 533.

10. Kirk, interview, 10 February 1983.

11. As Trilling wrote in *The Liberal Imagination* (1950): "It is the plain fact that nowadays there are no cónservative or reactionary ideas in general circulation. . . . [T]he conservative impulse and the reactionary impulse do not, with some isolated and some ecclesiastical exceptions, express themselves in ideas but only in action or in irritable mental gestures which seek to resemble ideas" (vii).

12. This is not to say, of course, that the Conservative Party in Britain or the Republican Party in the United States were not successful (nor even that conservative intellectuals such as Kirk did not prefer them to the alternatives)—but rather than they were not really "conservative" in the eyes of cultural conservatives. They did not "conserve," did not consistently champion "the permanent things," but rather supported (or at least colluded with) Big Business and the atheistic, secular trends of modernity. Kirk welcomed the re-election of Winston Churchill in 1951 (and the ouster of the British Labour Party); the Conservatives would remain in power until 1964. Moreover, although he was an advocate of Senator Robert Taft for the Republican Party nomination in 1952, Kirk supported the election of Eisenhower that November (and his 1956 re-election). But neither British Conservative nor American Republican leaders stood before cultural conservatives such as Kirk (or William F. Buckley and the *National Review*) as worthy tribunes for an authentic cultural conservatism. Not until Senator Barry Goldwater's candidacy in 1964 did American cultural conservatives have a standard bearer about whom they enthused—and not until Ronald Reagan's 1980 election did they have a victorious one.

13. Kirk, interview, 11 November 1984. *Partisan Review* discussed the book at length in two issues: November 1953 and January 1954.

14. Elwood Lawrence was also the author of *Henry George in the British Isles* (1957), among other books.

15. Kirk, interview, 11 November 1984. In *The Sword of Imagination*, Kirk discusses his relationship to Warren Fleischauer, whom he met in 1941 and who became an English professor and colleague of Kirk's at Michigan State College.

16. Kirk met the English trade union M.P. George Brown in autumn 1957 at a conference on promoting North Atlantic cooperation, which was held in Bruges, Belgium, and attended by political scientists, journalists, civic leaders, and business people.

17. Kirk, interview, 11 November 1984.

18. Ibid.

19. Ibid.

20. Russell Kirk, *The Conservative Mind*, 536.

21. Kirk, *Beyond the Dreams of Avarice*, 193.

22. The same was true for other *Modern Age* contributors. See for instance, Arthur Eckstein, "*1984* and George Orwell's Other View of Capitalism," *Modern Age* 29, no. 1 (Winter 1985): 11; and Leslie Mellichamp, "George Orwell: Terrible 'Simplificateur,'" *Modern Age* 28 (Spring/Summer 1984): 121.

23. Kirk, *Enemies of the Permanent Things*, 139.

24. Kirk converted to Catholicism in 1964, the year he married Annette Courteman-che. They had met in New York in 1960, when she, then a nineteen-year-old student at Molloy College, a Catholic institution for women on Long Island, appeared on a panel de-voted to one of his books, *The American Cause*, at a conservative conference.

25. Kirk, interview, 22 March 1985.

26. Ibid.

27. Christopher Hollis, *A Study of George Orwell* (London: Hollis and Carter, 1956). Hollis reviewed *Randolph of Roanoke: A Study in Conservative Thought* (Chicago: Univer-sity of Chicago Press, 1951) in the London *Tablet*, which brought Kirk to the attention of some of the most influential Catholic thinkers in Britain.

28. Kirk, interview, 22 March 1985.

29. Ibid. Before his death, Robert Aickman (1914–1981) was generally deemed the most accomplished writer of classic supernatural tales in English. Aickman's "strange stories"—his preferred term—are not the ghost stories of an antiquary, but rather enig-matic, disorienting spiritual journeys. Kirk himself wrote two Gothic novels: *Watchers at the Strait Gate: Mystical Tales* (1984) and *The Wise Men Know What Wicked Things Are Writ-ten on the Sky* (1982). Kirk also penned *The Princess of All Lands*, a science fiction collec-tion, along with a number of works of mystery, suspense, and fantasy in publications such as the *London Mystery Magazine* and *Fantasy and Science Fiction*.

Orwell and Kirk shared common ground here: Orwell's interest in the "demonic" or supernatural bears some affinities with Kirk's fascination with the Gothic tradition. The resemblance manifested itself in the two men's enthusiasm for popular culture: Kirk's popular fiction and Orwell's popular culture criticism reflected similarities of tempera-ment, vision, and values. Both men appreciated high culture but were not "spooked" by low culture.

30. Kirk, interview, 22 March 1985.

31. Ibid.

32. Ibid. Or, as Kirk wrote in *The Sword of Imagination:* "Kirk had a hand, along with a larger hand of George Orwell, in bringing about fresh attention to George Gissing. In 1950, Kirk published an essay on Gissing and talked of writing a life of Gissing."

33. Ibid.

34. See Leslie Mellichamp, "George Orwell and the Ethics of Revolutionary Politics," *Modern Age* 9 (Summer 1965): 272.

35. Kirk interview, 10 February 1983. Kirk was speaking at a short-lived moment of possible political realignment in Britain. But the Social Democratic Party soon disinte-grated after shocking British political observers in the early 1980s. In December 1981, a Gallup survey placed support for the Liberal-SDP alliance at more than 50 percent, with

the Conservatives and Labour languishing behind at 23 percent each. By 1987, the SDP had died, and its leaders (including Shirley Williams) had moved on.

36. Kirk, *Beyond the Dreams of Avarice*, 186.

37. Religion, in Kirk's view, is the very basis of culture and civilization. When Richard Nixon asked him in the late 1960s to recommend one book to read that would throw light on the modern world's disorders, Kirk recommended T. S. Eliot's *Notes toward the Definition of Culture* (1948).

38. Although staunchly conservative throughout his life, Kirk never endorsed the radical Right. He once called Robert Welch, founder of the right-wing John Birch Society, a "likeable, honest, courageous, energetic man" who nevertheless was "the kiss of death" for the conservative cause because of his "silliness and injustice of utterance." Both Orwell and Kirk were fiercely independent. Just as Orwell defended socialism from Stalin and his apologists, Kirk resisted McCarthyism. When Senator McCarthy's activities were treated as the work of a conservative, Kirk demurred, arguing that conservatism was a coherent tradition that predated anti-Communism. Kirk, like Orwell, was an intellectual outsider who scrutinized his own side just as vigorously as he attacked his ideological foes.

39. Kirk's central conviction was one that he believed Orwell shared: "The 20th-century conservative is concerned, first of all, with the regeneration of spirit and character with the perennial problem of the inner order of the soul, the restoration of the ethical understanding, and the religious sanction upon which any life worth living is founded." Kirk's conservatism sought to preserve "the old motives of morality and diligence that conservatives always had believed in: religious sanctions, tradition, habit, and private interest restrained by prescriptive institutions."

40. *Enemies of the Permanent Things*, 133. Kirk even used Orwell to defend Eliot against charges of anti-Semitism. Kirk admitted that Eliot was insensitive when he referred slightingly to "free-thinking Jews" in *After Strange Gods* (1934). But he argued that Eliot himself disavowed both any anti-Semitic intent and the book itself. (Eliot never reissued *After Strange Gods* after its first edition and denied permission to any writer or publisher seeking to quote from it.) Kirk quotes a letter from Orwell to Julian Symons (29 October 1948): "In the early 'twenties, Eliot's anti-Semitic remarks were about on par with the automatic sneer one casts at Anglo-Indian colonels in boarding houses. On the other hand, if they had been written after the [Nazi] persecutions began, they would have meant something quite different." Kirk, *Eliot and His Age* (New York: Random House, 1971).

CHAPTER FIVE

1. In the early 1930s, however, Orwell received several positive notices from the *Nation*. Wrote an anonymous reviewer of *Down and Out* in September 1933: "No writer submitting himself for the nonce to a horrible existence, for the sake of material, could possibly convey so powerful a sense of destitution and hopelessness as has Mr. Orwell, on whom these sensations were, apparently, forced. If we are correct in this conclusion, if this book is not merely a piece of 'human nature faking,' it is a restrained and all the more damn-

ing indictment of a society in which such things are possible" (Meyers, *George Orwell: The Critical Heritage*, 45–46).

2. Orwell virtually ceased contributing to the *New Republic* (*TNR*) after 1946, when Henry Wallace became editor. Orwell reported to Dwight Macdonald that year: "I have stopped sending my things to the *New Republic*, because what I am now doing is topical English stuff that wouldn't interest them. I seldom see the *N.R.*, and I'm not sure how far it has gone as a fellow-traveler paper. From their frequently swapping articles with *Tribune*, and being anxious to have my stuff, I thought they couldn't be very much so, but I was rather taken aback when I heard Wallace had become editor-in-chief." Letter to Dwight Macdonald, 5 November 1946. See *Complete Works*, vol. 18, 508. Seconding Orwell's disaffection with *TNR*, Macdonald replied that Orwell should develop ties with the *Nation*, but Orwell's worsening health and the struggle of completing *Nineteen Eighty-Four* prevented his doing so.

Wallace was editor of the *New Republic* in 1946–1947. In 1948, he became the presidential candidate of the Progressive Party, which advocated a policy of reconciliation and close cooperation with the Soviet Union. Macdonald had airmailed Orwell his recent book on Wallace, with the hope that, "since Wallace is now in England, [Orwell] might care to tell his readers about it." *Complete Works*, vol. 19, 127. Orwell responded, "Very good, and I am urging Gollancz to publish it over here. I am afraid Wallace may well cause 'our' man [Truman] to lose the election, and then Lord knows what may happen."

3. Orwell spoke positively about the *Nation*, but he wrote only two book reviews for them in his lifetime: on Louis Fischer's *Empire* in *Nation*, 13 May 1944, 572–573; and on Henry N. Brailsfort's *Subject India* in *Nation*, 20 November 1943, 588–589. After the magazine's laudatory notice of *Down and Out* in 1933, it paid Orwell no further attention for thirteen years until the publication of *Animal Farm*. When *Dickens, Dali and Others* appeared in America in 1946, literary editor Randall Jarrell wrote an enthusiastic personal letter to Orwell, inviting Orwell to contribute to the *Nation*. See Gordon Bowker, *Inside George Orwell* (New York: Palgrave Macmillin, 2003), 344.

After Orwell's death, however, the *Nation* devoted frequent attention to him. See for instance: Unsigned review of "Such, Such Were the Days," 15 April 1953; Allan Seager, "Review of John Atkins's book *George Orwell: A Literary Study*," 5 November 1955; Allan Seager, "Review of Lawrence Brander, *George Orwell*," 5 November 1955; Jacob Korg, review of Christopher Hollis's book *George Orwell*, 22 December 1956.

4. Wylie Sypher in Meyers, *George Orwell: The Critical Heritage*, 221.

5. Rosenfeld in ibid., 201.

6. Eliot told Orwell in his rejection letter for Faber that the pigs should have run Animal Farm since they were the most intelligent animals, and that Orwell's criticism should not have been that they were pigs, but that they should have been more "public-spirited" pigs. See Crick, *George Orwell*, 420.

7. Herbert Matthews, "Homage to Orwell," *Nation*, 27 December 1952. Matthews's review provoked a rejoinder from Lionel Trilling, who had introduced Orwell's book and

regarded Orwell as not just a "virtuous man" but an intelligent, clear-sighted one. See Lionel Trilling, "Was Orwell Shrewd?" *Nation*, 24 January 1953.

8. Meyers, *George Orwell: The Critical Heritage*, 149. Similarly, reviewing the American edition of *The Road to Wigan Pier* in August 1958, Robert Hatch exalted Orwell's reportage as "the writing of an artist with his blood up." *Wigan Pier* "can stand with Hogarth and Dickens." Yet a few sentences later, Hatch characterized the second half of *Wigan Pier* as "too angry to be just." Hatch allowed that Victor Gollancz and the Popular Front spokesman falsely "operated on the assumption that they grasped the issues of their day." Hatch concluded with an apology cum backhanded defense of the *Nation*'s pro-Stalinist enthusiasm: "It may have been an illusion—indeed, you can cite events to show that it was certainly an illusion—but it may be one that we cannot do without" (Meyers, 114–115).

9. Ibid., 259. Mrs. Trilling's provocative review of *Nineteen Eighty-Four* is worth quoting at greater length:

This assimilation of the English Labor government to Soviet communism is surely from any immediate political point of view, unfortunate. On the other hand, whatever our partisanship for the present English revolution as against the present situation in Russia, we must recognize that the generalization in the lesson Mr. Orwell is teaching is a proper one. Even where, as in his last novel, *Animal Farm*, Mr. Orwell seemed to be concerned only with unmasking the Soviet Union for its dreamy admirers, he was urged on by something larger than sectarianism. What he was telling us is that the basis of the path the Russian Revolution has followed to the destruction of all the decent human values have been the best ideals of modern social enlightenment. It is this idealism he has wished to jolt into self-awareness. In the name of a higher loyalty, treacheries beyond imagination have been committed; in the name of Socialist equality, privilege has ruled unbridled; in the name of democracy and freedom, the individual has lived without public voice or private peace—if this is true of the Soviet Union, why should it not eventually be equally true of the English experiment? In other words, we are being warned against the extremes to which the contemporary totalitarian spirit can carry us, not only so that we will be warned against Russia but also so that we will understand the ultimate dangers involved wherever power moves under the guise of order and rationality. . . . With this refusal to concentrate his attack upon Soviet totalitarianism alone, Mr. Orwell reasserts the ability, so rare among intellectuals of the left, to place his own brand of idealism above political partisanship. It is very difficult to pin a political label on the author of *Nineteen Eighty-Four:* if one has heard that Mr. Orwell is now an anarchist, one can of course read his new novel as the work of an anarchist—but one can just as easily read it as the work of an unfashionable, highly imaginative democrat or of an old-fashioned libertarian. (Ibid., 259–261)

10. Ibid., 158–159.

11. Ibid., 159.

12. Ibid.

13. The split also included differing estimates on the worth of Orwell's fiction and non-fiction, with the latter usually valued much higher. For example, Wylie Sypher praised Orwell's literary criticism in *Dickens, Dali and Others* after he had dismissed *Animal Farm*. Wrote Sypher:

> He is not doctrinaire; he undoubtedly feels that he is, as he said earlier, a liberal writer at a moment when liberalism is coming to an end. Orwell judges literature by its social bearings, but his socialism is not a mystique. With Dickens, he belongs in a nineteenth-century tradition of "free intelligence," not much liked by what he calls "the smelly little orthodoxies" of the left. His fighting in the Spanish war—where he discovered that intra-party politics is a cesspool—and his conviction during the London blitz that "bourgeois democracy is not enough, but it is very much better than fascism" have not dulled his sense that the fruits of the war must be revolutionary or else the war has been lost. (Ibid., 222)

14. Quoted in Dinitia Smith, "A Pig Returns to the Farm, Thumbing His Snout at Orwell," *New York Times,* 25 November 2002. The second quote is from Cockburn's introduction to Leonard Reed's *Snowball's Chance* (New York: Roof Books, 2002), 7. Reed has stated in interviews that he intends his novel to be not only a parody of Orwell, but an attack on Orwell's "championing of free-market capitalism." "I really wanted to explode that book," Reed told Smith. "I wanted to completely undermine it."

Cockburn's introduction to *Snowball's Chance* reminds readers at length that Orwell turned over to Britain's MI6 the names of people he suspected were communists. What Cockburn does not mention is that his father, Claud, a British journalist and member of the Communist Party, was an adversary of Orwell's. In *Homage to Catalonia*, Orwell exposed the Stalinist lies of Claud Cockburn, who was the *Daily Worker*'s correspondent in Spain during the Spanish Civil War. The elder Cockburn wrote under the pseudonym of Frank Pitcairn and spread the falsehoods of the Spanish Communist Party, one of which was that other left-wing militias (such as POUM) were working for Franco and the fascists.

Elsewhere Alexander Cockburn has remarked of Hitchens himself:

> I suppose Hitch's departure [from the *Nation*] has been inevitable ever since the *Weekly Standard* said he was more important than George Orwell. I think it was becoming increasingly bizarre for *The Nation* to publish his column. But people only very slowly take in these changes, much like Dorian Gray changes slowly in front of you. Hitch is no longer the beautiful slender young man of the Left. Now he's just another middle-aged porker of the Right. (Quoted in Lloyd Grove, "The Reliable Source," *Washington Post,* 26 September 2002)

Cockburn added that he has received "lots of letters from people saying Hitchens is still on our side," but that he began "drifting away years ago." "Is he a Tory?" Cockburn asks. "Well, he has stated publicly that Bush is his favorite politician and he'll vote for him. Poor Hitchypoo is under attack but he has been viciously rude, often at the personal level, about leftists in general." (Quoted in Christopher Reed, "Battle of the Bottle Divides Columnists," *Observer*, 2 March 2003.)

After Hitchens testified against Clinton advisor Sidney Blumenthal, a onetime friend, Cockburn dubbed Hitchens (who had been his own friend) "Hitch the Snitch." In one column, Cockburn wrote:

> Now, as a Judas and a snitch, Hitchens has made the big time. Orwell is Hitchens' idol, and Hitchens lost no time in defending Orwell in *Vanity Fair* and the *Nation*. Finally, I wrote a *Nation* column taking the line that Orwell's snitch list was idle gossip, patently racist and anti-Semitic, pre-figuring McCarthyism. Hitchens seemed surprised by my position that snitching is to be shunned by all decent people.

See Alexander Cockburn, "Why Hitch the Snitch Betrayed a Trusting Friend," *Irish Times*, 13 February 1999.

But Hitchens saw his disclosures about Blumenthal as the intellectual integrity of an Orwell, not a *trahison des clercs*. As he wrote ten years earlier in his regular column, "Minority Report": "The real test of a radical or a revolutionary is not the willingness to confront the orthodoxy and arrogance of the rulers, but the readiness to contest illusions and falsehoods among close friends and allies" (*Nation*, July 1989, 325). (Hitchens was commenting on the contrarian politics of C. L. R. James.)

Notably, because Hitchens was clearly attacking Clinton from the Left, Cockburn never derided Hitchens for his criticism of Clinton, only for his betrayal of Blumenthal. Since 9/11, however, Cockburn (and many other leftists, such as Chomsky) have regarded Hitchens as a man of the Right. (On this point, see note 21.) Since 2002, apart from geopolitical events associated with 9/11, Hitchens has also been more outspoken in his love for the United States—in sharp contrast to the anti-Americanism often expressed by Cockburn, Chomsky, and the far Left. (After 9/11, Hitchens even announced that he intended to apply for U.S. citizenship; he has done so and it is reportedly pending.)

See also: Alexander Cockburn, "St George's List," *Nation*, 7 December 1998, and "Orwell and Koestler," *Nation*, 7 December 1998; Patricia J. Williams, "*Animal Farm:* The Republican Version," *Nation*, 23 February 2004.

For Hitchens's replies see: "1984 and All That," *Nation*, 24 August 1998, 8; "Was Orwell a Snitch?" *Nation*, 14 December 1998; "Minority Report," *Nation*, 14 December 1998 and 24 August 1998; "Ignoble Ig-nazi-o?" *Nation*, 12 June 2000.

For other views of *Nation* contributors on Orwell, see: Eric Alterman, "Stop, Thief!" *Nation*, 16 October 2000, 10; John Leonard, "On Shooting at Elephants," *Nation*, 11 December 2000.

15. Occasionally, however, Pollitt lauds Orwell in order to lambaste Hitchens. She concluded one *Nation* column (titled "Letters to an Ex-Contrarian") with a stinging rebuke of her former colleague/comrade Hitchens, charging that he misrepresented anti-war protesters as apologists for terrorism: "Next time you put on your Orwell costume for TV cameras, I hope you'll put on his fairness and modesty too. You may have spent years as a man of the left in America, but I don't think you really knew the American left." Katha Pollitt, *Nation*, 25 November 2002. Hitchens replied to Pollitt: "You also know that, in

teasing me for donning an Orwell costume, you can hope to hurt my reputation without at all touching his. (My reputation being what it is, you can really hope to gratify only those who aim for the opposite effect.) My immediate question is this. Are you so sure that a covert sympathy for despotism and theocracy, or perhaps a glib and cultivated indifference to the menace, is a fringe rather than a mainstream problem in what used to be our family?" See Hitchens, "The Hitchens-Pollitt Papers," *Nation*, 16 December 2002.

16. One might characterize this as an "Orwellian" use of language. *Collaboration* is a derogatory term that surely cannot apply to someone working with a party and a government that he openly supported. See "The Orwell Files," unpublished manuscript, 2003.

17. Ian Williams adds:

In fact, George Orwell matters because he was so accurate in his depiction of so many of the people who are now his detractors. The socialist's clearly stated political and moral positions have been chucked down the memory hole so that he can be rewritten as a free market conservative, or in the case of Christopher Hitchens, somehow as simultaneously a Trotskyist and a retrospective neo-neoconservative supporter of current American imperial ambitions.

Of his erstwhile colleague, Christopher Hitchens, Ian Williams writes:

My worry is that Hitchens' time in the Fourth International dimension has affected his sense of relativity so that the constant ad-hominem attacks on him, which are indeed often of the specious sort leveled at Orwell, may have driven him into a political form of "synecdochism"—taking the part for the whole. The would-be Big Brotherhood who have reviled him may manufacture more vitriol than the real left, but they do not represent it. I suspect that a majority of *Nation* readers might actually agree with him most of the time . . .

Hitchens is right about the nature of the Iraqi regime, but I'd like to see a little more ambivalence from him about signing up for the obsessive crusade against it. The left needs contrarians: It doesn't need neo-neocons while the original breed have so much power in the White House. So I hope Hitchens sticks around. Orwell did.

Williams, "Why Hitchens Matters," *In These Times*, 23 December 2002, 24.

18. Ian Williams, "In Defense of Comrade Psmith," in *George Orwell: Into the 21st Century*, ed. Cushman and Rodden (Boulder: Paradigm, 2004).

19. See, for instance, *The Missionary Position: Mother Teresa in Theory and Practice* (London: Verso, 1995). See also *The Trial of Henry Kissinger* (London: Verso, 2001). *Letters to a Young Contrarian* (New York: Basic Books, 2001) is one of the most successful entrants in Basic Books' "Art of Mentoring" series.

20. One index of Hitchens's celebrity was the rumor that Hitchens had been the model for Tom Wolfe's hard-drinking British journalist Peter Fallow in *Bonfire of the Vanities* (1987).

21. Of course, another similarity between Orwell and Hitchens—as Alexander Cockburn and other leftists have pointed out ad nauseam—is that Orwell named names to the IRD and Hitchens signed an affidavit testifying that his friend Sidney Blumenthal committed perjury before Kenneth Starr's committee during the Monica Lewinsky investigation.

22. Despite periodic sharp clashes and bruised relationships with prominent fellow leftists (such as Alexander Cockburn, Edward Said, and Noam Chomsky), a perception of their common right-wing enemy (such as Kissinger, Mother Teresa, and the Ayatollah Khomeini) kept their alliance intact. This fact also induced fellow leftists to tolerate Hitchens's apostasies as those of a self-described "unaffiliated radical." The Blumenthal affair was the first major conflict between Hitchens and the Left; 9/11 and its aftermath triggered the break. Nonetheless, the war on terrorism is, for Hitchens, a war against theocracy and religious fundamentalism, which is why he can both support Bush on Iraqi intervention and castigate him as a born-again religious fanatic.

23. Hitchens, "Taking Sides," *Washington Post*, 14 October 2002. See also Grove, "The Reliable Source." One should emphasize, however, that the views of the *Nation* writers were not so monolithic as Hitchens's statement implies; as Ian Williams notes:

> Several of us on the *Nation* were appalled when so many of the so-called Left leapt to the defence of Slobodan Milosevic, in Bosnia and then crucially, over Kosovo. On the other hand some of the more liberal wing of the Left on the pro-Democrat side (as opposed to the Far Left) in the *Nation* were unhappy at Hitchens' deposition on Blumenthal.
>   . . . The break with the Left as such came, not just with his support for intervention in Iraq, but his support for the forms and finaglings of Bush and the NeoCons, like Wolfowitz, who seemed to have dazzled him. Orwell may have occasionally admitted that Churchill had a point, but he never went overboard like that!

Personal communication, 14 November 2004.

24. In *Salon*, the electronic magazine, the editors asked Hitchens: "If one were to look at your writing, say, since Sept. 11, there are threads of Orwell in it, aren't there? Whether or not they're cited." Hitchens answered: "Well if someone wanted to say that, I wouldn't feel I had to repudiate it."
    Cited in Scott Lucas, *The Betrayal of Dissent: Beyond Orwell, Hitchens and the New American Century* (London: Pluto Press, 2004).

25. It was also symbolically significant of Hitchens's trans-Atlantic voyage from English schoolboy to Washington journalist that, in the wake of September 11th, he filed papers for American citizenship.

26. Hitchens soon thereafter began a regular column for *Slate*, adding it to his several other prominent platforms, including the *Atlantic* and *Vanity Fair*.

27. Andrew Sullivan, the *Times* (London), 30 September 2000. Sullivan is a gay Catholic and a Tory radical. Like Hitchens, he tends rightward on numerous geopolitical issues, but he is a radical on most social issues, such as legalizing homosexual marriage.

28. Ron Rosenbaum, "The Man Who Would Be Orwell," *New York Observer*, 23 March 2002.

29. Certainly Hitchens is no antagonist of "the birth controllers," as Orwell was; but his severe criticism of Western sexual mores is most unusual on the Left. How many *Nation* contributors consider the separation of sex and childbearing morally problematic? Consider this passage:

> The post-1945 generation has been, at least until recently, free of the fear of untreatable disease and mass unemployment. It more or less grew up knowing that sex and procreation could be easily separated—the first generation in human history for which this was true. (Christopher Hitchens, "The Baby-Boomer Wasteland," *Vanity Fair*, January 1996)

Hitchens's mother reportedly aborted the fetuses that she had conceived before and after Christopher; some observers have suggested his moderate pro-life stand has an autobiographical basis. In any case, Hitchens—again like Orwell—is careful not to equate his criticism of sexual irresponsibility with support for the Church. See his "Minority Report," *Nation*, 24 April 1989, 546.

Elsewhere he writes about Orwell:

> Orwell clearly felt that the word "conception" meant what it said, but he never fell for the Catholic nonsense about hand-jobs being genocide and if he had lived to see the IUD he would have known better than to classify it as a murder-weapon. True, he didn't like contraception either—it was a purely rubberized business in those days— but he wouldn't have condemned it in the same breath as abortion. Think how much wretchedness could be avoided, or could have been avoided, if the Church would drop this dogma of equivalence.

Quoted by Andrew Sullivan in his blog at andrewsullivan.com, 30 October 2002.

30. In *Letters to a Young Contrarian*, Hitchens is careful to identify himself as an "anti-theist" rather than an agnostic or atheist. He writes: "I not only maintain that all religions are versions of the same untruth, but I hold that the influence of churches, and the effect of religious belief, is positively harmful" (55). Indeed, Hitchens explains about his cordial relationship with his conservative Tory brother Peter (who opposed the 2003 Iraq war strongly): "The real difference between us—and it's an unbridgeable one—is that he's a believing Christian. I have many political disagreements with all kinds of people, but they are irrelevant compared with the ones between me and anyone who is a religious believer" (quoted in Ginny Dougary, "Friendship and Betrayal," *Times* [London], 17 July 2002). Hitchens was baptized as an Anglican and educated at a Methodist boarding school with compulsory religious instruction, "but I also had a Jewish mother who was once married to a distinguished rabbi (whom I suspected to be a secret Einsteinian agnostic)" (59).

31. Hitchens has supported the Left's opposition to Zionism. He agreed with Edward Said on the Palestinian question (see their co-edited volume, *Blaming the Victim: Spurious Scholarship and the Palestinian Question* [London and New York: Verso, 1988]). In a posthumous review of Said's *From Oslo to Iraq and the Road Map*, Hitchens wrote:

It may well be . . . that the whole Zionist enterprise was a mistake to begin with and that Palestine should be a political entity that awards citizenship without distinction of ethnicity or religion. (For what it's worth, I think so too.) (Christopher Hitchens, "Polymath with a Cause," *Washington Post*, 15 August 2004)

32. See Hitchens's essay on Trotsky, "The Old Man," in the *Atlantic* (July/August 2004), where he writes with nostalgia: "Even today a faint, saintly penumbra still emanates from the Old Man."

33. Hitchens has occasionally expressed respect for Lenin, especially during the 1960s. But he was certainly no Leninist by the mid-1970s, though he has retained admiration for the socialism of Lenin's rival, Rosa Luxemburg. On Hitchens's youthful admiration for Lenin, see his review of Isaac Deutscher's little book on Lenin, "Prophet Silenced," *New Statesman*, July 1970, 811. Hitchens is also a vocal admirer of C. L. R. James, who was both a Trotskyist and a Leninist.

Martin Amis, a close friend of Hitchens's since their *New Statesman* days in the 1970s, has given wide circulation to the perception that Hitchens remains a defender of Lenin (and Trotsky). In the final pages of *Koba the Dread: Laughter and the Twenty Million* (New York: Hyperion, 2002), Amis addresses his friend as "Comrade Hitchens." Toward the end of the book is a long open letter to "Comrade Hitchens" in which Amis writes,

So it is still obscure to me why you wouldn't want to put more distance between yourself and these events than you do, with your reverence for Lenin and your unregretted discipleship of Trotsky . . . Why? An admiration for Lenin and Trotsky is meaningless without an admiration for terror. They would not want your admiration if it failed to include an admiration for terror. Do you admire terror? I know you admire freedom. (248, 250)

Hitchens replied to Amis in terms that underscore his frayed connection to Trotskyism and his attempt to associate Orwell with it:

There exists a historical tradition of Marxist writers—Victor Serge, C. L. R. James, Boris Souvarine and others—who exposed and opposed Stalin while never ceasing to fight against empire and fascism and exploitation. If the moral and historical audit is to be properly drawn up, then I would unhesitatingly propose the members of this derided, defeated diaspora, whose closest British analogue and ally was Orwell, as the ones who come best out of the several hells of the last century. A pity that you felt them beneath your notice. (*Guardian*, 4 September 2002)

Elsewhere Hitchens has explicitly insisted that he has never been a Communist Party supporter or (by implication) a Leninist: "As for myself, I always hated the Communist Party and considered myself to be operating from its left."

34. As one former comrade from their International Socialist (IS) days in the 1960s (who is still a member of the Socialist Workers Party and prefers to remain anonymous) wrote me in June 2004: "One thing I have always felt to be absent from his Orwell pose is any genuine sympathy for the underdog, for those at the bottom, the poor, the working

class, etc. I don't think Hitchens has ever had a *Down and Out* or *Wigan Pier* in him. Self-indulgence and self-advertisement have always seemed his hallmarks to me even when I have agreed with him."

35. Hitchens has told interviewers that his elder brother, Peter, another erstwhile Trotskyist but now an outspoken Tory, is very like his father—a naval commander who ended up working as a school bursar—while he takes after his mother. It was only after her death in 1973 that Hitchens discovered that she was Jewish. He now says that he was always particularly drawn to Jewish people—including, obviously, his second wife—and had, indeed, even felt himself to be Jewish. See Dougary, "Friendship and Betrayal."

36. Not long after, in 1973, his mother committed suicide with her lover in a hotel room in Athens. She had left a note, addressed only to Hitchens, with a postscript which read: "Give my love to your father and brother."

37. Hitchens was involved during the late 1960s and early 1970s with the International Socialists (IS) (forerunner of the Socialist Workers Party in Britain). Disgusted by the war in Vietnam and the Labour government's support for it, Hitchens was drawn to the IS when he was a student at Oxford. But he believes that, in the course of the 1970s, as the IS developed into the SWP, the international socialist movement took a wrong turn in evolving away from Luxemburg toward Lenin, which led him to "quietly cancel my membership." See "In the Bright Autumn of My Senescence," *London Review of Books*, 6 January 1994.

One recalls a passage from *Prepared for the Worst:* "Would Orwell have remained a socialist? He certainly anticipated most of the sickening disillusionments that have, in the last generations, led socialists to dilute or abandon their faith." Christopher Hitchens, "Comrade Orwell," in *Prepared for the Worst: Selected Essays and Minority Reports* (New York: Hill and Wang, 1988), 89. With these words, Hitchens acknowledges that Orwell also anticipated, as it were, Hitchens's own disillusionment with socialism and the Left.

38. See, for instance, "Words and History," *Nation*, 20 February 1982, 201, and "Minority Report," *Nation*, 20 September 1986, 239; 28 February 1987, 244; 30 April 1988, 596; 9–16 January 1989, 42; 4 December 1989, 671; 2 April 1990, 443; and 26 November 1990, 634.

39. See, for instance, Hitchens's review "Crick's Biography of Orwell," *New Statesman*, 28 November 1980, 20.

40. See Victor Navasky, *Naming Names* (New York: Viking Press, 1980).

41. Hitchens immediately became an active, highly visible presence on the American intellectual scene, while also retaining his connections to London magazines and publishers. In the 1980s, he became Washington editor of *Harper's* and book critic for the New York paper *Newsday*, as well as a regular contributor to the *London Review of Books*, *Granta*, *New Left Review*, and *Dissent*. He also began writing for *Vogue* and *Vanity Fair*. (His column in the latter is called "Fin de Siècle.") After publishing an early book on the Paris Commune and *Callaghan: The Road to Number Ten* (1976), he took up residence in Washington and wrote books such as *Hostage to History: Cyprus from the Ottomans to Kissinger*

NOTES TO PAGES 97–100

(1989), *Imperial Spoils: The Case of the Parthenon Marbles* (1989), and *Blood, Class, and Nostalgia: Anglo-American Ironies* (1990). Many of his columns and articles for the 1980s are collected in *Prepared for the Worst* (1989) and *For the Sake of Argument* (1993).

42. Here again, one notes that Hitchens repeatedly cites "Stalinism"—rather than "communism." In *Orwell's Victory* (London: Penguin, 2003), Hitchens pointedly writes that three great subjects of the twentieth century were fascism, imperialism, and "Stalinism."

43. Hitchens, "Orwell Missed America," *American Enterprise*, October–November 2002.

44. Indeed, unlike the case with many other contemporary intellectuals whom Hitchens has admired and toward whom Hitchens has felt a fraternal bond, Orwell is the only intellectual who has been both an intense and an enduring admiration for Hitchens. Contrast Hitchens's decades of esteem for Orwell—notably, a long-dead hero—with his responses to other contemporary writers and intellectuals whom he once esteemed and subsequently crossed swords with and/or grew disillusioned about, such as Edward Said (with whom he edited a 1988 book on the Palestinians), Noam Chomsky, Gore Vidal, Conor Cruise O'Brien, and Salman Rushdie (to whom he dedicated *Unacknowledged Legislation*).

45. See Hitchens, "Crick's Biography of Orwell," *New Statesman*, 28 November 1980, 20.

46. See my *Scenes from an Afterlife*, chap. 1, "Orwellmania in 1984."

47. Podhoretz was aiming here at nothing less than providing neoconservatism with an unimpeachable intellectual pedigree. He was well aware of what he was doing, noting that to have "the greatest political writer of the age on one's side" gave "confidence, authority, and weight to one's own political views." By emphasizing Orwell's hatred for "the left-wing intelligentsia" of his time, Podhoretz was also skillfully providing the present-day Left with an undesirable family tree, traceable to the British pacifists and communists (such as Claud Cockburn) of Orwell's day.

48. Hitchens, "Letters," *Harper's*, February 1983.

49. See also "Comrade Orwell," in Hitchens's collection *Prepared for the Worst*. The essay was originally published in *Grand Street*, Winter 1984.

50. Hitchens has been fiercely and relentlessly critical of Podhoretz in particular. See, for instance, "Born-Again Conformist," in *Prepared for the Worst:* Podhoretz is a "born-again conformist, with some interesting disorders of the ego" (113–114). On Williams, see "George Orwell and Raymond Williams," in *Unacknowledged Legislation*.

51. Hitchens, *Orwell's Victory*, 36.

52. Hitchens might wear my characterization proudly. As he writes in *Letters to a Young Contrarian:* "That is why so many irritating dissidents have been described by their enemies as 'self-appointed.' Self-appointed suits me fine" (81).

But Hitchens would certainly dispute the designation of Orwell as his "model." He opened *Letters to a Young Contrarian* with this observation: "The flattery is in your suggestion that I might be anybody's 'model,' when almost by definition a single existence cannot further any pattern (and, if it live in dissent, should not anyway be supposed to emulate)." Or later: "Our current culture, with its stupid emphasis on the 'role model' . . . Those who need or want to think for themselves will always be a minority; the human race may be inherently individualistic and even narcissistic, but in the mass it is quite easy to control. People have a need for reassurance and belonging" (93, 95). For a related point, see note 84.

53. Hitchens, *American Enterprise*, July 1999.

54. Ibid.

55. The preface concludes: "So this was an amazing and wondrous month [March 1999], perhaps the best of my life. (I finished my centennial study of George Orwell in the same period. Much more civilized to be writing about him than any of the above.)" Hitchens, *Letters to A Young Contrarian*, x.

56. Ibid., 29, 1.

57. Ibid., 138.

58. Hitchens, Review of *Orwell in Spain*, *Nation*, 10 November 2000.

59. *Orwell's Victory*, 39.

60. Ibid., 133.

61. See "George Orwell and Raymond Williams" in *Unacknowledged Legislators* (London: Verso, 1999), which also appeared under that title in *Critical Quarterly* 41:3 (October 1999).

62. *Orwell's Victory*, 102.

63. Ibid., 154. Hitchens's heaviest attack is targeted at Raymond Williams: "It is a fact that Williams despised Orwell, and devoted a lot of time to misunderstanding and misrepresenting him." Hitchens adds that Williams's *Orwell* (1971) "is a sly rather than oblique argument that Orwell would have done better to be someone else, and would have been a better author if he had written different, or at any rate other, books."

64. In his introduction to *Orwell's Victory*, however, Hitchens does acknowledge the wide and deep appreciation for Orwell: "The value of his work is debated only by his fellow socialists and anti-imperialists." But this point is obscured by the overall emphasis on Orwell's reception on the Left in the book.

65. Lucas, a Birmingham University (U.K.) professor of American Studies who grew up in Alabama, has written a book-length diatribe condemning both Orwell and Hitchens. See *The Betrayal of Dissent: Beyond Orwell, Hitchens, and the New American Century* (London: Pluto, 2003).

66. Orwell kept a private list of suspected communist fellow-travelers. In 1949, on his sickbed, he shared this personal notebook with Celia Kirwin, a friend who had begun to work for the Intelligence Research Department (IRD), which had recently been formed to counter Soviet propaganda.

News of Orwell's controversial "list" exploded into the headlines in 1996. The controversy reinvigorated criticism of his Cold War positions by giving his detractors a new line of attack on him. Moreover, it furnished them with a specific, complicated issue to use against him, rather than just general complaints or ad hominem derision.

67. David Brooks, "Orwell and Us: The Battle over George Orwell's Legacy," *Weekly Standard*, 23 September 2002.

68. Hitchens, *Orwell's Victory*, 73, 79, 84.

69. Ibid., 115.

70. Orwell, "Charles Dickens," *CW*, vol. 10, 165.

71. See Lucas, *The Betrayal of Dissent*. Lucas adds elsewhere:

For most of his writing, Orwell had patrolled the borders of Socialism as a lone ranger of decency. He had established himself as the authoritative voice of dissent, in part to limit the dissent of others. . . . What is unsettling is that Orwell and Hitchens are also joined in an effort to diminish, ridicule or even shut out completely the views of others. . . . Orwell and Hitchens, for all the proclamations of their individualism, never operated as maverick intellectuals when they defined the limits of acceptable opinion.

"What Would George Do?" *New Statesman*, 2 June 2003.
Nor is Lucas alone in his view of Hitchens's relationship to Orwell. Luke Slattery writes that *Orwell's Victory* "ripens the process of self-identification beyond the point of maturation." Slattery also maintains that Hitchens's "insistence on Orwell's intellectual integrity and independence is like a form of rhetorical cross-promotion for his own, especially after his highly public falling out with the American Left in the wake of September 11th" (Slattery, "The Author as Hero," *Australian*, 24 July 2002).

72. John Giuffo, "Why Hitchens Matters," *Village Voice*, Fall 2002.

73. Andy Croft, "Ministry of Truth," *Guardian*, 25 May 2002.

74. Geoffrey Wheatcroft, "Saved from Friend and Foe," *Spectator*, 8 June 2002.

75. Cheryl Miller, "Orwell's Example," *Policy Review*, October 2002.

76. As Hitchens mentioned to me in May 2003, both his British and American publishers rejected his own original, preferred title: *George Orwell: A Power of Facing*. That subtitle derives from a line in Orwell's "Why I Write" (1946), and it forms the theme of Hitchens's closing reflections in his book.

77. Judith Shulevitz, "What Would Orwell Do?" *New York Times*, 8 September 2002.

78. Hitchens's single gesture toward predicting the posthumous Orwell's stands is, rather, an attempt to deny the neoconservative claim to him:

> Would Orwell have remained a socialist? It may not be the decisive question, but it is an interesting one. He certainly anticipated most of the sickening disillusionments that have, in the last generation, led socialists to dilute or abandon their faith. To this extent, he was proof against the disillusionments rather than evidence for them. He hated inequality, exploitation, racism, and the bullying of small nations, and he was an early opponent of nuclear weapons and the hardly less menacing idea of nuclear blackmail or "deterrence." He saw how an external threat could be used to police or to intimidate dissent, even in a democracy. The spokesmen for our renovated capitalism, then, can barely claim that their pet system has developed to a point beyond the reach of his pen.

79. See chap. 16 in my *Scenes from an Afterlife*.

80. Elsewhere, however, Hitchens drew comparisons in the "If Orwell Were Alive Today" spirit that approached such claims. For instance, in October 2002, Hitchens wrote that Orwell "would have seen straight through the characters who chant 'No War on Iraq.'" Quoted in Lucas, *The Betrayal of Dissent*, 84).

81. On Rees's characterization, see the Epilogue to my *Scenes from an Afterlife*.

82. See Posner, *Public Intellectuals*. Posner refers to Orwell as "the exemplary figure" of "the best public-intellectual work of the last century" (73).

83. Hitchens, *Why Orwell Matters*, 216.

84. As I suggested in the introduction, certainly one could make a case that Hitchens is in the process of a sharp shift rightward and will soon pen his own version of "Why Lucky Jim Turned Right" (Kingsley Amis's 1973 manifesto announcing his new politics)—and follow Amis in developing his "Tory growl" into full-fledged Blimpism. Hitchens's contrariness reminds me somewhat of the perverse pleasure that the late Kingsley Amis (whom Hitchens befriended) seemed to derive from his numerous unpopular positions. (Hitchens remains a close friend of Martin Amis, Kingsley's son.) In fact, as I noted in Chapter Two, Kingsley Amis's contrariness led Martin Green to observe once that "it seemed as if he [Amis] could have no orthodoxy except an unrespectable one like Toryism"—a contrariness that one also often spots in the author of *Letters to a Young Contrarian*.

Indeed, Hitchens's curmudgeonly hatred of fashion reminds one not just of George Orwell but also—in fact, even more so—of Hitchens's other English literary hero from that generation, Evelyn Waugh. (Or as Hitchens once observed about ex-friend Gore Vidal: "It's impossible to know how conservative as well as how radical he can be." Christopher Hitchens, "The Cosmopolitan Man," *New York Review of Books*, 22 April 1999. Reprinted in Hitchens, *Unacknowledged Legislation: Writers in the Public Sphere* [London: Verso, 2000], 59.) Hitchens relishes this feisty unpredictability. One notes, in fact, that Hitchens has never hesitated to defend Waugh, a reactionary Papist, insisting on several occasions that Orwell's politically tinged literary criticism of Waugh was too narrow and one-sided.

Consider also these lines from *Letters to a Young Contrarian:* "But many is the honorable radical and revolutionary who may be found in the camp of the apparent counterrevolution. And the radical conservative is not a contradiction in terms" (100).

85. But even such an acknowledgment of Orwell's experience with "the broadcast media" via his BBC wartime stint during 1941–1943 is easily misleading. For it was broadcasting as we hardly know it today. His contributions were all read from prepared scripts. To that extent Orwell's wartime BBC was only technically a medium apart from the world of letters—it was an extension of it. Moreover, his broadcast scripts were closely screened for approval; no script was aired unless it had passed the scrutiny of the BBC and Ministry of Information censors. There was little or no unscripted and uncontrolled discussion on the radio as there is today.

86. On this point, see Diana Trilling's recollections in *The Beginning of the Journey: The Marriage of Lionel and Diana Trilling* (New York: Harcourt Brace, 1993) on the significant cultural status accorded *Nation* book reviews in the 1940s.

87. For Orwell's conception of a "true intellectual," see my *Politics of Literary Reputation,* 244.

88. Hitchens would doubtless take exception to these terms as well. "Our remaining expressions—maverick, loose cannon, rebel, angry young man, gadfly—are slightly affectionate and diminutive and are, perhaps for that reason, somewhat condescending. It can be understood from them that society, like a benign family, tolerates and even admires eccentricity. Even the term 'iconoclast' is seldom used negatively, but rather to suggest that the breaking of images is a harmless discharge of energy" (*Letters to a Young Contrarian*). But I do not condescend—I simply seek a language for describing Hitchens beyond the nomenclature of "contrarian."

89. See, for instance, Hitchens, *No One Left to Lie to: The Triangulations of William Jefferson Clinton* (London: Verso, 1999) and *A Long Short War: The Postponed Liberation of Iraq* (New York: Plume, 2003).

90. Hitchens has described himself as "a recovering Marxist, not ashamed, not unbowed, but thoughtful." Quoted in Sean O'Hagan, "Just A Pretty Face?" *Observer,* 11 July 2004.

91. My own judgment is that Hitchens is a radical who possesses what Conor Cruise O'Brien called Orwell's "Tory growl." From *Letters to a Young Contrarian:* "I have not, since you asked, abandoned all the tenets of the Left. I still find that the materialist conception of history has not been surpassed as a means of analyzing matters; I still think that there are opposing class interests; I still think that monopoly capitalism can and should be distinguished from the free market and that it had certain fatal tendencies in both the short and long term" (102).

He does see himself as a "materialist" and a "radical." Hitchens retains a lingering allegiance to Trotskyism. "Radicalism is humanism, or it is nothing" (115).

92. It is worth mentioning that this phrase, so often voiced about Hitchens today, was first used by Martin Green in the 1970s to describe Raymond Williams's anxiety of influence toward Orwell. See Rodden, *The Politics of Literary Reputation*, 218.

CHAPTER SIX

1. But an interesting shift from the intellectuals profiled in Part One is notable. Whereas intellectuals such as John Wain, Kingsley Amis, Dwight Macdonald, Irving Howe, Russell Kirk, and Christopher Hitchens are independent intellectuals first and foremost (even if they occasionally did teaching stints), the majority of my interviewees in Part Two are scholar-intellectuals (whether literary academics or academic historians) based in universities. Literary journalists such as Hitchens and Ian Williams, or avant-garde writers such as Richard Kostelanetz, are now the exceptions. This change reflects a shift in Orwell's audience from the general public to the university English and humanities departments, with his most avid readers consisting of literary scholars and historians rather than politically minded intellectuals writing for little magazines.

2. The responses from Richard Rorty, Richard Kostelanetz, Marshall Berman, and Bernard Crick are taken from interviews conducted in writing after the conference.

3. When I mentioned Morris Dickstein's observation about Orwell's artistic limitations to Gordon Bowker, author of *Inside George Orwell* (2003) and Orwell's most recent biographer, Bowker replied:

> I can agree that Orwell cannot be classed alongside Shakespeare (who on earth can?); I'm not altogether sure about Milton. Milton had a Christian vision which affords it a cosmic dimension; Orwell's vision was secular and therefore restricted to the known world, but it was as great as, perhaps greater than, that of almost any other British writer of the twentieth century that I can think of. I don't know, but I suspect that Orwell's vision has helped frame the modern mind in at least as important a way as Milton's helped frame the Christian-liberal tradition of which Orwell himself was an inheritor.

4. As I suggested both in the introduction and in note 1 of this chapter, the difference today between the literary/political intellectuals featured in Part One and the interviewees in Part Two is this: unlike the case in the first several postwar decades, during which coherent intellectual groups (often associated with little magazines) identified (or disidentified) with Orwell, that no longer prevails. Today, individuals of all political stripes—such as Christopher Hitchens, Alexander Cockburn, Andrew Sullivan, Leon Wieseltier, and Geoffrey Wheatcroft, rather than the *Nation*, the *New Republic*, and the *Spectator*, respectively—acknowledge Orwell as a strong literary or political presence. Moreover, unlike the situation of those intellectuals spotlighted in Chapters One through Four, we are now several generations removed from Orwell's day. So Orwell tends not to animate entire groups of intellectuals, but only those readers who have developed a special identification with him.

For an extended look at Orwell's influence on diverse groups of early postwar intellectuals and writers, see also Part Two of my *Politics of Literary Reputation: The Making and Claiming of "St. George" Orwell.*

CHAPTER SEVEN

1. Patai's comments in the interview further elaborate on her presentation at the George Orwell Centenary Conference, where she discussed her thoughts on Orwell since the publication of her book, *The Orwell Mystique: A Study in Male Ideology* (Amherst: University of Massachusetts Press, 1984). In her conference talk, "Third Thoughts on Orwell," she made clear that her view that Orwell was a misogynist has not changed, nor has her criticism of Orwell's attraction to the warrior ideal and idealized masculinity, his exaltation of working-class men, and his homophobia. Yet she also forthrightly admits, in light of her negative experiences with academic feminism, that *The Orwell Mystique* represented an indulgence "in a dogmatic or quasi-religious statement rather than one based on evidence. . . . I let my feminist politics dictate the results of my analysis."

See Daphne Patai, "Third Thoughts on Orwell," in *George Orwell: Into the Twenty-First Century* (Boulder: Paradigm, 2004).

2. This point warrants emphasis. As her critique of U.S. women's studies programs and the feminist academic Establishment reflects, Patai is a contrarian in the spirit of Orwell, Hitchens, and even Amis. She is unafraid to criticize what she perceives as "smelly little orthodoxies"—whether of the Left or the Right. Among my interviewees, her remarks formed the lone discordant note from the choirs of approval that the (mostly male) intellectuals in these chapters have accorded Orwell. Although I myself agree with them in the main, I also acknowledge that the great majority of Orwell's admirers (and adversaries) have been men. And this fact suggests much about how writers become figures—that is, not just because they stand as political or generational exemplars, but for unstated, less visible reasons too: for instance, because they are also inspirational gender models. Male critics have been particularly silent as to the significance of Orwell's reputation among male intellectuals and his special masculine appeal. For my assessment of the feminist critique of Orwell, see *The Politics of Literary Reputation,* 211–226.

CHAPTER EIGHT

1. Russell Jacoby, *The Last Intellectuals: American Life in the Age of Academe* (New York: Basic Books, 1987).

2. Since the rise of theory in the literary academy in the late 1980s, the chasm has become deeper. The concept of the public intellectual has emerged in reaction against academic specialization and jargon. (Some intellectuals have, however, reacted against the term itself, worrying that the adjective *public* has overwhelmed the noun *intellectual*).

3. Allow me here to share with you how our connection began—which is both typical and highly unusual of how readers encounter you, George. I was so inspired by *Animal Farm* that I began to read *Nineteen Eighty-Four* and an old copy of the *Collected Essays.* The figure of Winston Smith intrigued me, and in fact I soon had my own slight brush with Big Brother after I wrote a high school essay titled "Big Brotherhood."

I've kept this piece of juvenilia, which really represents the origin of my deeper relationship with you, George. A number of East German political prisoners who suffered terrible fates told me stories about their experiences of reading your work that began similarly to mine.

Permit me here, then, to share the rest of my own little episode. In that high school essay of 1972 I wrote that government wiretapping and bugging violated Americans' civil liberties. In the post-Watergate climate of late autumn 1972, I received three phone calls from F.B.I. agents about my essay, which I had delivered as a speech in various high school and community activities. The speech criticized the Safe Street and Crime Control Act of 1968, which contained many loopholes that allowed government agencies to wiretap and bug. A court order was required, but I argued that the history of court approval revealed widespread rubber-stamp approval without real judicial consideration. (As the widespread fears since 9/11 about the restriction of civil liberties and the expansion of police power and government surveillance authority demonstrate, the warnings in *Nineteen Eighty-Four* [and my little speech!] haven't lost their relevance.)

4. And perhaps this is why socialism, as a public policy, is misconceived. It locates its aims at an altitude too high for the general public. In so doing, it embraces Unreality. Most people will not cooperate with or respond to incentives that are several steps beyond them. Or as Yeats phrased it in another context: "I must begin where all ladders start/in the foul rag and bone shop of the heart." For me, that means that one ought to begin with capitalism and realistic economic incentives before advancing to socialism.

The point, once again, is this: It's useless and dangerous to dangle ideals above people, ideals that will only discourage them because they can't get near to reaching them. That is what leads to the cynical abuses of socialism, the self-righteousness of the people who promote these ideals, and so on. The ideal becomes a forced, hated abstraction—there is no gentleness, no pleasure, no real understanding of limits and the need to downscale the grandiose idea to something reachable and work upward step by step.

So that is why I am not a radical or a socialist—but rather a gradualist, a parliamentary social democrat. On a public policy level, I support positions that embrace reality. And reality is the diet on which all growth of the body politic must feed, a nourishing, health-supporting diet. It is pointless and even alienating and debilitating to urge that people embrace a strict, self-denying diet—it may not be suited to them and, regardless of how healthy it may be in the abstract scientific sense, it may represent a level of virtue that they cannot attain given their present habits. People feel discouraged if they keep failing at an ideal. But they feel encouraged if they make a couple of small steps on a regular basis—and then consolidate those steps into lived practice as they go.

So the neocons and leftists are both right—and wrong. Yes, choose the best of the available options as the neocons urge, but do not fix your gaze on them. The radical humanist is right, too: aspire to something higher. But it is wise to aspire not to the distant ideal, beyond what exceeds both our grasp and our reach—but rather to pursue something within our grasp or even perhaps within our reach.

To be a social democrat means to start from reality and yet to aspire to realistic ideals. It is realistic to aspire to something higher but not stratospheric, an impossible level of aspiration that my friends and I in graduate school used to call "nosebleed idealism."

Might the Orwell who supported Attlee's Labour government have shared such reservations about leftist ideals as mine?

Quite possibly. Part of the problem here is nomenclature and the history of Left sectarianism. Marx's own party in Germany called itself Social Democrat, and indeed the official name of the Bolsheviks at the time of the 1917 revolution was the Russian Social Democratic Party. One needs to remember that, in the 1930s, both the Comintern and the Popular Front made *social democrat* and indeed even *socialist* into terms of opprobrium among many leftists. Leaving aside the Left's sectarian debates, I believe that *socialist, democratic socialist,* and *social democrat* are all political designations that Orwell could ultimately have accepted as his own.

5. To mention, for example, my Catholicism once again: As a result, I oppose right-wing views of Catholicism that overemphasize authority, hierarchy, and obedience. I identify with the Thomist tradition, as exemplified in Leo XIII's encyclical *Rerum Novarum* (1891), which supported popular sovereignty, urged just government limitations on wealth, and called for economic reform and aid to the poor and working classes.

6. Orwell's six rules from "Politics and the English Language" are as follows:

1. Never use a metaphor, simile or other figure of speech which you are used to seeing in print.
2. Never use a long word where a short one will do.
3. If it is possible to cut out a word, always cut it out.
4. Never use the passive where you can use the active.
5. Never use a foreign phrase, scientific word or a jargon word if you can think of an everyday English equivalent.
6. Break any of these rules sooner than say anything outright barbarous.

EPILOGUE

1. Empson's letter is quoted in Bernard Crick, *George Orwell: A Life* (London: Secker and Warburg, 1980), 430.

2. Ibid., 430. And not just "Tory propaganda"—even official Nazi wartime propaganda. Indeed, not only has Orwell been used on all sides since the publication of *Animal Farm* and *Nineteen Eighty-Four,* his work was even used on both sides during World War II. Britain's use of a few seemingly unvarnished, patriotic passages in works such as *Homage to Catalonia, Coming Up for Air,* and *The English People* is well known. But the Nazis also selectively quoted and abridged Orwell (in passages of works such as *The Lion and the Unicorn*)—along with Carlyle, Ruskin, Shaw, Aldous Huxley, H. G. Wells, and several others—in their anti-British propaganda. German undergraduates drafted for the Wartime Propaganda Service were often assigned to collect suitable quotations from English literature for propaganda purposes. Such examples of British authors deriding Britain were valuable to the Third Reich because they came from non-German sources. Needless to say, the Nazis usually bowdlerized and misrepresented the intentions of the British authors whom they quoted.

So here we have yet another example of Orwell serving as an author (in his phrase about Dickens) "well worth stealing." (It is even possible that Orwell himself was aware of the Nazi exploitation of his work because of his wartime BBC broadcasting or his extensive contact with German refugees in London.)

For detailed treatment of these issues, see Gerwin Strobl, *The Germanic Isle: Nazi Perceptions of Britain* (Cambridge: Cambridge University Press, 2000), especially chap. 7, "'The Land without Music': Culture and Propaganda," 184–201.

3. Letter from Orwell to Julian Symons, 29 October 1948, in *The Complete Works of George Orwell*, ed. Peter Davison (London, 1998), 19: 461. Fyvel is not alone in this judgment. Nor is Daphne Patai, who voiced it in Chapter Seven. Orwell wrote extensively and critically about anti-Semitism, yet the idea that Orwell was anti-Semitic has supporters currently as it did during his lifetime. Muggeridge wrote of his surprise that so many of the mourners at Orwell's funeral were Jewish. "Interesting, I thought," he writes, "that George should have so attracted Jews because he was at heart strongly anti-Semitic." D. J. Taylor, Orwell's biographer, has written that anti-Semitism was Orwell's "dirty secret."

According to Les Adler, characterizing Orwell as a bigot misses the complex way in which he took his own cultural legacy as the starting point for critical reflection. Orwell complicated any simple or comfortable separation between racism and anti-racism, and he showed the emotional need of racists to believe their dogmas. On these points, see Les Adler, "Orwell's Anti-Semitism" (unpublished essay, 2004). See also Anthony Stewart, "Vulgar Nationalism and Insulting Nicknames: George Orwell's Progressive Reflections on Race," in *George Orwell: Into the Twenty-First Century*, ed. Thomas Cushman and John Rodden (Boulder: Paradigm, 2004), 145–159.

4. It may be useful here to speak of Orwell's "casual prejudice" toward Jews (at least until the mid-1930s) and feminists (not women generally), rather than of his anti-feminism or misogyny—attitudes that entail an overt, public, actively pursued hostility toward Jews and women. Orwell's bias derived from his class background and social upbringing, neither of which he completely outgrew (though he matured beyond their cruder manifestations in his later years). Orwell's class biases were largely a matter of perfunctory and careless asides, or even on occasion a shock tactic—not a species of racism.

The phrase "casual prejudice" is in Richard S. Levy, *Antisemitism in the Modern World: An Anthropology of Texts* (Lexington, Mass.: D. C. Heath, 1991), where he contrasts it with overt, antagonistic anti-Semitism. (Admirers of T. S. Eliot, such as Russell Kirk, might seek to defend Eliot on the basis of similar distinctions—though I find the case of Eliot, and both Dawson and Chesterton as well, far more problematic and doubtful.)

5. See my discussion of Campbell and Patai in *George Orwell: The Politics of Literary Reputation* (New Brunswick: Transaction, 2002 [1989], chap. 4). Writes Peter Davison in his *George Orwell: A Literary Life*.

Orwell (relatively rarely in his day, especially in a working-class family) was not the kind of man who would not wash up; he willingly changed young Richard's nappies at a time when few men did such things. But he was writing about a society which was dependent on the man working and, in working-class society, orientated to that end far more than was the world of the middle-class. Examination of a number of books of the first half of the twentieth century that have obvious parallels with *The Road to Wigan Pier* reveals few working women. (Harmondsworth: Penguin, 1962, p. 219.)

Davison's conscientious scholarship in all his writings about Orwell exemplifies the point of my first precept: "honor the context," which is to respect the politics of comparison. The life and work of an ancestor must be evaluated both in the context of its time and place and in relation to his contemporaries.

6. Milan Kundera, *Testaments Betrayed: An Essay in Nine Parts* (New York: Harper-Collins, 1995), 240.

7. To what extent is Orwell's "relative clear-sightedness" about the direction in which the big "isms" of History were heading a matter of personal character, attributable to Orwell's purported "decency" or to Trilling's "virtuous man"? I would say: no more so than the supposed "blindness" of the figures whom Kundera cites was necessarily and totally a matter of their ethical lapses or corruption.

Yet here again, it is important to draw some fine distinctions. For instance, in a recent essay, Richard Rorty quite fairly notes that it is by no means always a matter of "moral virtue" that caused Orwell to be on "the right side" of History, "as if luck had had nothing to do with it." But Rorty overemphasizes the component of luck—as if moral virtue had nothing to do with it.

Orwell did indeed possess, as he put it, "a power of facing unpleasant facts." This prevented him numerous times from making what Rorty casually refers to as "honest mistakes." As if vociferous support for Stalin into the 1940s and 1950s—when the facts about the Gulag were there for all to see—were merely "an honest mistake"!

Like Kundera, Rorty is entirely right that "the morally relevant facts" are not always there "for all to see." The Left is indeed much too apt to sling charges such as "renegade" and "sell-out." This "piggishness" on the Left is indeed a moral failure in its own right. When Rorty writes, "Orwell happened to have been in the right places at the right times, to have gotten switched onto the right political tracks," it is not just a matter of "sheer, dumb luck" that Orwell was always "on the right side." That puts far too much emphasis on Rorty's notion of "contingency," implying that history is always and necessarily radically contingent.

Perhaps, as Rorty says, *honesty* is not the best word to characterize Orwell's political choices. That word accents too heavily the subjective—unlike the word *integrity*. The fact is that Orwell possessed a high degree of political acumen, a capacity for discernment that inoculated him from ideologies of both the Right and the Left—to which so many intellectuals of his day and thereafter were susceptible. To say that Orwell simply "guessed right," that he "lucked out," overlooks this political acumen. It was a form of discernment that had a moral dimension, because Orwell could often see from a great distance the seeds of catastrophe. "All people who are morally sound have known since about 1931 that the Russian regime stinks," he once wrote. The self-congratulation was justifiable. This form of far-seeing vision is not a matter simply of luck or radical contingency.

(I also think that Rorty does an injustice to his parents, who broke with the Communist Party at the early date of 1932. "I think of them as lucky," he says. "They had occasion to work closely with the Party's leaders as most fellow travelers did not, so they learned things that other people only learned later." But it is not what they learned, but rather how they responded to what they learned, that makes all the difference. Almost everyone who was close to the Party's leaders had so much to lose or was so blinded that they continued to parrot the Party line. To their great credit, Rorty's parents did not.)

Certainly Rorty is right that "being honest, being true to one's ideals, has nothing in particular to do with the story History will tell about you, for historians are more interested in the consequences of your actions than in your motives." Yes, but sometimes your actions reveal your motives. Moreover, the range and scope of your vision—whether you are willing and able, in Matthew Arnold's phrase, "to see things steadily and to see them whole"—has everything to do with this far-seeing vision and the story that History will eventually tell about you. It has to do with "honesty" to the extent that honesty with oneself is a form of intellectual integrity. Implicitly divorcing motives and actions—as if one's motives do not lead to certain kinds of actions or inactions—is misconceived. *Pace* Rorty, "the moral" is that being truly realistic—indeed being "wise" about the direction in which events are likely to go if power is used and/or abused—has everything to do with the story History will tell about you.

See Richard Rorty, "Whittaker Chambers and Alger Hiss: Two Men of Honor," unpublished essay, 2004. The Orwell quotation is from a letter he wrote to Humphrey House on 11 April 1940 that can be found in *The Complete Works of George Orwell* (vol. 13, 141).

8. Kundera, *Testaments Betrayed*. Of course, therefore, such an ethics of detraction also necessarily entails that one argue a case on its merits, rather than shift the argument to ad hominem attacks or simply impute base motives.

9. Scott Lucas, *The Betrayal of Dissent*.

10. Kundera, *Testaments Betrayed*, 266–267.

11. *CEJL*, vol. 4, 30.

12. One tactic in this standard practice of intellectual grave-robbing is the use of selective quotation (rather than simply fabricating Orwell's posthumous politics by mere assertion), which is especially common among Orwell's admirers and detractors. Indeed, a key principle of the ethics of admiration should be to "honor the text"—and thus avoid what might be termed the "politics of the ellipsis." For instance, we saw in Chapter Five how Christopher Hitchens (rightly) condemned Norman Podhoretz and Raymond Williams for their misleading quotations from Orwell.

It ought to be noted, however, that their use of the politics of the ellipsis pales compared to its abuse by C. M. Woodhouse in the 1956 introduction to the paperback version of *Animal Farm*. Woodhouse misquoted Orwell's essay "Why I Write" to "rectify" Orwell into a Cold Warrior. Woodhouse cites a passage in which Orwell declares how the Spanish Civil War defined his political faith: "Every line I have written since 1936 has been against totalitarianism. . . ." Woodhouse halts there: the ellipses are his own. And thus he vaporizes Orwell's closing words ("and for democratic socialism, as I understand it") and, along with them, Orwell's radicalism.

It is germane to mention that Woodhouse was a chief cultural official in Britain's version of the CIA—he worked for both the Secret Intelligence Service (SIS) and the Information Research Department (IRD) in the early Cold War era, during which time he coordinated joint projects with the CIA. Among his IRD activities were to oversee clandestine participation by British intelligence in the sponsorship of the Congress for Cultural Freedom and *Encounter*, both of which were discovered in the mid-1960s to have been largely financed by CIA front organizations. Woodhouse also arranged with Orwell's publisher, Fred Warburg, to lend Secker & Warburg's name as the distributor of *Encounter*—and Warburg no doubt helped smooth the way for Woodhouse to contribute the introduction to *Animal Farm*'s Signet edition, which went on to sell several million copies in the next three decades. On these points, see my *Scenes from an Afterlife*, chap. 4.

13. Louis Menand, "Honest, Decent, Wrong: The Invention of George Orwell," *New Yorker* (27 January 2003).

14. Leon Wieseltier, "Aspidistra," *New Republic*, 17 February 2003.

15. Lionel Trilling, "Reality in America," in *The Liberal Imagination: Essays on Literature and Society* (New York: Viking, 1950).

16. And such a proper skepticism will never mean that, because George Orwell voiced a certain opinion, that opinion is valid just because he said it—especially when one is extrapolating about events from Orwell's day to our present. Just because Orwell said or did something does not make it right or wrong—as if his stature justified a certain conclusion: Q.E.D. That would be most foolhardy, a classic example of what the Stalinists once called "citationism." Surely Orwell himself would have said: "Don't give me the name of a so-called Authority. Give me an argument!"

Here again there are uses as well as abuses of Orwell's legacy—and it is important to draw the proper distinctions and not to confuse one with the other.

And the fact is that, especially in the instance of Orwell, they are indeed frequently confused—and utterly divorced from political ethics or an ethics of rhetoric. Terry Eagleton has summarized the case for and against Orwell in stark terms that point up how ideologically motivated assertions, whether pro or con, are often treated as if they were legitimate persuasive arguments. Eagleton's encapsulations would be amusing if they did not so accurately mimic the rhetoric of numerous Orwell admirers and detractors:

The case for the defence is that Orwell was a magnificently courageous opponent of political oppression, a man of unswerving moral integrity and independence of spirit who risked his life fighting Fascism, narrowly escaped death at the hands of Stalin's agents in Spain, and denounced an imperialism of which he had had unpleasant first-hand knowledge as a young policeman in Burma. In the meantime, he managed to pioneer what is now known as cultural studies. In a remarkable feat of self-refashioning, he turned his back on a life of middle-class privilege and chose for his companions tramps, hop-pickers, Catalonian revolutionaries, louche artists and political activists.

Eagleton then beautifully summarizes the prosecution's case:

> Orwell was a self-mythologizing romantic toff who went in for the odd bit of sentimen-
> tal slumming, sometimes adopting a ludicrous cockney accent in the process, and
> ended up in political defeatism and despair. A second-rate novelist and a furtively
> fabricating social commentator, he was a homophobic, anti-feminist, unsociable, anti-
> intellectual authoritarian and latently violent. He was also an anti-semitic, sexually
> promiscuous, self-pitying Little Englander, whose later fantasies about Big Brother
> and pigs running farms (they haven't the trotters for it) bequeathed a set of lurid ste-
> reotypes and convenient caricatures to the Right.

Terry Eagleton, "Reach-Me-Down Romantic," *London Review of Books*, 19 June 2003,
7–8.

17. Revelations about Koestler's mistreatment of women—his alleged rape of Jill Crai-
gie, among other assaults—have destroyed his reputation as a humanist and champion
of the dispossessed. Silone's radical credentials have been soiled by evidence that he was
an informant to the fascists in the 1930s as well as knowledgeable about CIA funding of
Cultural Freedom (and other anti-Soviet postwar activities of the Western intelligence services in the "cultural cold war").

18. That is the already-cited verdict of Richard Posner in his *Public Intellectuals*, to
which I referred in the introduction.

Bibliography

Alexander, Edward. *Irving Howe.* Bloomington: Indiana University Press, 1998.

Annan, Noel. "The Intellectual Aristocracy," in *Studies in Social History,* ed. J. H. Plumb. London: Longmans, Green, 1955.

Atkins, John. *George Orwell: A Literary Study.* London: Calder and Boyars, 1954.

Bowker, Gordon. *Inside George Orwell.* New York: Palgrave Press, 2003.

Brander, Laurence. *George Orwell.* London: Longmans, Green, 1954.

Branson, Noreen, and Margot Heinemann. *Britain in the Nineteen Thirties.* New York: Praeger, 1971.

Brown, Gordon. *Maxton.* London: Mainstream Publishing, 2002.

Brym, Robert J. *Intellectuals and Politics.* London: George Allen and Unwin, 1980.

————. "The Political Sociology of Intellectuals: A Critique and a Proposal," in *Intellectuals in Liberal Democracies: Political Influence and Social Involvement,* ed. Alan G. Gagnon. New York: Praeger, 1987.

Calder, Angus. *The People's War: Britain 1939–45.* New York: Ace, 1972.

Cockburn, Alexander. "Why Hitch the Snitch Betrayed a Trusting Friend," *Irish Times,* 13 February 1999.

Collini, Stefan. "The Grocer's Children: The Lives and Afterlives of George Orwell," *Times Literary Supplement,* 20 June 2003.

Collins, Randall. *The Sociology of Philosophies: A Global Theory of Intellectual Change.* Cambridge, Mass.: Belknap Press of Harvard University Press, 1998.

Connolly, Cyril. *Enemies of Promise.* London: Routledge, 1938.

Crick, Bernard. *George Orwell: A Life.* London: Secker and Warburg, 1980.

Crick, Bernard, and Audrey Coppard. *George Orwell Remembered.* London: Ariel Books, 1984.

Davison, Peter. *George Orwell: A Literary Life.* New York: St. Martin's Press, 1996.

Davison, Peter (ed.). *The Complete Works of George Orwell.* London: Secker and Warburg, 1986–1997.

Eagleton, Terry. "Reach-Me-Down Romantic," *London Review of Books* 25:12, 19 June 2003.

Fyvel, T. R. *Intellectuals Today.* London: Faber, 1968.

———. *George Orwell: A Personal Memoir.* London: Macmillan, 1982.

Gagnon, Alain G. "The Role of Intellectuals in Liberal Democracies," in *Intellectuals in Liberal Democracies: Political Influence and Social Involvement,* ed. Gagnon. New York: Praeger, 1987.

Gollancz, Victor (ed.). *The Betrayal of the Left: An Examination and Refutation of Communist Policy.* London: Gollancz, 1941.

Gross, Miriam (ed.). *The World of George Orwell.* London: Weidenfeld and Nicolson, 1971.

Havighurst, Alfred F. *Britain in Transition: The Twentieth Century,* 4th ed. Chicago: University of Chicago Press, 1985.

Hennessy, Peter. *Never Again: Britain, 1945–1951.* New York: Pantheon, 1993.

Heppenstall, Rayner. *Four Absentees.* London: Barrie and Rockliff, 1960.

Hitchens, Christopher. *Letters to a Young Contrarian.* New York: Basic Books, 2001.

———. "Orwell Missed America," *American Enterprise,* October–November 2002.

———. *Unacknowledged Legislation.* London: Verso, 2001.

———. *Why Orwell Matters.* New York: Basic Books, 2002.

Hollander, Paul. *Political Pilgrims: Travels of Western Intellectuals to the Soviet Union, China and Cuba.* New York: Oxford University Press, 1981.

Hollis, Christopher. *A Study of George Orwell.* London: Hollis and Carter, 1956.

Howe, Irving. "George Orwell: 'As the Bones Know,'" reprinted in *Decline of the New.* New York: Horizon, 1970, 269–279.

———. *A Margin of Hope.* San Diego: Harcourt Brace Jovanovich, 1982.

———. Preface to *1984 Revisited: Totalitarianism in Our Century.* New York: Harper and Row, 1983.

Howe, Irving (ed.) *Nineteen Eighty-Four: Text, Sources, Criticism.* New York: Harcourt Brace, 1963.

Hynes, Samuel. *The Auden Generation: Literature and Politics in England in the 1930s.* London: Bodley Head, 1976.

Jacoby, Russell. *The Last Intellectuals: American Life in the Age of Academe.* New York: Basic Books, 1987.

Katz, Wendy. "Imperialism and Patriotism: Orwell's Dilemma in 1940," *Modernist Studies: Literature and Culture* 3 (1979): 99–105.

Kazin, Alfred. "Not One of Us." *New York Review of Books,* 23 January 1984.

Kirk, Russell. *Beyond the Dreams of Avarice.* Chicago: Regnery, 1956.

———. *The Conservative Mind.* Chicago: Regnery, 1960.

———. *Enemies of the Permanent Things.* New Rochelle, N.Y.: Arlington House, 1969.

———. *The Sword of Imagination: Memoirs of a Half-Century of Literary Conflict.* Grand Rapids, Mich.: William B. Eerdmans, 1995.

Kogan, Steve. "In Celebration of George Orwell on the Fiftieth Anniversary of 'Politics and the English Language,'" *Academic Questions* (Winter 1996–1997): 15–29.

Kundera, Milan. *Testaments Betrayed.* New York: HarperCollins, 1985.

Lucas, Scott. *The Betrayal of Dissent: Beyond Orwell, Hitchens, and the New American Century.* London: Pluto Press, 2004.

———. *Orwell.* London: Haus Publishing, 2003.

Lutman, Stephen. "Orwell's Patriotism," *Journal of Contemporary History* 2(2) (1967): 149–158.

Macdonald, Dwight. *Discriminations: Essays and Afterthoughts 1938–1974*. New York: Grossman, 1974.

Menand, Louis. "Honest, Decent, Wrong: The Invention of George Orwell," *New Yorker*, 16 January 2003.

Meyers, Jeffrey. *Orwell: The Wintry Conscience of a Generation*. New York: Norton, 2000.

Meyers, Jeffrey (ed.). *George Orwell: The Critical Heritage*. London: Routledge and Kegan Paul, 1975.

Nadel, Ira Bruce. *Biography: Fiction, Fact and Form*. London: Macmillan, 1984.

New, M. "Orwell and Antisemitism: Toward 1984," *Modern Fiction* 21:1 (1975).

Newsinger, John. *Orwell's Politics*. New York: St. Martin's Press, 1999.

Patai, Daphne. *The Orwell Mystique: A Study in Male Ideology*. Amherst: University of Massachusetts Press, 1984.

Posner, Richard A. *Public Intellectuals: A Study of Decline*. Cambridge, Massachusetts: Harvard University Press, 2001.

Rees, Richard. *George Orwell: A Fugitive from the Camp of Justice*. London: Secker and Warburg, 1961.

Rodden, John. *The Politics of Literary Reputation: The Making and Claiming of "St. George" Orwell*. New York/Oxford: Oxford University Press, 1989.

———. *The Walls That Remain: Western and Eastern Germans After Reunification*. Boulder, Colo.: Paradigm, forthcoming.

———. *Scenes from an Afterlife: The Legacy of George Orwell*. Wilmington, Delaware: ISI Books, 2003.

———. "The Separate Worlds of George Orwell," *Four Quarters*, Summer 1988.

Rodden, John, and Thomas Cushman (eds.). *George Orwell: Into the Twenty-First Century*. Boulder, Colo.: Paradigm, 2004.

Rose, Jonathan. *The Intellectual Life of the British Working Classes*. New Haven and London: Yale University Press, 2001.

Rose, Jonathan (ed.). *The Revised Orwell*. East Lansing: Michigan State University Press, 1992.

Rosenbaum, Ron. "The Man Who Would Be Orwell," *New York Observer*, 23 March 2002.

Rossi, John. "George Orwell's Conception of Patriotism," *Modern Age* XLII, no. 2 (Spring 2001): 128–132.

Samuels, Stuart. "English Intellectuals and Politics in the 1930s," in *On Intellectuals*, ed. Philip Rieff. New York: Doubleday, 1969.

———. "The Left Book Club," *Journal of Contemporary History* 1 (1966).

Shelden, Michael. *Orwell: The Authorized Biography*. London: Heinemann, 1991.

Sorin, Gerald. *Irving Howe: A Life of Passionate Dissent*. New York: New York University Press, 2002.

Spurling, Hilary. *The Girl from the Fiction Department*. London: Hamish Hamilton, 2002.

Stansky, Peter, and William Abrahams. *Orwell: The Transformation*. London: Constable, 1979.

———. *The Unknown Orwell*. London: Constable, 1972.

Steinhoff, William. *George Orwell and the Origins of 1984.* Ann Arbor: University of Michigan Press, 1976.

Stevenson, John. *British Society 1914–45.* Harmondsworth: Penguin, 1984.

Sumner, Gregory D. *Dwight Macdonald and the Politics Circle: The Challenge of Cosmopolitan Democracy.* Ithaca: Cornell University Press, 1990.

Swingewood, Alan. "Intellectuals and the Construction of Consensus in Postwar England," in *Intellectuals in Liberal Democracies: Political Influence and Social Involvement,* ed. Alain C. Gagnon. New York: Praeger, 1987.

Symons, Julian. "Orwell: A Reminiscence," *London Magazine* 3 (September 1963): 35–49.

Taylor, D. J. *Orwell: The Life.* London: Chatto and Windus, 2003.

Thompson, E. P. "Outside the Whale," in *Out of Apathy.* London: New Left Books, 1960.

Trilling, Diana. *The Beginning of the Journey: The Marriage of Lionel and Diana Trilling.* New York: Harcourt Brace, 1993.

Trilling, Lionel. "Reality in America," in *The Liberal Imagination: Essays on Literature and Society.* New York: Viking, 1950.

Tyrell, Martin. "The Politics of George Orwell (1903–1950): From Tory Anarchism to National Socialism and More Than Half Way Back," *Cultural Notes* 36, 1997.

Wadhams, Stephen. *Remembering George Orwell.* Harmondsworth: Penguin, 1984.

Wain, John. "Here Lies Lower Binfield," *Encounter,* 17 October 1961.

Walton, D. "George Orwell and Antisemitism," *Patterns of Prejudice* 16:1 (1982).

Westbrook, R. "The Responsibility of Peoples: Dwight Macdonald and the Holocaust," *Holocaust Studies Annual 1.* Florida: Greenwood, 1983.

Wieseltier, Leon. "Aspidistra," *New Republic,* 17 February 2003.

Williams, Ian. "In Defense of Comrade Psmith," in *George Orwell: Into the 21st Century.* Boulder, 2004.

Williams, Raymond. *George Orwell.* Englewood Cliffs: Prentice Hall, 1974.

Wood, Neal. *Communism and British Intellectuals.* New York: Columbia University Press, 1959.

Woodcock, George. *The Crystal Spirit.* London: Jonathan Cape, 1967.

Young, John Wesley. *Totalitarian Language.* University of Virginia Press, 1991.

Zwerdling, Alex. *Orwell and the Left.* Yale University Press, 1974.

Index